Dear Reader,

I am very pleased to offer this, the third edition of *The Everything® Guide to Investing in Your 20s & 30s*. I've been involved with the financial market since 1987, and I've seen a lot of things.

The investment landscape is always changing in response to politics, government policies, interest rates, and scientific advances—that's just the way of the world. However, one thing remains constant: Once you know how investing works, **you can succeed**.

In this book, I will show you how to make sense of all things investments, how to be prepared, **how to adjust and adapt** by investing in stocks and related investments, and how to add real estate to reliably produce current income and simultaneously build long-term wealth. And because I expect you will have some extra money coming in after your first investments, I will also offer insights into alternative routes like cryptocurrencies, collectibles, and private equity.

I sincerely hope you enjoy this book and that it helps you to start or continue your **journey to financial success**.

Sincerely,

J. Duarte, MD

Joe Duarte's Smart Money Passport (smartmoneypassport.substack.com)
Joe Duarte's Sector Selector (buymeacoffee.com/wsdetectivx)

Welcome to the Everything® Series!

These handy, accessible books give you all you need to tackle a difficult project, gain a new hobby, comprehend a fascinating topic, prepare for an exam, or even brush up on something you learned back in school but have since forgotten.

You can choose to read an Everything® book from cover to cover or just pick out the information you want from our four useful boxes: Questions, Facts, Alerts, and Essentials. We give you everything you need to know on the subject, but throw in a lot of fun stuff along the way too.

QUESTION
Answers to common questions.

FACT
Important snippets of information.

ALERT
Urgent warnings.

ESSENTIAL
Quick handy tips.

We now have more than 600 Everything® books in print, spanning such wide-ranging categories as cooking, health, parenting, personal finance, wedding planning, word puzzles, and so much more. When you're done reading them all, you can finally say you know Everything®!

PUBLISHER Karen Cooper
ASSOCIATE COPY DIRECTOR Casey Ebert
PRODUCTION EDITOR Jo-Anne Duhamel
SENIOR CONTENT EDITOR Lisa Laing
EVERYTHING® SERIES COVER DESIGNER Erin Alexander

THE
EVERYTHING®
GUIDE TO
INVESTING
IN YOUR
20s & 30s
3RD EDITION

YOUR STEP-BY-STEP GUIDE TO:
Understanding Stocks, Bonds, and Mutual Funds •
Maximizing Your 401(k) • Exploring Strategies
for Alternative Investments • Taking Advantage
of Investment Apps • Investing Sustainably •
Becoming Financially Independent

JOE DUARTE, MD

Adams Media

New York   Amsterdam/Antwerp   London   Toronto   Sydney/Melbourne   New Delhi

Adams Media
An Imprint of Simon & Schuster, LLC
100 Technology Center Drive
Stoughton, MA 02072

An Everything® Series Book.

This Adams Media trade paperback edition June 2025
First Adams Media trade paperback edition November 2014

For information about special discounts for bulk purchases, please contact Simon & Schuster Special Sales at 1-866-506-1949 or business@simonandschuster.com.

The Simon & Schuster Speakers Bureau can bring authors to your live event. For more information or to book an event, contact the Simon & Schuster Speakers Bureau at 1-866-248-3049 or visit our website at www.simonspeakers.com.

Interior design by Colleen Cunningham and Maya Caspi

Manufactured in the United States of America

1 2025

Library of Congress Control Number: 2025001012

ISBN 978-1-5072-2401-4
ISBN 978-1-5072-2402-1 (ebook)

Contains material adapted from the following title published by Adams Media, an Imprint of Simon & Schuster, LLC: *The Everything® Guide to Investing in Your 20s & 30s* by Joe Duarte, MD, copyright © 2019, ISBN 978-1-5072-1030-7.

Contents

CHAPTER 10

The Large Universe of Mutual Funds **153**

CHAPTER 11

Combining Funds for Performance **165**

CHAPTER 12

Exchange-Traded Funds— Made for Trading **179**

CHAPTER 13

ESG Investing **195**

Introduction

Over the last few years, the investing world has changed drastically, spiking interest rates and causing issues with affordability across the globe. These changes make investing carefully and strategically even more crucial. Plus, as the world evolves, so does the investing scene; as a future investor, you'll need the most up-to-date information to make the right decisions for your nest egg(s). And, while investing is worthwhile at any age, it's especially important in your twenties and thirties so that you get the most out of compounding (having your money make more money off itself over time).

In *The Everything® Guide to Investing in Your 20s & 30s, 3rd Edition*, you'll learn about the modern financial world, where you'll discover plentiful ways to grow your wealth. Within these pages, you'll find information about the traditional asset classes, such as stocks, bonds, mutual funds, commodities, and currencies, and you'll also be introduced to the growing world of cryptocurrencies, options, exchange-traded funds (ETFs), and more. Luckily, you only need to master a few of these asset classes and combine them to simultaneously create current income and build your long-term nest egg. Additionally, you'll learn why financial advisors may be useful and how to DIY your investing portfolio. So, regardless of how you choose to invest, this book breaks down each asset, strategies for investing with it, and much more. You'll have access to the most up-to-date information in an easily understood way.

While investing can be chaotic, with the information found in this book, you can seize your opportunity to make powerful financial changes. So, if you're wondering which stocks are safe and which may be too risky, which can offer you the best return on investment, which investments are best for you, or even how to plan for investing in retirement, you'll find all the answers here. After all, the best asset is knowledge, and grasping and learning how to take advantage of the state the market is in—regardless of what that state is—will lead you toward success.

In addition to everything mentioned previously, you'll also learn:

- How you can afford to invest, given your current income and financial restrictions
- How willing you are to take risks with your money
- How to manage that risk to make money now and in the future
- How a financial advisor can walk you through your options and help choose the best asset classes (stocks, bonds, cryptocurrencies, and more) for you

Most importantly, you'll learn how to develop a plan for your current income, allowing you to safely build your wealth. Whether you've invested and are looking for more information or you've never invested, if you are in your twenties and thirties, time is on your side. Starting to invest in your twenties and thirties will give you ample opportunities to build the kind of financial future that you are looking for. Turn the page, and let's get started.

CHAPTER 1

Are You Ready to Become an Investor?

When thinking about investing, it's best to understand the big picture. Investing is traditionally the long-term process by which you build wealth. During periods of inflation, it's also a process through which you build current income. Either way, it has two basic components—saving and compounding. You save with the purpose of investing that saved money. Compounding is what money does for you by earning interest, by the price appreciation of your investments, or both. Together, these two processes grow your money. Once you understand these concepts, you are ready to get started.

In this chapter, you will learn all about the current world of investing, setting achievable goals for your investments, and how to adjust your expectations of growing your wealth. You'll also understand if you have everything you need to invest by using the "Ready to Invest" test toward the end of this chapter.

Setting the Scene to Invest for Now and for Later

Investing has two time frames: the present and the future. The first step is to ground yourself in the present; ask yourself whether you can afford to invest, and if not, how you can take steps to afford it. The rest will follow.

FACT

Compounding and saving make your money grow faster. If you start with $1,000 and add $50 per year, you will end up with $1,250 after five years. If you earn just 5% interest on your money and still add $50 per year, after five years, you will have an extra $276.28.

The Stock Market Is for the Present and the Future

Inflation takes a bite out of your finances, but investing in stocks offers a double-edged solution for the short and long term. For the long-term income, invest in your 401(k) plan and individual retirement account (IRA). For short-term income, work a side job and trade in stocks and related instruments. As you build capital, you can further provide short-term income via real estate investments that, along with your targeted stock trading, will increase your current income.

What Cash Flow Is and How to Manage It

Your short-term income goal is to have positive cash flow, or money left over after you pay your bills. You can then use that excess cash flow to pay down your debt and eventually build working capital to invest in real estate, which will expand your opportunities for current income.

FACT

Successful companies focus a great deal of energy on their cash flow. That's because positive cash flow is the lifeblood of key areas of their business, such as expanding operations and offering performance bonuses.

There are two ways to increase your cash flow. You may pay down your debt as quickly as possible, or you may increase the input into your working capital fund. For the second option, work some side hustles and/or fine-tune your stock trading skills. Over time, you'll see steady progress.

How Will You Finance Your Investing?

The money you use for investing can come from anywhere—a savings account, an inheritance, or even a lottery win. For most people, investment money is money earned from a side gig or profession. However, those with good credit and sound savings plans can prudently borrow money to invest in tangible assets to generate income, such as real estate. If you've got some money set aside, you're ahead of the game; the more you have, the better your starting point, especially if you use those assets as loan collateral. At the same time, it's good to never borrow money for investing until you gain experience, have solid finances, and know your way around the markets— one bad decision could put you in a difficult place.

ESSENTIAL

Maximize your contributions to 401(k) plans and IRAs to set up your future nest egg. Traditionally, billionaires built their fortunes by owning and managing their businesses and then leveraging the business proceeds into stock investments. During periods of inflation, however, it's necessary to use the power of the financial markets to build up a business prior to leveraging it to build wealth. During periods of inflation, it's best to trade stocks and use the proceeds to pay down debt and use excess cash flow to build a business.

With lagging inflation, retirement plans and passive income vehicles (like real estate) are the ground floor for building wealth. Additionally, side hustles and short-term trading in the financial markets help generate current income and expand your investment capital.

To figure out if you can afford to invest, count how much money you have left at the end of the month after all your bills are paid. Even $100 is a good start. Build your solid foundation by saving the excess money in a bank account or a money market mutual fund. A mutual fund, which is similar to a savings account, invests in short-term-interest-paying bonds (maturity of less than ninety days) such as US government Treasury bills or commercial paper (short-term bonds issued by corporations). A money market mutual fund is a holding tank for your money as you plan your investments. The more you save, the faster you can move into more aggressive investments. If you have less than $100 at the end of the month, you should work a little harder to control your expenses or figure out how to make more money, such as a side hustle or working overtime, while balancing family and other important aspects of your life. Don't fret, $100 is a great start.

When you have at least $1,000 or more saved, buy some shares in a mutual fund that invests in stocks or bonds, a good entry-level place for investors. Always go for more. So, if it was easy to save $100 the first month, get greedy and go for $200 the next month, so you can grow your nest egg faster and benefit more from compounding.

ALERT

Before investing, pay off as much debt as possible. Think of debt as a big sack of potatoes that you carry on your back everywhere you go that drags your future down. Being lighter makes you move faster.

If you don't have extra money at the end of the month, review your expenses and trim them where you can. If you're trying to make money without some kind of reliable backing, you're asking for trouble. So don't put your rent or food money into a mutual fund; you may find yourself without a place to live or going hungry.

Details Are Important

Successful investing requires paying attention to the details of what you do and how you do it. For example, plan what you will set aside for both current income and long-term wealth building, how often you will invest it, and how you will monitor your progress. Over time, as your investments grow, adjust based on your needs and your progress. Revisit your goals and expectations at least every three months. Work your way from $100 per month to $1,000 per month. And, as you save money, research different mutual fund companies to find the ideal one for you. Well-known, reliable mutual fund companies include Fidelity Investments, Vanguard, and T. Rowe Price.

ESSENTIAL

The reasons most small investors give up are a lack of cash and risking too much too soon. That causes difficulties during tough times. Markets will always rise and fall, so to stay in the game, set aside as much as you can in your money market fund before you try to put it to work. Then add as much as you can as often as possible to maximize compounding. Eventually, you'll use the stock market to fund your current income and build future wealth.

Know Your Risk Profile

Knowing how much you are willing to risk in investments depends on both your personality and your ability to be objective based on your circumstances. If you are willing to jump out of an airplane without a parachute, you might like to trade options and futures without doing your research or doing some paper trading without risking real money. Of course, that course of action is certainly not recommended. However, people who don't like to leave their house if there are clouds in the sky don't make good investors either.

Still, it makes sense to know how much of a risk-taker you might be. Once you know, you can explore the different kinds of investments and methods that may make sense for you. Regardless of your risk profile, as an investor, there is no substitute for planning, study, risk understanding, and patience.

ALERT

Trading options is risky, but selling options produces income. This technique is useful and worthwhile after you've gained some stock market experience.

To gauge your risk profile, ask yourself these three questions:

- How much can I afford to lose?
- How much do I need to reach my goals?
- How do I react to losing?

If you have only a few hundred dollars to your name, and you need them to get by, you should avoid high-risk investments and concentrate on saving money that you will invest in the future. If your goal is to have a million dollars by the time you retire and you are only twenty-three years old, you're in good shape, as time is on your side. But it won't happen without planning, work, and execution, as everything depends on how much money you can save over time and how well that money can be invested to maximize both current income and wealth building. If you get sick to your stomach when your favorite sports team loses a game, lower-risk investments may be the way to go for you, especially when markets become volatile in response to an unexpected event that is well beyond your control.

Setting Realistic Goals and Timetables

Your timetable starts when you decide to start investing. First, note that you have two goals: current income and building wealth. Then, decide when you will open your account(s) and how much you will allocate to each goal. If you have money set aside, you're ahead of the game. If you have less than $1,000, your best bet is to put that money in the bank or a money market mutual fund and continue adding to the account until you have enough to start investing. If you're looking to invest soon, avoid putting that money in a CD (certificate of deposit) or another type of account that won't allow you to add to it or that will limit how often you can put money in or take it out.

Put It in Writing

Wishing for something won't help you get it, but writing your goals on paper, reading them frequently, and reviewing and refining them will get you places. Note your goal(s), the time frame to reaching them, the amount of money you'll need, how much you have now, and what you are willing to do to get to your goals.

If your long-term goal is to retire early, write down the age of retirement, where you'd like to live, and how much money you think you'll need. Write it in such detail that you can see yourself doing it. "I want to retire when I'm fifty. I want to move to Cape Cod and live in a house by the shore with a great view of the sea. I plan to do a little consulting work on the side and run along the beach with my dog every day." If you have shorter-term goals, like owning a home or visiting a particular foreign country, include those as well and divide your savings and investing capital among them. Also, be specific about how much money you will allocate toward producing current income and the amount you will allocate toward building wealth.

Break the process down into stages. Set monthly, quarterly, and yearly goals. Be specific. Write down exactly how much you'll put into your IRA or 401(k) every month and how much you will deposit in your current income-generating account. Decide how much you'll pay in debt every month and to whom, and how much money you will dedicate to each area. Know that this process will require a great deal of time and planning, and it's likely to require adjustments along the way.

Review and Refine Your Plan

Keep a set of lists with clear and concise objectives and revise them frequently, sometimes every day, but at least monthly. The time interval between checkups and changes is up to you. The key is to get in the habit of making your financial situation something you monitor and adjust frequently, especially when your situation and your needs change. Most of all, keep track of your progress.

Moreover, consider getting help as needed. For example, is your spouse or significant other participating in the plan? Does that person understand the goals? If it's not going the way you planned, take a step back and review the situation alone, then as a couple. Give yourself credit for what you've accomplished and review where things didn't go as you planned. If your goals change, it's not a setback; it's just a reboot. Go through the same process of planning for your next goal.

Simply talking things over with friends or relatives may be helpful. If what you're doing isn't working, it may be time to get a second opinion. By raising the issue with someone who's been there, you may be able to reevaluate the situation. The answer may be something as simple as finding a good financial advisor or shifting your priorities.

Research good online resources for retirement planning, building wealth, and personal finance, like MarketWatch.com's personal finance and retirement sections. The personal finance section offers great ideas for budgeting, saving money on credit cards, and finding bargain trips, as well as great general tips on how to increase your current income and save money. The retirement section is terrific for getting organized and staying updated on changes in mutual funds, IRA rules, taxes, and what to do with your 401(k) plan.

Discount brokers are great resources for baseline savings and investing information. The key is to continue to build capital. So even if you're stuck, continue to put money in that savings account or money market mutual fund as you figure out your next move. You can use *Joe Duarte's Smart Money Passport* Substack (https://smartmoneypassport.substack.com) to trade stocks for current income.

How Much Will You Need to Get Started?

Theoretically, you can start with a nickel. But in the real world, the more you have when you start investing, the better off you'll be. What's even more important is gauging how much you'll need to save and invest over time and to adjust this as your financial situation changes. A rule of thumb used by some mutual fund companies is that you should save eight times your annual ending salary, the money that you have after taxes and expenses, to retire. This is a great guideline for your 401(k) plan or IRA. It's not likely that a young person can do that right away, so it can be done in a stepwise fashion.

ALERT

Searching through the free content on a mutual fund or bank website can give you a fair amount of useful information. Just be aware that their goal is to get you to invest your money with them. Make sure that you use any sensible information without necessarily buying into a sales pitch.

For example, if you start at age twenty-five and you save one time your ending salary by the time you're thirty-five, the next goal should be to save three times your ending salary by the time you're forty-five, five times by the time you're fifty-five, and so on. Remember, this is just a formula. Life isn't always this neat, but you do have a benchmark. You can modify this formula by starting to save earlier, adjusting the amounts more frequently, or changing your retirement age goal. You can also try to put extra money away every chance you get as long as you add it to the original goal amount. Become a savings machine for your retirement and future wealth. If you have a 401(k) plan as your main retirement source, max that out and start a separate IRA to add more money to your retirement.

When Getting Started, Always Think Liquid

You've got some savings, you've got a plan, and you're looking for ways to get things moving. One of the most useful things to do when investing is to consider the flexibility or liquidity of any investing vehicle. Liquidity is the ease of moving the money around—cash in hand is the most liquid of assets. Liquidity certainly comes in handy if something changes, such as a sudden short-term price drop in the stock market that gives you an opportunity to buy shares at lower prices. Let's say that you get a side gig that pays quickly, or you get a bonus or a raise at work. Suddenly you have extra money. That extra money could take you to your $1,000 initial investment target, letting you start your investing plan sooner than you might have intended. If your savings is locked up in an illiquid CD that won't let you move the money around for six months or a year, you'll be stuck and will have to wait until the CD matures before you can get started on your longer-term investment plan.

Bank Accounts versus Money Market Mutual Funds

Bank accounts and money market mutual funds are the most liquid savings and investing vehicles. And although they are similar, they are not the same. You set up a bank account with a bank and you open the money market mutual fund with a brokerage or mutual fund company. Savings accounts pay interest rates, but usually not as much as a money market fund through a brokerage firm. Checking accounts sometimes pay minimal interest.

Money market mutual funds pay interest rates and may have check-writing privileges, but they often require as much as between $1,000 to $2,500 minimum balance, and some may limit the number of checks you can write from the account.

Therefore, it is a good rule to have a bank account for savings, a checking account for paying bills, and a separate money market mutual fund as the central holding area for investment capital. A good operating rule is that when your savings account reaches a certain milestone, you should move money into your money market fund. That's because your money market fund is the first leg of your current income strategy.

Open a money market mutual fund account as your initial investment decision. This account will serve as your central investment account. From there, you can switch money to mutual funds, stocks, and other investments with a phone call or a click of your mouse.

Next, you'll decide how much money to set aside for investing and how often you will add to your investments. A good method is to add a constant or nearly constant amount every month. If your goal is $100 every month, but you only have $50 this month, add the $50. Try to add $150 next month. No matter what, just keep adding to your account.

Even if you check your balances every week or month, give your accounts a thorough checkup every three months. If you're not where you thought you should be, ask yourself why and do your best to make it right.

You can adjust your timetable to conform to your circumstances. Things happen, so if you lose your job or a health emergency pops up, things may be difficult for a while. Stay patient and do your best to stay on track. But if you get a promotion and a raise, give your investment account a raise, too, and modify your addition schedule.

When you reach a milestone, like when you get to your first $10,000, see what you can do to get to $20,000 faster than what it took to get to $10,000. Then do it again when you get to $30,000. Always give yourself room for error, but always make changes and look for ways to make your returns better. Investing is a fluid process. And those who keep up with what they are doing in a systematic fashion do better.

Know Before You Invest

Once you've opened your investment account, keep that money in the money market mutual fund as long as it takes for you to decide what to do with it. Remember, as you start, you'll need time to become familiar with the stock market and how you can use it to give yourself occasional paychecks, which you can use to pay bills. Shares in a money market mutual fund do not fluctuate in price. Although you are buying shares, each share is worth $1. That won't change unless very difficult financial circumstances develop. It has only happened once in the history of investing, during the 2008 financial crisis.

FACT

The Federal Deposit Insurance Corporation (FDIC) does not insure money market mutual fund accounts. Money in these accounts is "at risk" of loss. The good news is that even though it can happen, the odds of losing money in a money market account are almost zero.

Take your time and try out some trading strategies on paper before committing to real-time investing. In the beginning, you can buy shares in a growth mutual fund on paper and follow the share price over a few weeks. Correlate how the fund does in relation to the stock market. If conditions remain the same and the fund does well over the period, pull the trigger in real time and keep an eye on things. You can do the same thing with any stock.

Once you've done some research, it may make sense for you to invest in a well-managed mutual fund that invests in stocks, bonds, or both (a balanced approach). This is a well-suited strategy for your 401(k) or IRA. If you know someone who had good results with a particular mutual fund, research it for yourself. Here's where talking to your parents, an uncle, or wealthy family friend may come in handy.

ALERT

A mutual fund prospectus tells the story of what to expect when you buy shares of the fund. Not only will it describe the fund's investment philosophy, its current holdings and allocation, and its overall approach to investing; you will also get a snapshot of past performance. And while history isn't everything, knowing how a fund performs during a bad market is essential if you are trying to decide whether to hold shares for several years, especially during bear markets.

Don't bank on their ads too much, though. Get the prospectus and see for yourself. Monitor the share price. Compare the fund's performance to the stock market and see how it has behaved during similar periods of economic activity and interest rates in the past. Explore how well the fund has done both recently and over time. Start following its price on a weekly or daily basis for a few weeks. Always compare your funds, or stocks, to the appropriate benchmark and the general market. When you read a mutual fund prospectus, it will always tell you which major stock index it is trying to emulate or beat. Most diversified growth or growth and income mutual funds will use the Standard & Poor's 500 Index (S&P 500) as a benchmark.

Once you get better at investing and start to invest in individual stocks, the process is similar to what you did with a mutual fund, just with more detail. With a mutual fund, you're investing in a management style, expertise, and investment strategy. With an individual company's stock, you're investing in the potential for profits of one entity. However, the fundamental idea of doing research on the company, its products, its strategies, its plans, and people's experiences with it are all necessary. For example: If you go to a coffee shop on a regular basis, it's always crowded, and it's part of a major chain like Starbucks, research the company. See how it's doing, and consider investing in it.

ESSENTIAL

When investing in individual stocks, it's good to "kick the tires" before you buy. That means going to the supermarket and seeing if anyone is buying products made by that company, seeing how many cars are parked in the parking lot of a certain company that retails specific products, and listening for which companies get a lot of press in financial circles. Use this method as the starting point for your research, then follow it by reviewing prior earnings and research reports, asking questions, and getting a long-term view of the company from a stock chart. You can find excellent stock charts on the web at StockCharts.com.

The Basics of Market Analysis

Individual investors have a responsibility to their future and their families. Investing is not a game, especially if you'll be doing short-term trading to help pay the bills. It's a serious activity that should be taken up only by those who wish to take it seriously. It's almost a second occupation, and you should be prepared to make a serious commitment.

The Global Economy Has Changed

After the 1980s, national economies became synchronized and turned into a global economy. Commerce among companies, individuals, and countries functioned to a great degree as a single entity. That initially changed after the 2016 US presidential election, and the pandemic and the war in Ukraine further accelerated the change. Aside from a renegotiation of the North American Free Trade Agreement (NAFTA) among the US, Mexico, and Canada, the world has split into several trading blocs, with Brazil, Russia, India, China, and South Africa (BRICS) on one end and the US and Europe on the other. Plus, trade tariffs are now common and often higher than they were before. Globalization hasn't fully reversed, but what was once considered standard in global trade is no longer guaranteed. And while the US dollar remains the global exchange currency, it now has more intense competition from the Chinese yuan and other regional currencies.

The take-home message from this emerging dynamic is that markets don't always respond to international trade news as they once did. Additionally, supply chains have been altered in multiple ways. Unfortunately, the bottom line is that prices for many products have risen significantly and may never be fully reversed.

Central Banks and Markets

Central banks are government banks that must monitor and respond to the economies of their country by raising or lowering interest rates. Within recent years, their importance for investors has only increased. Now, interest rates are the most important influencers of economic activity because their level dictates how easy it is to borrow money to finance investments such as real estate. Thus, understanding central banks and how they affect your pocketbook is extremely important. In general, weakening economies lead central banks to lower interest rates. Economies that show so much strength that inflation is starting to rise lead to higher interest rates.

The trend of interest rates directly influences the cost of your business decisions. The US Federal Reserve (also known as the Fed) is considered the world's most influential central bank. The bond market moves in response to the actions of the Federal Reserve and other central banks, and the other markets, stocks, commodities, and real estate eventually follow.

In general, lower interest rates are good for stocks and bonds because stock and bond prices tend to rise in response to lower interest rates. Higher stock prices improve your financial condition and your chances of getting loans. Commodities, such as gold, oil, wheat, corn, and coffee, and gasoline prices respond less to interest rates and are more influenced by supply and demand as well as the general state of the world's political climate and how these factors affect trade policy. Real estate responds to both interest rates and supply and demand for land and housing. However, after the 2007–2008 subprime mortgage crisis and the presence of zero interest rates for nearly a decade, the housing market became much more sensitive to interest rates than in the past. The persistently low supply of housing has increased the affinity between interest rates and real estate.

Be that as it may, even though interest rates rule the roost, each market also responds to its own dynamics and should be individually understood before you invest in it.

Political Influences

Politics often lead to market volatility. Wars, trade disputes, and military agreements among nations can affect all four markets because the global markets are still financially interconnected despite the changes in crucial policies that began after the 2016 US presidential election and are likely to continue after the 2024 election. Indeed, it is still possible for any investor to invest in just about anything, anywhere, at any time through direct investments such as stocks and bonds or through mutual funds.

Keep in mind that events anywhere in the world can and will affect your personal investments. News still travels fast. Money still moves at the touch of a button or a signal from a robot trader. All markets are still interconnected and still tend to move in a coordinated fashion over time. Therefore, risk can go from a very low level to a place of extreme danger in a few minutes at any time;

sometimes in response to the stroke of a pen at 1600 Pennsylvania Avenue, in Beijing, or elsewhere. Thus, all investors should become "experts" in their chosen investment fields to the extent that they can be aware of the risk of losses.

Evaluate and Adjust Your Approach

Do not rush; because you are young, you can afford to sincerely consider your options. This chapter has discussed creating your road map for making decisions, getting basic information, and taking your first steps to start your investing career. You should have the tools now to know if you're ready to become an investor and how to get started.

Remember, there is an orderly method for getting started with investing, with a beginning, middle, and end point. All along the way, the three basic steps are asking questions, letting the answers lead to the next step, and getting used to the notion that frequent evaluation is the way to keep things going in the right direction.

Writing your plan down, keeping it handy, and reading it regularly reinforces your goals and lets your subconscious mind do its job, which is to process information and eventually help you to make better decisions. By paying attention to the markets on a regular basis, you will improve your understanding of how they work, and by checking how your investments respond to the action in the markets, you will get a good feel as to what works and what doesn't.

The "Ready to Invest" Test

Before investing, make sure you've got these areas covered:

1. Have a steady income
2. Have money left over after meeting your obligations
3. Consider the effect of possible upcoming personal changes such as marriage, children, illness, or divorce before investing

4. Build savings before establishing an investment capital fund
5. Use a money market mutual fund as your platform for investing
6. Know your risk profile
7. Do your homework and work everything out on paper before investing in anything in real time
8. Invest in mutual funds and ETFs, especially in your 401(k) before investing in individual stocks

Once you've checked off the items on this list (and then double-checked it), you're ready to dive into the world of investing.

It's a New World

To set the stage for your investing journey, you need context. Before the pandemic, interest rates were relatively low. A thirty-year mortgage with a rate of 3.5% was common, and work and life were much different than today—and work and life may change even more in the coming years. Before 2020, an average person in their twenties and thirties with a steady job could plan on having a family, buying a home for a reasonable price, and working steadily toward retirement.

Unfortunately, things have changed dramatically since then—record low interest rates sparked inflation, leading to a rapid rise in interest rates and ultimately changing the entire global economic equation. When interest rates fall too far, inflation usually results because too much money in the economy is chasing too few goods, and this raises prices. The higher rates climb, the harder it is for an economy to grow.

How Pandemic Interest Rates Shifted the Market

The pandemic caused a migration out of cities into suburbs, rural areas, and the Sunbelt states. This demographic change and the economic and inflationary earthquake that followed fueled a unique round trip in interest rates, from close to zero during the height of the pandemic (2020) to a dramatic rise to 5.5% by 2022.

This shift in interest rates was caused by the Federal Reserve's quantitative easing policies (creating money out of thin air) and the simultaneous infusion of money into the economy via stimulus checks by the US Treasury. The net result was an inflationary wave, as supply chains could not keep up with the demand for goods spurred by the newly created money. Moreover, this series of seismic events simultaneously disrupted global supply chains, the housing sector, and the jobs market, creating an entirely new set of rules; a complete redesign of both expectations and the reality of how to provide for current financial and future needs.

Financial Markets Overtook the Economy As Wealth-Building Tools

During this tumultuous period, investors did better than non-investors because the stock market entered a multiyear bull market. Those investors who leveraged their stock holdings into other asset classes, such as cryptocurrencies and real estate, outpaced those who did not. Plus, many companies shifted locations from places like China to India, Vietnam, Thailand, parts of Eastern Europe, and the US.

It's Time to Think Differently

Financial markets are now a major source of income. The better the markets, the better the economy seems to operate. Because society has structurally changed, we won't be returning to how things were anytime soon. Furthermore, wars, the realignments of relationships among countries, and the growth of artificial intelligence (AI) have reshaped the employment landscape to one in which professions and occupations that were once seen as guaranteeing steady livelihoods suddenly became less reliable as the centerpieces in a financial plan.

In the past, most of a person's income came from wages, but due to inflation, many have resorted to supplementing their income by combining traditional income with alternative income-generating activities like investing in stocks, becoming landlords, or having a side hustle. Partaking in these activities creates a more engaged income stream.

Investing this way opens new opportunities to anyone who can adjust to them, and when interest rates begin to fall, investments will help those who invest wisely as the stock market rises.

The Four Pillars

There are four major components (pillars) of the plan.

1. Funding your investments via multiple income streams
2. Maximizing your 401(k) and IRA to increase long-term wealth
3. Leveraging stock market gains while developing passive income streams to deliver current income
4. Mastering the art of positive cash flow and credit management

Throughout this book, you'll learn a systematic, multistage approach designed to manage your current and future financial needs. Over time, you'll be in a more comfortable situation than if you had relied on traditional means alone for your present and future income.

Though results are not guaranteed, this approach is sensible, actionable, and practical. Moreover, this plan is attainable for just about anyone who puts in the time and effort to make it work. This approach will require efficient planning, consistency, and time management.

CHAPTER 2

Steps to Grow Your Nest Egg(s)

Every investor needs a source of investment capital. This is often called the *nest egg*, and it is the lifeblood of your investment plan. Thanks to inflation and the post-pandemic economy, it is important to have two nest eggs, one for current income and one for building future wealth. This chapter is about starting, growing, and using your nest eggs. Money will come into these eggs, earn interest, and be deployed to individual short- or long-term investments. The good news is that you can build each egg separately and then use what you've learned while developing the first one, which should be your retirement fund, to help build your second, or current income, nest egg.

Give Your Finances a Physical

Optimize your nest eggs by first taking an honest inventory of your finances. Make two lists: "Sources of Income" and "Expenses." Be as specific as possible in both. First, list your sources of income:

- Wages from your job(s)
- Bonuses
- Child support or alimony
- Rental income
- Interest income
- Dividend income
- Capital gains income
- Other income

Next, list your expenses. This list may be longer than the income list. Be brutally honest with yourself and include every possible expense that you can think of on this list. You can always pare it down later. Here are some sample expense categories:

- Savings
- Mortgage or rent
- Utilities
- Car payment
- Other
- Public transportation
- Credit card payments
- Student loans
- Any other loan payments
- Home maintenance
- Childcare
- Child support or alimony
- Insurance: car, health, home, etc.
- Out-of-pocket medical expenses
- Health insurance if self-employed
- Computer expenses
- Cell phone
- Entertainment/recreation
- Food: dining out/groceries
- Clothing and shoes
- Gifts and donations
- Hobbies
- Interest expense
- Household/personal care products
- Federal, state, and local income tax
- Social security tax
- Property tax
- Retirement contributions
- Investments
- Pet expenses

You'll be surprised at how much you spend and where you spend it. With this checkup, you'll find expenses that can be cut or savings that can be increased to create a sound budget and free up money for investments. Consider what you spend on subscriptions and gifts. Given the amount of free information online, some magazine or streaming subscriptions may not be needed. Maybe you're too generous with your online shopping for friends, family, and yourself.

> **ESSENTIAL**
>
> Do you really need both Prime Video and Netflix? Probably not. Be creative and detailed. Use as many sources of data as possible to do your financial physical exam. Include credit card statements, loan statements, receipts, and your checkbook. By including as many expenses as possible, you will get the most complete picture of where your money goes, and you'll give yourself the best chance of success when you start preparing your budget.

Savings and investments are included as expenses to illustrate how much of your money is already committed to this side of the ledger. Pay close attention to how much you are already putting into savings, your 401(k) plan, or an IRA. If you have zeros or minimal amounts next to these bullets, then you have your work cut out for you. But don't be discouraged. Every negative situation is just an opportunity for improvement. Consider making a reduction in one of your "luxury" areas, such as expensive coffee and chocolates, and putting that money in your retirement savings. You don't have to torture yourself, but maybe doing something like this every other month or once a quarter will help.

The Great Analysis

Once you've made your list, evaluate its strengths and weaknesses. Ask yourself if you're putting your money in the best possible places and, if not, consider the best use for it. Be fearless and honest. Keep what makes sense and dump what doesn't.

For example, if you're spending big bucks on a gym membership but don't have time to go, cancel it. You can jog or walk in the park for free. How about that "healthy" food vendor delivery that tastes like cardboard? Consider cooking simple meals instead. It's bound to cost less. Even one or two changes along these lines can make a big difference, and the fact that you've spotted a pluggable hole in your finances is huge.

It's a good idea to update the list you've made every month and see what's working and what isn't. Other areas that can easily be trimmed include entertainment expenses, such as movies. Go to a matinee, and skip the luxury theaters. Buy small popcorns and drinks, which are better for your wealth (and your health) than the larger ones. For a cheaper option, try YouTube movies. They're free, and you can mute the commercials. Also, books are cheaper—free at the library—and can be more fun than movies. Be creative, and be true to yourself and your plan. Once you've analyzed your income and expenses, it's time to make your budget.

Artful Budgeting

Budgeting, like medicine, is part art and part science, and it depends on the factors that affect your life, income, spending habits, and overall circumstances. The goal of budgeting is to trim expenses to pay off debt and leave money for saving, investing, or other financial objectives, such as maxing out your retirement and developing ways to make current income.

What Is Cash Flow and How to Manage It Successfully

Cash flow is the lifeblood of your budget and your investments. Your budget should revolve around positive cash flow, with the goal being paying your bill installments for the month and having enough cash left over (this is positive cash flow).

To achieve this, simultaneously increase your paycheck (work overtime, grab a side hustle) and reduce the number of bills you pay. For example, if you owe $1,000 on one credit card and $3,000 on another, focus on paying off the $1,000 card first. Once that's paid off, then focus on paying off the $3,000 card. Meanwhile, work on developing your side hustle, while avoiding adding new expenses.

Making Your Side Hustle Work for You

Your side hustle can be anything from driving for Uber or delivering for DoorDash a couple of nights per week. If you're a good writer, try your hand at tutoring. In the summer, mow a few lawns for extra money. In the winter, shovel some snow. Whatever you do, take that extra money and work on paying off your debt as you work toward positive cash flow. When you reach that milestone, take the extra money and save it as you develop your investment fund.

QUESTION

How do I find balance among my side hustle, career, and personal life?

Make sure your family is aware of what you're doing and why you're doing it. Most of all, if possible, don't let the side hustle detract from your other important responsibilities.

How Much Money Do You Have?

A good budget starts with knowing how much money you have available each month. You get this number from your thorough investigation of your finances after subtracting expenses from income. It's a good idea to calculate this for at least three to six months so that you can see some trends. Once you analyze a few months' worth of data, you should have a pretty good idea of where your money is going and how you can redirect it to better use.

Where Is Your Money Going?

You may discover that your finances are dying a slow death courtesy of small expenses such as grocery shopping, cups of coffee, beer, wine, and going out for food with friends. You should be sure to live life, but don't let these little things add up to big expenses, like rent or mortgage, car payments, and loans.

A daily $5 latte is $35 per week, $140+ per month, and $1,820 per year. You can make espresso at home for less than $250 per year plus $50 for an old-fashioned espresso maker. Toll road expenses can add up to the hundreds per month. If you work from home, you can avoid those fees. The "little" things add up in a hurry, and by finding things you can replace or do away with, you can make a big difference in your spending.

Realistic Targeting of Expenses

Once you know where you are spending your money, you can start making some decisions about where to adjust. Divide your expenses into sections. Look at the big expenses first, then look at the medium expenses, and finally look at the smaller costs. The numbers will be different for everyone. The "bigs" may be those expenses that total above $400 per month and are likely to include rent or mortgage costs, car payments, and maybe some credit cards. The "mediums" may contain insurance and student loans—these would be the $100–$400 group. Finally, the "smalls" should be those expenses below $100. The "smalls" will likely be the largest section and will include your bills for dry cleaners, babysitters, groceries, movies, and other things based on convenience.

FACT

Consider transferring balances to a zero-interest-rate credit card and paying it off before the rate rises (usually twelve to eighteen months). You will pay a "fee" up front, but you will usually have time to pay off the card balance at a much lower interest rate. This will free up money that can be used to pay other expenses, put toward savings and investment, or both.

Separate the three groups of expenses and add them up as individual categories. By separating them into categories, you will get a better idea of the effect each group is having on your finances and how to attack them. Some areas (mortgages, student loans, car payments, etc.) will be difficult to reduce or replace. But there are plenty of other expenses that have the potential to be adjusted. That means that your biggest chances for spending cuts are likely to come from the "smalls." But that doesn't mean that you shouldn't spend time exploring the "bigs" and the "mediums." Here are two examples of how to look at your groups, ranging from big to small:

In the "big" column, a $2,000 credit card balance at 20% interest per year, on which you're only making minimum payments every month while you continue to charge, could turn into a $5,000 balance in five years if the interest rate stays the same. If interest rates rise, you would pay more. Consider targeting the credit card debt first to free up money for saving and investing. If you pay that credit card off and save $5,000, it could grow to nearly $6,250 in five years at 5% compounded interest.

> **ALERT**
>
> Here's a tax tip that can help you save money and improve your budget. If you own a home-based business, your coffee, utilities, transportation (if business related), rent, homeowner association fees, and grocery expenses may be at least partially tax deductible.

In the "small" column is grocery shopping. A larger-than-expected "surprise" here may be from buying prepared foods, which cost more. Try buying fresh food and cooking it yourself more often. Snacks are also expensive and can be cut back. Sodas, flavored water, and coffee drinks add up too. Consider going to the grocery store more often and buying only what you need each time, instead of making one big monthly trip where you might buy more than you really need of any one item. One trick to help control your grocery spending is to pay cash and never spend more than what you have in your pocket. Sometimes that might mean putting something back on the shelf. Never have more than $100 in your pocket when you go grocery shopping, and you won't overspend. Set concrete spending targets on your choices and pinpoint the things that won't hurt as much as others. If nightly dining out is too expensive, cut the five nights of dinner per week to one or two per month and use the nights out as treats for making a good decision.

Intangible Benefits

Think outside the box, as there may be more benefits besides freeing up some money when you make some spending cuts. In turn, those "extra" benefits may have a positive impact on your budget. By cooking your own food, you can eat healthier. These healthy choices may later be reflected in lower medical costs.

If you spend $50 per month on public transportation, consider walking. Do you really need to ride with Uber or Lyft? Consider walking one stop farther before taking the train. Walking is good exercise, and the ticket may cost less if you buy it three blocks farther along. Try walking to work to wind down and transition to homelife.

FACT

It pays to shop and read the label. A 31-ounce jar of store-brand salted peanuts costs $8.99, while the 32-ounce jar of a popular brand costs $12.99. Four dollars is a lot of money to pay for an ounce of peanuts. If the store peanuts are just as good as or close to the national brand in flavor and consistency, this is an easy choice. It makes sense to compare similar products and to try different strategies.

Look for free stuff when you treat yourself. If you buy Starbucks coffee by the bag at the grocery store, there may be a coupon for a free cup of coffee at the bottom. That can add up to twenty or more free cups of coffee per year if you're a regular customer. You can order your coffee online and possibly get free shipping. By doing this, you save about $1–$2 per bag compared to the grocery store.

Shop around for your cell phone plan. You may find significant savings as often as twice per year when the plans do updates or service upgrades. Sometimes they'll throw in a free phone. A $20 per month savings will bring you $240 per year.

See the Difference

Next, compare how much money you will actually spend before and after your analysis and your targeted cuts. Whatever is left is your free cash flow—what you will put in your bank account or your money market mutual fund to build your savings and investing capital fund. Track this figure over three months and see where things stand. Get greedy when you can and add in more every chance you get.

And while you're at it, internalize the concept of free cash flow, as it will serve you well when you start investing, especially in real estate.

> **ALERT**
>
> You need a name for the money you will use to invest. Consider calling it your "investing capital fund." It's a good descriptive term, but it's also a sign that you are starting to get in the right mindset and becoming a more serious investor.

If you've made good decisions based on your financial checkup and your analysis of the data, you'll start budgeting effectively and should see your debt shrink, while what's left in your pocket grows every month. Even if it's a small amount, such as $50, it's progress. As you pay more things off, like credit cards, and you control your expenses while adjusting your objectives, your free cash flow should start to grow along with your investing capital fund.

Personal Finance Software and Apps

There are many ways you can track your personal finances. You can spend money on software like Quicken, or you can use an Excel spreadsheet. If you're trying to save money, the spreadsheet may be the way to go. If you want to plan or centralize your finances, software often lets you do your budget, do your taxes online, as well as write checks and pay bills. You may want to do a spreadsheet at first and then move up to the software as you get more organized. What's important is having the ability to track your budget and gauge your successes and failures so that you can make changes as needed.

ALERT

Your bank or investment firm may have free financial and budgeting software available on its website. This may be all you need to get started before you spend money on other software or apps.

Start with simple entries and add details as you progress. Balancing your checkbook and paying bills is a good beginning. It will get you comfortable with the software and help you to develop a routine. The data you enter into the software will also become the basis for your budgeting.

ALERT

Be skeptical of free online software from sources that you can't verify, especially if they ask you to provide your name, social security number, and other personal data. Now, more than ever, these programs are linked to identity theft scams or data brokers. Either way, you lose. A good example of a scam of sorts involved the popular Robinhood brokerage app. This issue has been resolved. But it serves as a great example of what could go wrong. In September 2018, the Securities and Exchange Commission, which oversees most of the financial world, accused the company of allegedly selling data about stock trades placed on its platform to high-frequency traders on Wall Street. Computer programs would then take the data and place trades ahead of the customers to make money off the transaction even before it took place on behalf of the Robinhood customers. More recently (September 2024), Robinhood settled with the state of California for $3.9 million in response to complaints about its cryptocurrency withdrawal and policy disclosure policies.

Personal finance software that you pay for or that your bank or other trusted institution provides free of charge is likely to be more reliable and help you get better organized, as it has built-in templates that can save you time and effort as you plug in data. It also has graphing and trending functions, which let you see your progress over time.

You can buy Quicken at www.quicken.com. Another popular software for budgeting is Mint, found at www.mint.com; for Moneydance, hit www.moneydance.com. For straight budgeting consider Goodbudget. As you develop your business, CountAbout may fit the bill. Unfortunately, as with all apps, there is always a risk of getting hacked. Also make sure that you look for hidden costs and consider any privacy issues, such as what the app does with your personal data.

Get Some Apps

Smartphones are great for keeping tabs on your stocks and gathering information. Indeed, for smartphone and mobile fans, there are plenty of apps to help you get started with investing.

Rocket Money offers both simple and more complex budgeting and personal finance tools. You can even set up automatic transfers to saving accounts with it. The simple version is free, and the advanced version costs $6–$12 per month.

If you're detail-oriented, check out YNAB (You Need a Budget). It's built on the principle that every dollar has a job. It can be cumbersome for beginners and costs $109 per year.

Pocket Guard focuses on getting your bills paid, lowering your debt, controlling your spending, and increasing your savings. It costs $74.99 per year.

Personal finance apps change, so consider visiting CNET.com for the latest information and app reviews. *CNET* is a highly reliable technology review site that describes and rates apps, software, and hardware, similar to *Consumer Reports*. If you can't find what you're looking for in the headlines, you can search for your topic. It really makes it easy to find the right app.

Develop a Progress Checklist

Update your budget every month, as early as possible after you have all the data. By starting early, you have a chance to revise it and meet your objectives sooner. Include data from your checkbook, your bank and credit card statements, and your receipts. Make the changes in your spreadsheet or budgeting software and consider graphing the categories over time. A picture really is worth a thousand words.

Adjust the List As Needed

Making a budget and investment plan is a fluid process. You may miss your targets in some areas and exceed them in others. If you miss the numbers altogether, don't be discouraged. Just reexamine what you're doing and adjust your goals. You may have too much detail and may need to combine some categories or rethink your priorities. There is no absolute way to do this, especially if your circumstances change. Small changes can add up, so look for easy places where you can cut spending without causing yourself too much pain.

Whenever something changes in your life, it will affect your budget. Life events like getting married, switching jobs, salary changes, having a child, caring for a loved one, and many other inevitable events can affect how you spend your money and will have to be adjusted for.

Leaks and Consequences

When adjusting your list, look for leaks, those little expenses that can add up without you noticing but can cause a good deal of damage to your budget. Spending leaks come mostly from impulse buying of things that you thought you needed at the time. Much of the time, this kind of buying is influenced by advertising and is best avoided because it can ruin your budget. If you fall prey to impulse buying on a regular basis, it will make reaching your goal more difficult.

The best way to plug the leaks is to only buy what you need. Make your grocery list beforehand and stick to it while trying to use only cash and limiting the amount in your wallet. Stay disciplined. If you buy things online, go to the item you need and don't fall for the "people who bought this also bought" ploy. If you're buying a book that costs $20 and there is an offer for buying a second book for $15, it's best to avoid the second book. Even though spending $35 for two books may sound good, in real terms, you spent $15 on impulse. That's $15 that could have gone elsewhere, like your investment capital fund. If you fall for this kind of thing on a regular basis, it will add up. Be strong.

Don't Quit

Making a budget and sticking to it can be discouraging, but it helps if you channel your inner Scrooge. When your goal is to invest, it's natural to want to jump right to it. But the hard truth is that you need capital, first to save and second to invest. And unless you win the lottery, the most likely source of capital is your income and what you do with it.

That means that you need patience, planning, and motivation.

FACT

Single people can make budgeting and investment decisions faster. Those with families must consider their family's needs. Ask for their input. Sometimes it makes more sense to buy the store brand of an item than to cut it out completely. Just by making this change, the savings can be significant.

Try to make the budget as simple as possible. If you have a family, make it a team effort. Reward yourself for hitting a milestone, such as when you make your stated goal for investing at the end of the month or when you pay off a credit card. There is a good feeling when you've made progress, and success tends to bring more success.

Remember that your budget is a means to an end. It's a useful tool. Don't lose sight of the goal, which is to have enough money left over at the end of the month to start an investing plan that will eventually lead to current income.

CHAPTER 3

A Quick and Dirty Overview of the Twenty-First-Century Economy and Investment Vehicles

The economy is a complicated structure with a nearly infinite number of moving parts. Still, as an investor, you need to understand how economies generally work. You won't need a PhD in economics, but you should have a good grasp of the big picture regarding economic activity at any time. Plus, you should understand how a particular activity will affect interest rates and the return on your money, whether it's invested in stocks, bonds, mutual funds, real estate, commodities, or a combination of asset classes.

How Markets Affect the Economy

Economists were stumped when a recession didn't materialize during the post-pandemic period of higher interest rates (2022–2024), despite traditional signs of a slowing economy, such as falling home sales and job cuts in the technology sector. This was because the stock market kept rising.

Traditionally, the economy has been viewed as a money-generating machine and its accompanying distribution system. After the pandemic, the financial markets became at least equal partners and, in some cases, led the economy. This is because, after the pandemic, more people relied on the financial markets for income than in the past.

Still, no matter where you live or invest, things are made, grown, harvested, distributed, and eventually bought and sold by someone at some point. The economy is essentially the sum of all those activities and transactions and how the money that travels through each transactional point is deployed. However, due to inflation, more people traded in the financial markets to improve their current income. For example, as illustrated in the section on stocks, if you make one good trade per month, you may net a few hundred dollars with that trade. Thus, depending on your finances, that sum may be the difference between positive and negative cash flow.

ESSENTIAL

Economies are still cyclical, which means that general trends can reverse at any time. More than ever, because of their effects on the markets via the changes in the amount of money in circulation, changes in interest rates and government policies are the most important factors. These changes are reflected in the price action of financial markets, which in turn circle back to the economy.

Whether you are investing via stocks, bonds, or mutual funds anywhere in the world, the basic behavior of all economies is generally similar. What's different is that when financial markets do better, so do the economies they are connected to, as people feed their stock market gains into purchases, which in turn fuel the economy. When the market rises, economic expansion generally occurs. It generates jobs. Jobs lead to paychecks. Paychecks lead to purchases. Purchases lead to business expansion, more jobs, more paychecks, and so on. A weak stock market causes the economy to contract, as people have less money to spend. This leads to job losses and, in general, the reverse of what you see during good times.

FACT

During the Great Depression, there was widespread unemployment, with the peak unemployment rate reaching 25% in 1933. In comparison, during the Great Recession (between 2007 and 2009), the unemployment rate peaked at 10% in October 2009.

Some facets of the economy remain constant, thus economic activity can rise or fall excessively with significant consequences. For example, because of record-low interest rates combined with extraordinary fiscal policy (such as stimulus checks), if an economy expands too rapidly, inflation develops. Inflation is when there's an excess of money available and not enough goods for purchase. That leads to increased demand and higher prices. The flip side is a recession, a period during which the economy contracts. This tends to be a time when there is too large a supply of goods. It is also a period when money, at least money in circulation that can be used to buy things, expand businesses, create jobs, and so on, is scarce. Prices for goods and services often drop, or remain fairly stable, during a recession. When a recession goes on for longer than a few years and job losses mount, it's often called a depression. A depression is a grim period of history where there is a great deal of suffering. The hallmark of a depression is people's inability to find work and the widespread loss of property in the face of rising poverty. After the pandemic, rising markets kept the economy going, but once markets roll over, expect a slowing of the economy.

Economic Forecasting Is Inexact

Economic forecasting is very difficult, which is why economists are often referred to as "dismal scientists." This inexactness, or apparent unwillingness of the economy to follow the "rules" in a precise fashion, is easy to understand because at the very root of how economies function is human behavior. Human behavior is predictably unpredictable, and economists, whose jobs are difficult under the best of times, often use computer models that can sometimes fail due to inadequate assumptions based on past performance of economic trends. For example, during the acceleration of the US economy after 2016, economists continued to predict low gross domestic product (GDP) growth for months when in fact, the GDP was growing at a much faster rate. Also, in the post-pandemic period, few economists have factored in the effect of a long-term bull market in stocks.

FACT

A bull market is when stock prices generally rise for extended periods, usually months to years. A bear market is the opposite. Generally, bull markets last longer than bear markets.

Moreover, while the Fed and private sector economists wait for data to make decisions, the real economy and markets respond rapidly and decisively to events. Events such as changes in interest rates and other economic data can affect the markets more quickly than economists can react due to the rapid dispersal and amplification of news via social media. This creates financial market volatility, which trickles into the performance of retirement funds and cash management accounts and influences financial decisions such as buying a new home or car. Therefore, economic trends, which in the past might have taken years to develop, can now become evident within weeks or months. On the other hand, if there's no major stock market disruption, economies tend to be more resilient.

Indeed, behaviorally speaking, when people feel good about life, such as when the stock market is rising, they spend money, fueling economic activity. When things aren't going so well, they spend less, and economies tend to slow. The hardest part of economics is pinpointing the exact transition points from one trend to the other. That's why it's best to keep your economic analysis in general terms while appreciating that it's nearly impossible to base your investments solely on economic forecasting. Staying practical and staying in touch with the markets and the economy is the best approach.

FACT

Bull and bear markets come in two versions: cyclical and secular. Generally, a cyclical market is one where prices are going up or down over the course of a year or less, while a secular market is one that lasts several years. A bull market in stocks began in March 2020 and was still active as of September 2024, making it a classic example of a secular bull market.

Above all, remain patient and don't fight the general market price trend. The economy is the hardest to gauge when the trend is changing. Markets can either anticipate or respond to a change in the economy and change direction accordingly. Thus, depending on the majority opinion of the market's participants and the prevailing economic data, a rising market will eventually become a falling market, and a falling market will eventually find a bottom before rising back up. Thus, the direction of the stock market matters because of its effect on the economy.

Ultimately, economic events develop in an unpredictable fashion and trends take time to develop and change. For instance, job losses when economies soften usually start slowly and may remain undetected for some time. Meanwhile, investment trends, such as rising stock prices, often overshoot the general trend of the data. But at some point, when the market realizes that the economy has changed, the price trend may change suddenly. The point is that the timing of economic cycles and markets is imprecise. It might take several months before a key change in the economy is noticeable, thus the reaction in stock prices may be sudden as the unknown becomes apparent. On the other hand, if stocks begin to falter, the odds of an economic slowdown rise.

Interest Rates Should Interest You

Interest rates are set by the Federal Reserve in the United States and by other individual central banks around the world. Each central bank sets the rates for its own country or region, and traditionally, the trend for all interest rates was very similar. However, after the 2016 election, and especially after the pandemic, central banks have been acting more independently. This is because, starting in 2008, and again in 2020, the Federal Reserve lowered interest rates aggressively to reverse the deep recession caused by the subprime mortgage crisis and to address the pandemic. In 2020, other countries followed the lead of the Fed. But while the US economy held up as the Fed raised interest rates to curb inflation, other economies in Europe, Canada, and Asia did not fare as well.

Because of the post-pandemic disparity in different economies around the world, the interest rate climate changed in mid-2024 as central banks in Europe and Canada lowered interest rates starting in the spring. By September 2024, the Federal Reserve joined the party with a 0.5% rate cut, reversing four years of rising interest rates in the US. With this cut, the Fed pulled the trigger without a full-fledged recession and while inflation was flattening out but not decreasing. This raised some eyebrows, as the possibility of the Fed's move reigniting inflation became likely. In the short term, however, the rate cut was a positive because it raised the possibility that borrowing costs would fall.

Congress mandates the US Federal Reserve to "fight inflation" and "maintain full employment." Economists, mathematicians, and professionals at the Federal Reserve study the economy and create reports that are used by the decision-makers at the central bank to determine how to adjust interest rates.

Although there is no set formula for when the Federal Reserve decides to raise or lower interest rates, the central bank generally changes interest rates when the rate-setting committee, known as the Federal Open Market Committee (FOMC), agrees that the economy has slowed to the point where lower rates are needed or when there is a danger of inflation and it needs to raise rates. The FOMC usually meets six to eight times per year to review data and make interest rate decisions.

Interest Rates Make the World Go Round

Interest rates, set by the Federal Reserve and other central banks, have a ripple effect through the economy, the markets, and your daily life. When the Fed changes any of its key interest rates, markets respond by adjusting asset prices. This can lead to changes in the rates charged for car loans, student loans, credit cards, and mortgages. The interest rates you pay when you buy on credit depend on the decisions made by the Federal Reserve.

FACT

The FOMC reports its decision on interest rates after every meeting, and the chair holds a press conference after the decision is released. This decision and the press conference receive heavy press coverage and usually influence stock and bond prices. Catch the action on CNBC.com. For more information and details on the Fed, go to www.federalreserve.gov.

The Federal Reserve has two important rates that you may hear mentioned in the news. The federal funds rate tells banks what interest rates to charge one another for short-term overnight loans, which they use to balance their books. The discount rate is the rate the Fed charges banks to borrow from the central bank. Changes in either or both rates usually lead to important moves in the stock and bond markets, with ripple effects on the economy. The first day after the September 2024 rate cut by the Fed led to a major rally in the US stock market.

How Interest Rates Affect Stocks and Bonds

As a beginning investor, the most important thing to understand is that the Federal Reserve and the major central banks in China, Japan, and the European Union have the power, by making changes to interest rates, to affect the value of your investment portfolio and your cash flow.

FACT

The price of a stock often rises in expectation of good things, such as future earnings, and falls when the company actually reports excellent earnings. This is often referred to as "buying on the rumor and selling on the news."

Interest rates have a dominant influence on stock prices, more so than the state of the economic cycle. Generally, stocks tend to do well when interest rates are low or falling, whether the economy is very strong or just getting by. This is because interest rates are determined using projections for market factors in the future. If interest rates are low or stable, stocks usually follow along, as investors buy to participate in the trend toward rising earnings and profits of companies. But if the projections say that interest rates should rise soon, stock prices might begin to fall even if the market is doing well overall. This is not a perfect relationship, however, as we saw in the post-pandemic period when stocks continued to rise along with interest rates. As a stock investor, your job is to invest in stocks, not in the economy. Thus, a big key to success for stock investors is to know the trend of interest rates and their relationship to the economy, and most importantly, the effect that relationship is having on market prices. In other words, if stocks are rising, you should have some money in the market regardless of what interest rates are doing.

Bonds, on the other hand, tend to do better when the economy is slowing or not doing so well. That's because inflation reduces the net return on bonds. The interest earned by bonds remains fixed, and fixed returns can't compete with rising inflation. If a bond pays an interest rate of 5% and inflation is running at 2%, the net interest rate is 3%. If a bond pays 3% and inflation is rising faster, say, at 4%, the return has been reduced to −1%.

Savings Accounts Don't Mind Higher Interest Rates

Rising interest rates aren't necessarily a bad thing. If you have a fair amount of money in a savings account or a money market mutual fund, the interest you earn on those savings will be higher as rates increase. Generally, money market mutual funds and savings accounts are low-risk investments, and earning a higher return with lower risk is a positive. If you have $1,000 in a money market mutual fund that is earning 3% per year, your return would be $30 per year. At 6%, it would be $60 per year.

Mixed Blessings in Real Estate

Real estate also responds to interest rates. Lower interest rates lead to lower mortgage rates, which usually attract buyers. Higher interest rates do the opposite. Supply and demand for homes, especially new homes, also respond to interest rates. Builders borrow money to finance their business. As a result, lower interest rates tend to spur home building while higher interest rates tend to do the opposite. If you are a rental property owner, higher interest rates may be a good thing, as fewer people tend to buy homes and may decide to rent. In the post-pandemic period, the combination of rising home prices and higher interest rates increased the public's willingness to rent in many cases.

FACT

The average investment portfolio has both stock and bond investments. The purpose of allocating the money to different asset classes is to protect the investor against changes in the economy. The goal is to have the stock part of the portfolio rise in value during a strong economy and for the bond portion of the portfolio to decrease any potential losses from the stock portfolio if the economy and the stock market turn lower. The amount of bonds in any portfolio depends on how much interest a bond pays and any person's risk tolerance. Remember: During inflationary times, bonds lose their value and may not be as attractive as stocks.

Crypto Comes of Age

Cryptocurrencies are here to stay, and they can be useful both to deliver current income or as long-term wealth-building tools. Bitcoin and Ethereum are where much of the money lives in this space. You can buy cryptos in fragments (called *satoshis* for Bitcoin) or as entire coins. They are still a long way from being fully legal tender in the entire world but are likely to become so in the next few years.

When you start, it's best to consider trading or investing in crypto via Bitcoin ETFs, as they are the most liquid. You can trade both spot ETFs, which follow the trend of Bitcoin in the spot market, or via ETFs that invest in Bitcoin futures. Spot ETFs are based on the current Bitcoin price, while futures-based ETFs trade on the expected price of Bitcoin at some point in the future, depending on the expiration date of the futures contract. The price trend is the same. It may make sense to pick either one based on which has a lower price per share.

When you become proficient at technical analysis, you can pick precise entry and exit points in these ETFs and set targets. When you hit your profit target, you can sell the ETF and use that money to pay bills. For long-term wealth building, you can invest in crypto ETFs via your 401(k) plan or IRA.

Important Numbers and Reports to Watch

There are many economic reports released daily. Taken as a whole, cities, counties, and states release reports on a regular basis. The stock, bond, and commodity markets usually focus on the national reports released by key agencies of the federal government. There are five essential reports that no investor should be without knowledge of.

The Employment Situation Report

This is the granddaddy of them all. Also known as the Jobs Report, this key set of data is released by the Bureau of Labor Statistics on the first Friday of every month and usually leads to some kind of significant move in both the stock and bond markets. It is especially important near elections or during heated political periods, as all political parties, including minor parties such as the Green Party or Libertarians, often make use of the data reported to further their political agendas.

The two big components of this report are the number of new jobs created and the unemployment rate. More new jobs signal a growing economy. The unemployment rate is a fuzzier number with some statistical nuances that tend to be negligible for most investors. Generally, a low unemployment rate is a positive. The Federal Reserve's September 2024 rate cut was influenced by evidence of the job market slowing, even as inflation wasn't completely tamed.

Consumer Price Index

Every month, the US Department of Labor's Bureau of Labor Statistics reports on inflation at the consumer level—or, what you pay when you buy things. The Federal Reserve uses the Consumer Price Index (CPI) as a data point for making changes in interest rates. If the CPI number starts to move above where the Fed thinks it should be, it may signal that higher interest rates may be on their way in the future. A lower-than-expected CPI may signal a slowing economy. And a falling CPI may be a signal that the Federal Reserve will decide to lower interest rates. The stock and bond markets pay very close attention to this number if it is above or below expectations. A slight fall and flattening out of the CPI's growth rate preceded the September 2024 rate cut by the Fed.

An important aspect of the CPI is that the monthly reports highlight the growth rate of inflation, not the full amount of inflation. For example, a 0.2% month-over-month increase may be seen as a positive, but that does not account for how much inflation has grown nominally since it last bottomed. In other words, what may be seen as a bullish growth rate is not the full picture, as inflation may have risen by 10% or more since it last bottomed out.

Gross Domestic Product

The gross domestic product (GDP) is a report released by the US Department of Commerce's Bureau of Economic Analysis on a quarterly basis, with revisions often following the initial report. The GDP is a big-picture item that reports on the sum of all the goods and services produced in the United States. It's a snapshot of how much the economy grew or contracted on a quarterly and yearly basis expressed as a percentage. A figure of 4% or above is considered a sign of a strong economy, while 2% or below is seen as steady or slowing, depending on the trajectory of the trend in the numbers. A GDP between 2% and 3.99% is considered sustainable, although that may change in the future. Two consecutive quarters or more of negative growth is the definition of a recession.

FACT

Due to the pandemic, the GDP in the US fell by 32.9% in the second quarter of 2020. This prompted the Federal Reserve to embark on a historic interest-cutting cycle coupled with quantitative easing (the printing of new money to increase the money supply and spur the economy).

The GDP is not always as big a market mover as the Jobs Report or the CPI unless there is a surprise. For example, if the markets were expecting 3% growth, but the actual figure is 5.2% growth, that means the economy is growing at a much faster rate than expected. Stocks, bonds, and maybe even the Federal Reserve would respond to this type of number. The type of response would depend on where the market cycle is at the time. For example, if the economy had just emerged from a recession, the 5.2% figure would be considered a pleasant surprise and stocks would likely rally, while bonds would likely sell off. If that type of number had been released after a secular bull market, it would be interpreted as a sign that the economy was overheating, which could have a negative effect on all markets, as everyone would expect a round of interest rate increases from the Federal Reserve. The potential for an unexpected number and an equally unexpected response is a perfect example of the inexact nature of economic forecasting and the predictably unpredictable behavior of markets.

Institute for Supply Management Report

The Institute for Supply Management's (ISM) *Report On Business* is a highly anticipated private sector report that often moves the market. Investors usually focus on the Purchasing Managers' Index (PMI). If this index is above fifty, it's a sign of growth in the manufacturing economy. A number below fifty suggests a slowing economy. The PMI has ten components that are placed into the formula that gives the overall PMI number. The ISM index components are new orders, production, employment, supplier deliveries, inventories, customers' inventories, prices, backlog of orders, exports, and imports.

FACT

The ISM was established in 1915. Its purpose is to provide information, education, and guidance to supply chain management professionals. The importance of the *Report On Business* to the markets waxes and wanes, but it does offer useful information to investors. Ahead of the Fed's 2024 rate cut, this indicator showed the economy was weakening.

The Beige Book

This important report is a summary of the information gathered by the Federal Reserve about the economy for the previous six weeks. It's based on interviews and research done by the Fed staff in each of the central bank's twelve district banks. The full text can be found at the Fed's website upon release. CNBC, Bloomberg, and FOX Business News all spend a good deal of time reporting on the information in each installment. It's an interesting read if you have the time, as it often provides detailed quotes and observations regarding current economic conditions and how they may affect plans by business owners. During his September 2024 post–rate cut press conference, Fed chairman Jerome Powell cited the most recent Beige Book, which showed most Fed districts' economies as weakening, as a major influence on his decision to cut rates.

FACT

The ISM also produces a report focusing on the service economy called the ISM Non-Manufacturing® *Report On Business®*. This slightly lesser-known report can also be a market mover.

Stocks, Bonds, and Mutual Funds

Think of stocks, bonds, and mutual funds as three different ways to participate in the fortunes of a company or, in the case of a bond, in the fortunes of a company, government, or government entity. The difference between a bond and a stock is that bonds are IOUs while stocks are pieces of a company. A mutual fund is an investment company that invests in stocks, bonds, commodities, or a combination of several asset classes. On the other hand, cryptocurrencies continue to evolve, while their current role seems to be one of a storage of value for money. As time passes, cryptocurrencies will likely evolve further into more traditional money roles.

What Is a Stock?

Shares of stock are pieces of a company that give the holder the opportunity to participate in the fortunes of the enterprise, good or bad. Stocks rise and fall in price and may also pay dividends. It can be tough to determine what exactly causes a specific stock's price to rise or fall, but in general, the price of a stock rises and falls based on these general factors: sales of the company's products, the decisions made by management, interest rates, and external economic forces. Only the stock of public companies trades on exchanges or through some kind of over-the-counter arrangement, as in the shares of penny stocks.

Only investors with a good knowledge of the financial markets and a good-sized portfolio of at least $50,000–$100,000 minimum should consider investing in individual stocks. The reason for this is that individual stock prices tend to fluctuate more than mutual funds over time.

ALERT

A bad earnings report could ruin a small portfolio of stocks. If you own three hundred shares of XYZ stock and it misses its earnings expectations, XYZ could lose a large portion of its value in a hurry. If XYZ is 20% or more of your total portfolio, you could take a big cut. On the other hand, experienced investors may take advantage of such a dip in the price and buy, assuming they have a long-term time horizon. Moreover, nimble trading in stocks is a great way to enhance your cash flow.

What Is a Bond?

Companies or governments borrow money by selling bonds. While governments fund programs via bond sales, companies often sell bonds to expand plants, develop new products, buy back their own stock, or buy back bonds that pay higher interest rates in exchange for bonds that pay lower interest rates. By selling bonds to investors, companies avoid or decrease upsetting their earnings streams and cash flows and are thus able to continue normal operations.

Governments sell bonds to pay off debt and continue to fund their current and future obligations. The US government runs on money it gains by selling US Treasury bonds, which are considered the highest-rated bonds in the world. Government agencies also sell bonds to keep enough capital around to continue granting student loans and funding other programs without depending solely on taxpayers to directly foot the bill.

Why should anyone care about bond yields? Bond yields, especially the yield on the ten-year Treasury note (TNX), are benchmarks for mortgages, car loans, home equity loans, and many other interest rates. It's good to know when bond yields fall, as it could be an opportunity to investigate refinancing a mortgage or other loan. Plus, lower Treasury bond yields are often bullish for stocks. So, if you trade stocks, it's important to your cash flow to know the effect bond yields are having on the stock market.

What Is a Mutual Fund?

A mutual fund is an investment company that invests in assets on behalf of its clients. Investors buy shares in the mutual fund, not in individual assets or companies, and these mutual fund shares are critical components of most 401(k) plans. As a result, they play a key role in your retirement. Mutual funds have managers. Some mutual funds have a sole manager. Others are managed by committees of individuals and buy and sell assets based on the votes of the committee. Mutual fund managers are licensed by their states, and their actions are governed by the rules of the Securities and Exchange Commission. Fund managers are highly educated, often in finance as well as other fields of study. They must pass rigorous examinations and are required, like all investment advisors, to attend continuing education classes and seminars. Companies that sell mutual fund shares to the public are highly regulated by the federal government.

ESSENTIAL

Consider buying your first mutual fund shares from a larger fund company that has been around for a long time. These companies tend to have better online and phone support and often sponsor seminars and classes for beginning investors. It's also convenient to buy your funds through a brokerage account, as you will already be set up to trade stocks.

Mutual funds offer a document called a prospectus, which lists the kinds of assets they invest in, the rules they follow, how they analyze the markets, their past performance, and, most importantly, what they owned at the time the prospectus was filed.

Fundamental and Technical Market Analysis

There are two ways to analyze markets: technically and fundamentally. The latter is the most common method used by investors, but it is not always the best when used on its own. Fundamental analysis is all about facts and data. All earnings and economic reports, as well as news and events that affect prices, are considered parts of fundamental analysis. A mutual fund prospectus, an opinion piece that you read on a financial website, or even a look around a retail store of a company that interests you are considered fundamental analysis.

Fundamental analysis is essential, as it will build a knowledge base about your investments, which in the long haul is an excellent thing. The disadvantage is that company fundamentals don't always immediately correlate with the price of a stock or the direction of any market. That's where technical analysis can help you make better decisions regarding the timing of when to buy or to sell.

General Fundamentals of the Financial Markets

Fundamental data (the fundamentals) is the information that affects market behavior and direction: news items, economic releases, and events in general. Each market—stocks, bonds, and commodities—has its own set of fundamentals. And while all markets have their own rhythm, because of the rapid spread of news via the Internet, all stocks, bonds, currencies, and commodity markets around the world are linked to one another in terms of price. So, regardless of trade policy or geopolitics, what happens in one market can, and often does, have repercussions in other markets.

If a positive US Jobs Report leads to a rally in US stocks, investors may see similar moves in Asian and European markets on the next trading day. If you own a mutual fund that owns Japanese stocks, there is a good chance that it, too, will have a good response.

QUESTION

What should investors focus on?

Beginning investors should be aware that currencies exist and that they may influence their portfolios. That said, beginning investors should focus more on budgeting, paying off debt, building an investment capital fund, and deploying it within the scope of our two major goals: current income and future wealth.

What happens in stocks, bonds, and commodities can also affect the currency markets. At the same time, events that affect the US dollar, the euro, and other world currencies can have effects on financial markets worldwide.

Fundamentals of the Stock Market

The stock market is where stocks of companies trade. In the United States, it is composed of three major indexes: the Dow Jones Industrial Average (INDU), the Standard & Poor's 500 (SPX), and the NASDAQ Composite Index (NASDAQ). There are other well-known indexes, including the Dow Jones Transportation Average (DJT), the Dow Jones Utility Average (DJU), and others that detail prices in individual sectors of the overall stock market. For example, there are specific indexes used to gauge the prices in biotechnology, homebuilder, and financial stocks.

An index is a group of stocks whose prices are worked through a formula to provide the value of the index at any one time. The Dow Jones Industrial Average has thirty stocks, and the price of the index at any time is what an investor would pay for one share of the index. So, if the Dow's most recent quote is sixteen thousand, that's how much one share of the index would cost. The Standard & Poor's 500 (S&P 500) has five hundred stocks. The NASDAQ Composite Index houses over four thousand stocks.

Company earnings, interest rates, and company mergers influence stock prices. External events, such as wars, geopolitics, changes in commodity prices, and trends in the bond market, also influence stock prices.

Fundamentals of the Bond Market

The bond market is much bigger than the stock market in terms of how much money exchanges hands there at any given time. It also has a much greater influence on the global economy than stocks do.

ALERT

It is said that bond traders love bad news. Remember that bonds hate inflation. Inflation happens when economies grow too rapidly. A slowing economy is the best time to own bonds.

While stocks often respond to economic trends, the bond market directly influences major economic trends. That's because bonds are all about interest rates, and credit depends on the general direction of interest rates. Generally, rising interest rates slow economic growth, while falling interest rates tend to stimulate growth.

Fundamentals of the Cryptocurrency Markets

The simplest explanation is that cryptocurrencies (cryptos) have no fundamentals. That is to say that, unlike stocks, bonds, and commodities, there are no special events that move cryptos one way or another. They move to the beat of their own drum.

So, your best results as a crypto investor are achieved either through buying into them periodically and holding on through ups and downs or by becoming proficient in technical analysis and using those skills to trend trade them.

That said, if trading cryptos is your thing, then you should learn the ropes well before adding large sums to a crypto account. In other words, start small and build up your positions over time, knowing that they will have their ups and downs based only on the amounts of money that is flowing into them.

ALERT

In 2024, the Securities and Exchange Commission (SEC) approved ETFs based on the spot prices (current prices) of cryptocurrencies. You can now trade cryptos through ETFs. Check to see if this is allowed in your 401(k) plans, as it can add a new dimension to your wealth-building plan.

Technical Analysis

Technical analysis is fundamentally based on reading and analyzing price charts. Beginning investors should know the basics, but, as you gain experience, you will likely appreciate the importance of price charts as a tool to make precise entries and exits into stocks and other assets such as bonds, commodities, and cryptocurrencies. A picture, especially combined with a good knowledge of the fundamentals, is worth a thousand words (and often thousands of dollars). Here are the basic concepts you can complement with an excellent tutorial found at StockCharts.com, where a search for "ChartSchool" will get you started on the right path. For a more hands-on experience, you can check out *Joe Duarte's Smart Money Passport* (https:// smartmoneypassport.substack.com), where trade details are described using specific technical indicators.

ESSENTIAL

Becoming proficient in technical analysis is extremely useful if you choose to engage in short-term trading. Consider becoming a proficient technical analyst, as it will enhance your ability to accurately enter and exit short-term trades. It can also be useful if you choose to day-trade. Entering and exiting positions efficiently is crucial to enhancing your cash flow and your current income.

Price charts have three basic components: prices, moving averages, and other key points that let you get a grip on whether this is a good time to enter or exit either the market or any individual stock, bond, ETF (exchange-traded fund), or mutual fund. Price charts can seem confusing at first. But by learning each individual component and building on that knowledge, anyone can know enough about them to get a good feel for whether the chart is flashing good or bad news, whether to buy or sell, and when to do it. Think of price charts as providing a timing component to the fundamentals of any asset.

If you're new to the study of price charts, the following sections give you a tour of the essential information you'll need to glean useful information from them. Investors who focus solely or primarily on charts are known as chartists or technicians. It's best to combine price charts with fundamental analysis.

The First Look

Charts are divided into time periods. The most common periods cover the price action over one year with each period of the chart covering the price action for a day of trading. The first look at the chart is often revealing. Just by looking at the general direction—up or down—of prices, you get an idea as to what the action has been over any period you choose. A rising trend means money is going into the stock. A falling trend means sellers are in charge.

Moving Averages

Price charts are full of lines known as moving averages. Commonly used moving averages are the twenty-day, the fifty-day, and the two hundred–day moving averages. Each moving average plots the average of prices for the number of days, ending on the last day plotted. Moving averages smooth out price action. A rising moving average is a positive factor for any financial instrument, as it tells you that prices have trended higher for the past twenty, fifty, or two hundred days.

FACT

The two hundred–day moving average is often referred to as the line that divides bull and bear markets. Generally, when prices remain above the average, the market is in a bull phase. When prices remain below the average, the market is in a bear phase.

Support and Resistance

Prices have important starting and stopping points. These are generally known as support and resistance. Support areas are where buyers tend to come in and buy. Resistance points are areas where sellers get the upper hand. Plus, markets that find support are usually worth considering or buying into because buyers are putting money to work in that price area. Markets that find it difficult to move above resistance are usually worth avoiding or considering selling in, as sellers are using that price area to sell shares.

Volume

Price charts also have vertical bars at the bottom that count the trading volume for the stock pictured on the chart. This is the number of shares that traded for that stock on that day. Good charts have different colors for volume on up days (usually white or green) and down days (red).

Generally high volume, up or down, especially over time, is a signal that the market is continuing to head in the direction of the volume. At some point, volume reaches extreme levels, which can be a signal that the trend is about to reverse.

Investors that combine both fundamental and technical analysis have a more complete picture of where they are putting their money. Perhaps the best use of technical analysis is that it can be very helpful in choosing when to enter or exit any market. If you learn the few basic concepts of chart analysis, you will have a nice base to start from and will be able to make more informed decisions about your investments.

Robot Tricks

Every market cycle has its own wrinkles, and because technical analysis is a visual pursuit, it will help you spot key market phenomena. Many robot trading programs or algorithms are based purely on technical analysis and use moving averages and other forms of support and resistance levels as triggers for making trades. Around 2009, people began to catch on to the fact that the robots almost always bought stocks at key support levels. It became a well-recognized trading technique to wait for prices to fall to a key moving average, perhaps the fifty-day or the two hundred–day lines. This frequent occurrence, the buying of stocks when they traded near expected support levels, became known as "buying the dip." Thus, if you didn't use technical analysis during this period, you would have likely missed many opportunities to buy before prices resumed their upward climb.

ALERT

Prices often consolidate just above or below the twenty-, fifty-, and two hundred–day moving averages. Therefore, it pays to increase your awareness of the price trend but also to be patient as you buy and sell when prices approach these lines.

Interestingly, the nearly 100% automation of the stock market is an early and underappreciated example of AI. Expect more developments over the next few years in the way markets function, especially as the explosion of regional data centers progresses. We may even see the New York Stock Exchange in unexpected places such as Dallas or Miami.

CHAPTER 4

A Close Look at Stocks

Given the history of losses in stocks, such as what happened in 2008 and 2020, you may not be terribly keen on the stock market. Yet it pays to think of the stock market as a giant pool of potentially accessible funds for both your current income and future wealth building. All you must do is learn how to grab your share.

Stocks are a good place to start when you're a young investor because these are the investment vehicles that, over time, offer the most potential for portfolio growth. Specifically, becoming proficient in short-term trading can be a useful tool for current income and improving your monthly cash flow. However, because stock prices can be volatile, they should be viewed as one part of a diversified portfolio. As you learn more, you should also consider what kind of a stock investor you may become: a trader with a shorter time frame in mind, a buy-and-hold investor, or somewhere in between. You may also find that all three approaches can be useful. For example, short-term trading can produce current income, while the buy-and-hold method can deliver dividends. Intermediate-term trading, holding stocks for weeks to months, can be a little of both.

The Exchanges and Who Polices the Store

Stock exchanges are places where buyers and sellers meet to transfer shares to one another. The best-known stock exchanges are the New York Stock Exchange (NYSE), also known as the Big Board, and the NASDAQ. Most of the trading is now automated and handled by AI-programmed computers.

Other major stock exchanges around the world, such as the London Stock Exchange and the Frankfurt Stock Exchange, are also automated. Smaller exchanges such as Arca are in data centers located around places like Hoboken, New Jersey. They are where most of the trading happens.

To trade stocks successfully, you must be proficient with sophisticated analysis and tools, as you are mostly trading against high-frequency trading (HFT) computers or traders who use sophisticated software. However, online brokers also provide sophisticated tools for active traders. These programs are your best bet and are often free of charge based on your trading volume. Some brokers may charge a fee for access to their trading program to investors who don't qualify, often as low as $100 per month. You can also subscribe to online high-end charting and trading platforms, which in many cases allow you to route your own orders, also for a fee.

FACT

To learn more about high-frequency trading, check out Michael Lewis's book *Flash Boys: A Wall Street Revolt*.

The stock market, just like all large-money enterprises, is a risky place where fraud is not uncommon. The Securities and Exchange Commission (SEC) oversees enforcing the rules. The exchanges and industry associations such as the National Association of Securities Dealers (NASD) along with state securities boards also keep things clean. The SEC enforces federal securities laws, investigates possible violations, and recommends solutions.

Its focus is to protect small investors from scams and unscrupulous brokers. Still, bad things can happen to good people, so you should be very aware of the risks before you start trying to trade your account in individual stocks.

The SEC's website, www.sec.gov, provides free investment information through its EDGAR (Electronic Data Gathering, Analysis, and Retrieval) database. You can find the latest public company reports, such as 10-Q and 10-K forms. These forms often tell you about a company's upcoming plans, expectations, and, more importantly, its concerns and potential difficulties.

What Are Stocks?

Stocks are pieces of companies. When a company "goes public," the owners transfer ownership in shares of the company to the public in an initial public offering (IPO). After the IPO, stocks trade on exchanges. Stock owners share in the fortunes of the company, good or bad. Shares of common stock grant the shareholders rights, including the right to influence company policy and direction through votes at the annual shareholder meetings.

Stock Indexes

An index is a group of stocks whose values are pooled together using a mathematical formula. As each stock in the index trades, its most recent price is processed through the formula, leading to the value that is reported during the stock market trading day and when stocks stop trading at the close. An example of indexing is the frequent value quoting of the Dow Jones Industrial Average, the most quoted stock index in the world. A Dow quote of sixteen thousand means that it would cost $16,000 to buy one share of the index at that place in time.

Types of Stock Indexes

There are dozens of indexes that quantify the value of groups of stocks, but they can all be divided into two major categories: diversified and sector-specific. Diversified indexes house several types of stocks, while sector-specific indexes measure the value of stocks in the same sector of the economy.

FACT

The stock of a company may be included in several sector indexes simultaneously. For example, shares of Apple are found in five separate indexes, including the NASDAQ-100 Index and the S&P 500 Information Technology Index.

The Dow Jones Industrial Average (also referred to simply as the Dow) is composed of thirty large global blue chips, or high-quality corporations in different industries. Members of the Dow Jones Industrial Average include software giant Microsoft and banking giant JPMorgan Chase. The Standard & Poor's 500 Index (S&P 500) contains five hundred large companies. It's considered the market benchmark because it has more stocks than the Dow, offering a wider view of the market.

The NASDAQ Composite Index (NASDAQ) has over four thousand stocks. It's traditionally weighted toward technology companies but is considered a diversified index because it also has biotech, banking, and energy stocks.

ALERT

The more you know about individual market sectors, the better off you'll be. This knowledge is most important when some areas of the market are rising and others are not. Keep tabs on separate sectors to concentrate on those areas that offer the best potential returns.

Sector-specific indexes include the Semiconductor Sector Index (SOX), the Biotechnology Index (BTK), and the Bank Index (BKX). Each sector index contains stocks from that sector of the economy. For example, SOX includes Nvidia and other semiconductor manufacturers. You can find companies such as Amgen in BTK. Banks such as JPMorgan Chase and Bank of America are in the Bank Index.

Types of Stocks

There are two broad categories of stocks: growth stocks and income stocks. Growth stocks such as Amazon grow their sales, revenues, and earnings at rapid rates, offering investors the opportunity for capital appreciation. These stocks can make you money when you buy low and sell high and tend to be companies either in their early stages of being publicly traded or well-established companies that deliver products and services that are in high demand. As the company matures, growth may slow and the stocks start paying dividends, which produce income. Income stocks, such as oil and bank stocks, are primarily owned for their dividend payouts.

FACT

Dividends are portions of a company's profits that are passed on to shareholders. They are usually, but not always, paid out on a quarterly basis. Some companies pay both a quarterly dividend and extra dividends throughout the year depending on circumstances. To keep tabs on companies that pay, check out www.dividend.com.

Inside Growth Stocks

Growth stocks are pieces of companies whose sales, revenues, and profits grow at a faster rate than the market. For example, if the S&P 500 index has a sales growth rate of 10% per year, a dynamic growth stock could be growing its sales at a 20% clip or even faster. This makes the stock of these companies very attractive, often for extended periods. Perhaps the best example of a long-standing growth company is Amazon.com (AMZN). A relatively new member of the group is AI semiconductor company Nvidia (NVDA). Growth stocks usually pay no dividends and pour every resource possible into the company to continue their growth.

The Income Producers

Income-producing stocks, also known as yield stocks, are often those of older, established companies that pay out a high percentage of their earnings to shareholders through dividends. The most common yield stocks are those of electric utility companies. Blue chip stocks, like oil giant ExxonMobil and tobacco giant Altria Group, are also reliable dividend payers. Altria's dividend has remained very popular over time, attracting buyers to the stock. It's best to own both growth stocks and dividend-paying stocks in any diversified portfolio with a long-term time horizon. For current income via short-term trading, growth stocks tend to be more useful.

ESSENTIAL

Investors who are just getting started should consider a mix of growth and income stocks in their long-term, wealth-building portfolio.

Preferred stocks are a special type of dividend payer that offer a higher yield than the common stock of a company and have a lifespan defined by their redemption date. Their dividends are guaranteed and are paid no matter what the company's earnings do.

Preferred stocks are a separate class of shares, distinct from common shares, the class of stock with which most people are familiar. The share class of a stock, either common or preferred, is determined by the company when the stock is issued to the public. For example, if XYZ has both common and preferred shares, XYZ common has the symbol XYZ when it trades. Its preferred stocks may trade with the symbol XYZ.A or XYZ.B. Preferred stock holders have no vote at the annual company meeting and do not have any of the rights of holders of common shares. So, even if you want to vote for necessary change, you're left out of the loop—that's the price of a higher dividend.

> **ALERT**
>
> Beware of dividend-paying stocks with an extraordinarily high yield, or dividend rate. If either a common or preferred stock has an uncommonly high dividend yield, there is usually a reason to be careful. High dividends often mean that a stock's price has fallen significantly and the company has not cut its dividend—usually a sign of trouble. A good rule of thumb is to check the dividend yield of the S&P 500 online and use it for comparison. For example, if the S&P 500 yield is 2% and XYZ common is paying 8%, you should do some more research on XYZ before chasing that high dividend.

General Characteristics of Growth versus Income

Growth stocks can be hugely profitable but also very risky. They tend to be the section of the market where day traders and momentum traders make their living. Thus, when traded correctly, they offer the potential for current income. These stocks can move, up or down, in a big way in a short period. One way to cut risks and build long-term wealth is to own a growth stock mutual fund that owns large numbers of growth stocks and can cushion the risk of one or two stocks that happen to have a big move to the downside on any given day. These funds are highly useful in IRAs and 401(k) plans.

> **ALERT**
>
> Fast-moving growth stocks are also known as momentum stocks. Momentum stocks tend to rally over long periods and make huge gains over the period. Eventually, they all come crashing down. Trading them during up trends offers great opportunities for current income. For example, if you recognize that XYZ is in a rising trend ahead of its earnings, you may choose to buy the stock ahead of the report, sell it before the news, and use the proceeds for a car payment or other expenses.

Sizing Up Individual Stocks

There are three capitalization categories in the stock market: small, midsized, and large (also known as small-cap, mid-cap, and large-cap). Capitalization is the value of the company in dollars in the public market. To calculate any stock's market capitalization, multiply the current price of the stock by the number of outstanding shares.

ALERT

Stock quotes are best through your online broker. Free quotes when you don't have access to your broker can be found at CNBC.com, where you can build easy-to-refer-to watchlists of your favorites.

Small-cap companies are companies whose market capitalization is less than $3 billion. Mid-cap companies are between $3 billion and $6 billion. Anything above $6 billion is considered large-cap. Blue chip stocks are those with very large market values, such as Apple, Microsoft, and Alphabet (Google). The definitions of market capitalization size tend to shift based on whether the market is trading at a very high or low level. For example, if the market has been declining for a long time, the definition of a small-cap stock might differ from what it would be if the market happened to be trading near its all-time highs. In a declining market, small-cap may be defined as stocks with market caps at $1 billion or less, while large-cap may refer to stocks that are valued over $3 billion.

Small-Cap Stocks

Smaller stocks can be fast growers, but they may be small for a good reason, such as their products are very niche-specific or they are a development-stage company and don't have any products. Many speculative biotechnology stocks are in the small-cap sector. As a class, small stocks tend to be riskier than large-cap stocks. They usually don't pay dividends. By the same token, a small company, which is able to expand its sales, earnings, and scope, may become a mid-cap, a large-cap, or a blue chip stock at some point in the future. As with growth stocks, owning a well-managed, well-established small-cap stock mutual fund can help to reduce the risk. The benchmark index for small-cap stocks is the Russell 2000 Index (RUT).

Mid-Cap Stocks: The Sweet Spot in the Market

Because they are usually well-established companies that have a track record, have stable earnings, often pay dividends, and tend to grow at reasonable rates, mid-cap stocks are often referred to as the sweet spot of the market. Still, as with any area of the market, mid-cap stocks can be risky, so always do your homework. The benchmark index for mid-cap stocks is the Standard & Poor's MidCap 400 Index (MID). As with other areas and sectors of the market, a mid-cap stock mutual fund is worth considering for your long-term wealth building.

Blue Chip As Large-Cap Stocks

Blue chip stocks, a particular type of large-cap stock, are the names everyone recognizes when they think of the stock market. These are companies like Walmart, Procter & Gamble, and Amazon. The Dow Jones Industrial Average houses thirty select blue chip stocks. The S&P 500 also has its share of blue chip stocks, as well as housing the five hundred largest stocks in the US stock market. Blue chip stocks are usually near the top of their industry, deliver reasonably predictable earnings on a quarterly basis, and are often the backbone of conservative stock portfolios. Large numbers of mutual funds and institutional investors own blue chip stocks. A blue chip stock mutual fund can also be a staple for your IRA and 401(k) plan.

Cyclical, Defensive, and Value Stocks

Three other categories of stocks that you should be aware of are cyclical, defensive, and value stocks. These categories include small-cap, mid-cap, large-cap, and blue chip stocks that behave in similar ways to one another.

Cyclical stocks are companies whose price action tends to change with the business cycle. These include the steel, chemical, construction, heavy machinery, and mining companies. Generally, when the economy is expanding, these stocks tend to move higher. A great example of a cyclical stock is Sterling Infrastructure (STRL). Sterling builds roads, bridges, and data centers. When the AI megatrend took hold, Sterling became a highly traded stock as its sales grew rapidly due to the company's data center business. Cyclical stocks can be volatile and often pay dividends. Always check before investing.

Defensive stocks tend to be relatively stable and often have small price fluctuations. This category includes utility and healthcare stocks. They are not immune from long-term down trends in the market, but they may hold their value better during down periods than most growth and momentum stocks. The utility stocks became momentum stocks in 2024 as the demand for power in the world grew dramatically due to AI and data centers.

ESSENTIAL

When looking at stocks, whether growth, cyclical, defensive, or value candidates, compare them to the market. For example, if the overall market, as measured by the S&P 500, has rallied 5%–8% or more in a few weeks, consider waiting before you buy. Aggressive gains by the market are often followed by some kind of pullback. It's better to buy stocks when prices have fallen some and are starting to show signs of stabilizing.

Value stocks are those that are cheap relative to the overall value of the market. These are usually stocks of companies that are doing quite well but are being ignored by the market, which tends to focus on momentum stocks. Value investors are very patient and often wait for long periods before profiting. Value stocks tend to be companies that sell at less than two times their book value. For example, in September 2024, ExxonMobil (XOM) was selling at just 1.91 times its book value. This was a classic value scenario.

Important Market Sectors

The S&P 500 is divided into eleven sectors. Each sector is given a weighting in the index, which is the amount of influence it has on the overall price of the index. For example, in September 2024, these were the approximate weightings:

- Information Technology: 30%
- Healthcare: 12.2%
- Financials: 12.6%
- Consumer Discretionary: 10.2%
- Telecom Services: 8.6%
- Industrials: 7.5%
- Consumer Staples: 6.1%
- Energy: 3.3%
- Utilities: 2.6%
- Real Estate: 2.4%
- Materials: 2%

You can see the areas where people spend big money. Information Technology, Healthcare, Financials, Consumer Discretionary, and Telecom Services add up to nearly 74% of the index. If you were to construct your own S&P 500–inspired stock portfolio, this is the model that you would use. This weighting changes over time depending on the economy and the general state of the markets.

Penny Stocks

Penny stocks, stocks priced under $5, are the danger zone of the stock market, where you can lose a bundle of money fast. When you hear about how Apple and Microsoft were once penny stocks, consider that Google, Facebook, and Twitter were not penny stocks when they went public. Overall, this area of the market should be avoided.

CHAPTER 5

Choosing Stocks to Buy

The ideal stock is one that moves steadily higher over a long period, pays a good dividend, and has all the characteristics of a great company. Because you are putting real money into a financial instrument whose price rises and falls, often several times within a few minutes, evaluating and owning stocks is complex and requires patience. Moreover, to be a successful stock investor, you need careful thought and a well-put-together plan that lets you pick winners consistently and lets you know when it's time to sell.

Five Points That Make a Great Company

There are five characteristics of a great company:

1. Great products
2. Superb management
3. Excellent customer service
4. Adaptability to current trends and changes in current customer needs
5. Accountability to shareholders

A great company has great products, great corporate ethics, and excellent management, and can communicate its successes and failures in a timely and honest fashion. A terrible company is usually marked by shifty management, inconsistent returns, and a lack of direction.

Analyzing Amazon.com and Texas Instruments

Sometimes a team approach is called for, which is why two companies are combined in this section: Amazon.com and Texas Instruments, two companies that started from humble beginnings to become giants in their sectors. More important, their rise to greatness was not by accident but was achieved through attention to detail, especially regarding short- and long-term company management and paying attention to both the needs of their customers and understanding emerging trends.

Amazon.com is viewed by many as an online retailer that pioneered nearly instant delivery of purchases to its customers. But while it's the dominant force in that space, it's also a media company via its streaming services and program production units. More importantly, it's a major data storage and AI-related company that serves both the private sector and governmental clients, while researching trends like AI or the data centers required for storage before many others.

And while Amazon rules e-commerce, Texas Instruments (TI) is a global leader in analog and digital semiconductor chips, and a model of consistency, delivering credible results quarter after quarter while paying highly attractive dividends. Impressively enough, the chips aren't flashy—they don't run video games or fly spaceships. Instead, they do the things that assist other chips in doing the glamorous work. Without TI's chips, it's hard to imagine anything in the world, or space, running.

FACT

Both Amazon.com and Texas Instruments had humble beginnings. At Amazon, Jeff Bezos, like other tech entrepreneurs of his day (Steve Jobs, for example) started his company in his garage, and through the classic story of perseverance, literally built it from the ground up. For its part, Texas Instruments got its humble start with its first major product being the portable calculator. And hundreds of billions of dollars later, as they say, the rest is history.

And while some companies (like Intel) strayed from their path and couldn't adapt to new markets, Texas Instruments remained focused on its strengths: semiconductors that are crucial to the operation of all systems ranging from automotive and multimedia to simple things such as toasters and blenders. This company built upon those technologies while expanding its market share through adaptation.

Texas Instruments built plants in the US to accommodate the increasing demand for automotive chips used in electric vehicles, while recognizing that the global economy had shifted post-pandemic and that domestic production and demand for its products would change.

Great Products

There isn't a whole lot you can't buy on Amazon.com and have delivered to your door within 48 hours. However, that aside, a significant portion of its earnings comes from data center operations, streaming services, and government-related programs, many of which are classified and together are known as Amazon Web Services.

On the retail front, Amazon has just about anything any customer could want. This is especially true since it bought Whole Foods Markets, allowing you to get groceries delivered from the comfort of your home. In addition, Amazon has agreements with GrubHub for meal deliveries.

Texas Instruments engineer Jack Kilby, in conjunction with Robert Noyce of Fairchild Semiconductor, developed the first integrated semiconductor chip, also known as an integrated circuit (IC). ICs are the backbone of computer functions, where multiple components housed on a single silicon chip work together to deliver one outcome. ICs are in all functioning electronics ranging from cell phones and smartwatches to computers and peripherals like mice and joysticks.

Without these two companies, today might look very different.

Superb Management

Aside from the results evident via earnings reports, the most important aspect of management is succession (what happens when a successful CEO or founder leaves the company). When Howard Schultz left Starbucks, for example, he was temporarily brought back when things began to fall apart without him. Unfortunately, after his second departure, things got worse for the company.

QUESTION

How can I tell a good investment quarter is around the corner?

A fun investment exercise is to count the number of Amazon Prime trucks you see on the street. The more of them you see, especially as earnings season approaches, the more your expectations of a good quarter should rise. Often, the correlation between the number of Prime trucks you see and the company's quarterly results is quite strong.

In contrast, when Jeff Bezos left his CEO post at Amazon, his replacement, Andy Jassy, took over. Jassy was not as well known as Jeff, but he was instrumental in Amazon's growth. He helped to develop Amazon Web Services in 2003 and became the head of the division. Amazon Web Services is the company's fastest-growing unit. Additionally, Jassy also developed Amazon Music. So, he was well primed for the CEO job and didn't really miss a beat, although it took two years before his efforts began to pay off. When Jassy took over, the company was struggling, as the transition from e-commerce to technology had been rocky, especially in the post-pandemic period. But Jassy looked toward the future and implemented his business plan. The stock bottomed in 2023, but as of September 2024, it had risen nearly 60% from its bottom after a 10-for-1 split in the price.

Texas Instruments' management style focuses on promoting from its most outstanding executive pool. It's common to see someone who's been with the company for twenty-plus years chosen as the new CEO. Once a successor is picked, that person becomes executive vice president and chief operating officer of the company, thus becoming intimately involved with the company's daily operations in preparation for the job. As a result, investors experience no surprises as to when changes at the top will come or who will be in charge.

Excellent Customer Service

Amazon's customer service is state of the art and is central to the brand's success, as it is built on accessibility. You can even pick up packages at gas stations or Whole Foods on the way home from work. Merchandise returns are usually simple and can be handled in person at Whole Foods or other retailers with contracts with the company. As of this writing, one of them is Kohl's.

Texas Instruments serves corporate and government clients about as well as any company, which is why they remain a leading global technology company through the decades. One of their most unappreciated acts is their use of plain language during their investor presentations and announcements, where they usually under-promise and over-deliver.

Adaptability and Innovation

To survive, companies must adapt and remain relevant to maintain and grow revenues and earnings. Amazon transitioned from e-commerce to a diversified technology company. TI became a company that produced integral parts of a diversified technological revolution, adapting its chips to multiple areas of the technology market, especially focusing on the workhorse areas of the market, analog and digital microprocessors, without which the technology we take for granted today would not function.

ESSENTIAL

A good company tends to under-promise and over-deliver. Both Amazon and TI usually err on the side of caution during their earnings calls. This can lower the price of the stock even after the company has beaten expectations in its most recent quarter. Keep an eye on the shares for a few days after this, as it may be a great opportunity to buy the shares on the price dip.

Accountability to Shareholders

Aside from running a profitable company that is tuned into customer needs, a great company must take care of its shareholders. You don't want to buy stock in a company that does not have the shareholders' best interests in mind. That's where listening in on company earnings calls, reading earnings call transcripts, and keeping up with media and analyst coverage of the company pays off. Both Amazon and TI have excellent reputations for enhancing shareholder value.

Think Big and Know What You Buy

To build long-term wealth and trade successfully in the short term for current income, your best bet is to identify the dominant trend in the markets, also known as a megatrend. Megatrends are investment themes that last for years; the leading companies delivering the products that make the megatrend expand are the best to invest in. Each period in the market has its own megatrend. In 2024, the market fell in love with AI, and stocks involved in this megatrend took off.

There are two ways to invest in a megatrend—directly and indirectly. Direct participation means investing in companies that make the products used in the megatrend. Indirect participation requires investing in companies that support the megatrend.

For example, Nvidia was the leader in creating AI-related semiconductors. Investing in Nvidia was a direct way to participate in the AI megatrend. On the other hand, the utility sector became popular because of the increased power demand brought about by data centers and servers housing the AI.

Both Amazon and TI participated in the AI megatrend—Amazon because of its Web Services division that houses and maintains data centers; TI because its chips make everything work. In this case, TI's power regulation processors were popular because of their ability to reduce power consumption.

Once you've deciphered the megatrend and companies that are profiting from this phenomenon, consider these factors:

- Does this company meet the criteria for a great company?
- What are the current sales growth and earnings growth rates?
- How is the valuation?
- How is this stock behaving compared to the market?
- Does this company pay dividends, and is the dividend growing?

Answering these questions will help you decide if you want to invest.

Is This a Great Company?

This is an easy one. Let's say you just bought a new cell phone from a start-up company called XYZ that's trying to expand its market share. You like the phone, and you start seeing other people buying it. That's the signal to dig more into this company as you apply the "five point" approach. Check for the presence of each of the five key characteristics:

- Great products
- Superb management
- Excellent customer service
- Adaptability and innovation
- Accountability to shareholders

See what the answers are. If the company earns the five points that describe a great company, then it's time to do more homework. As you research the company's fundamentals, consider how long you want to own the shares in the long term. A quick view of a price chart may help. For example, if the stock is very volatile, it may be more suited to short-term income via tactical trades. If it tends to move sideways or moves higher for extended periods, it may fit the bill for a longer-term hold.

Checking Sales and Momentum

XYZ's sales presumably come from selling cell phones and accessories. A good rule of thumb for growth companies is that they should have at least three or more quarters of sequential sales growth. Great growth companies deliver 20% or faster growth year over year in the early stages of their growth phase. Exceptional companies maintain or accelerate their growth at a sustainable and consistent pace.

Amazon offers a great example of sustainable growth. For fiscal year 2024, Amazon grew its earnings at a 64% rate year over year, while growing its revenues (sales) at a 12% rate. Those are the types of companies that hit the home runs. Sales momentum is the one metric where the five characteristics of a great company come together. If sales rates are stale or decreasing—but you still see more XYZ phones around—it may be worthwhile to keep an eye on the company and see what it does over the next couple of quarters. You may be catching it at a period when the sales growth has not been reported. In this case, focusing on long-term wealth building by owning a small number of shares, especially if the stock is rising in price without any news, could make sense.

Earnings and Revenue Growth and Cash Flow

Revenue, also known in investment language as the top line, is the amount of money a company collects on its sales. Revenue growth signals that a company is selling larger quantities of its products, that it can collect on what it sells more efficiently, and that its customers pay their bills, all signs of a well-managed company. Earnings are also known as the bottom line, or what's left over after a company pays its expenses, including servicing its debt. Don't confuse earnings with cash flow. Cash flow consists of the funds left over *after* paying the bills (not including debt and taxes), and earnings are the funds you have *before* paying bills.

Cash flow is the amount of money left over per quarter after bills are paid, excluding long-term debt and taxes. Thus, a company may hold large amounts of debt and still be cash flow–positive if it makes its debt payments on time and in the prescribed amounts. The money left over can then be distributed as dividends or be funneled into the company for plant expansions, repairs, or product development. Free cash flow, which is the preferred metric used by TI, is what's left of the cash flow after the company has deployed a portion into expanding its operations.

Ideally, earnings, cash flow, and revenues grow simultaneously. If revenues are growing faster than earnings, the company may have a lot of debt and may not deliver earnings or earnings growth for some time. In that case, you want to make sure that they are cash flow–positive. This is acceptable for young companies but not for established companies. Great companies consistently show a strong top- and bottom-line growth rate, with excellent cash flow. Ten percent or above is excellent growth and is sustainable, while 20% is well above average and signals a company with even better potential. When revenues and earnings start to falter, it could be a sign that harder times are ahead, and evaluating whether you want to hold on to the stock makes sense. When cash flow goes negative, it's a sign that bigger trouble lurks.

Valuation

Valuation refers to whether a stock is cheap or expensive. There are many ways to express valuation, but price/earnings ratio and price-to-book are simple, accurate, and easy to find as part of stock quote information at stock market websites such as *MarketWatch* and *Bloomberg*.

ESSENTIAL

When researching stock valuations, look at what you're paying for. When reviewing growth stocks, explore the particulars of a company like Amazon, a monster company with an expensive stock, outrageous growth rates, and market dominance, to a struggling company such as Snap. In September 2024, Amazon was selling with a P/E ratio in the high 40s, while selling at nearly nine times book value. That's expensive by any measure. On the other hand, its year-over-year sales and earnings growth were well above the valuation, which means that even though the stock is expensive by traditional measures, it's still one to own, given its growth rates remain stable or rise.

Price/earnings (P/E) ratio describes how much you are paying for every dollar of earnings when you buy a share of stock. To calculate a P/E ratio, divide the price of the stock by the most recent earnings per share. A P/E ratio of 10 is considered "normal," while a P/E ratio above 20 is generally considered expensive. It's best to understand P/E ratios as a measure not just of how expensive a stock is but also of what investors are willing to pay for a stock and what they are getting in return.

For example, it's not uncommon to see P/E ratios in the high teens or much higher for growth stocks that are delivering consistent returns. Let's say that a popular growth stock (ABC) has a P/E ratio of 179, which at first glance makes it expensive. On the other hand, investors might be willing to pay up based on excellent growth rates such as 20+% year-over-year revenues and nearly 100% on earnings, as the company continues to gain market share. Compare this to a company (OUCH) with a P/E ratio of –10, a clear losing record. ABC might trade at $500 while OUCH might trade at $6.00. Meanwhile, a value stock (VALU) with a hefty and reliable dividend may trade at a P/E ratio of 16 with a share price of $60. Investors are willing to pay for ABC's growth rate, while the main reason to own VALU is the $3.20 yearly dividend—a 4.7% yield. OUCH should be avoided while ABC and VALU should be considered.

Price-to-book refers to the relationship between the price of the stock and the book value, which is the value of all the company's assets. Amazon's price-to-book ratio was a lofty 27.5, while Altria's was 7.28. You can see the wide difference in valuation between a fully energized growth stock and a reliable value stock.

Also consider that price-to-book value can be misleading. Some company shares sell below book value and may not be cheap. In fact, they may be failing enterprises with sinking earnings and revenues on the verge of bankruptcy. In this case, it's the assets, such as buildings and other things that the company may own, that give it any value at all. Thus, valuation is only a small part of the overall analytical survey that you should perform.

Relative Strength

Relative strength (RS) measures a stock's performance in comparison to the market. The most common comparison is between an individual stock and the S&P 500. The higher the number, the better, as it means that your stock's price is rising faster than that of the whole index. When this happens, RS is considered positive. A back-of-the-napkin method of calculating this metric is as follows: if XYZ stock is trading at 50 and the S&P 500 is trading at 1,800, divide 50 by 1,800. XYZ's RS is 0.028. You can graph this on a daily or weekly basis if you're a stickler for details and spreadsheets. Investors.com displays the daily RS for all the stocks it lists in its daily stock quotes.

FACT

Valuation measures are useful tools, but the ultimate truth when you own a stock is the price. When the price starts to falter even in the absence of news, it probably means that something is lurking in the future and that the smart money is selling before the news becomes public. Valuation is also a more useful measure when you're holding the stock for longer periods to build long-term wealth.

As with any other aspect of stock analysis, you should put relative strength in the proper perspective. If you own a bank stock that pays a steady dividend and the stock is rising at half the rate of the S&P 500, you are not necessarily in a bad position. This is especially true if your stock is rising steadily and you are getting dividends. On the other hand, if you own a growth stock and its relative strength is fading, it's likely a sign that you may have to consider selling it.

Dividends

Dividends are important, but they are more important when you are investing for the long term to build wealth. Think of them as getting rent for being patient with a stock that is not moving very much. By the same token, you should avoid stocks that are either falling or not holding their value. If a dividend isn't enough to keep stockholders in the stock, something must be going on behind the scenes. When the stock of an individual company falls, it's usually because someone with a lot of money knows something you don't. Always look at dividends within the context of how a company is doing, how it's running its business, and how it's managing its future.

To judge the quality of a dividend, compare it to the following benchmarks:

- The yield of the US ninety-day Treasury bill
- The yield of the ten-year US Treasury note
- The dividend yield of the S&P 500
- The dividend yield of other stocks in its sector

Altria Group (NYSE: MO), the tobacco stock, has been a historical leader in dividends to its stockholders. In January 2025, the company's dividend yield was 8.05%. In comparison, the US ninety-day T-bill was paying 4.20%, the ten-year US Treasury note was paying nearly 4.6%, and the S&P 500's dividend yield was 1.29%. In this case, from purely a dividend-paying standpoint, Altria was an excellent stock. But from a growth perspective, not so much, as its revenues and earnings were flat during this period.

Know Where You Are in the Market Cycle

The most difficult part of investing in stocks is knowing when it's best to buy, hold, or sell. If you are not in tune with this reality, you could lose large sums of money, sometimes in a hurry.

Bull versus Bear Market

The trend is indeed your friend. The official definition of a bull and a bear market is a price gain or loss of 20%. However, most traders simply refer to a period when stock prices are rising as a bull market and a period when stock prices are falling as a bear market, without too much concern for the exact percentage. In a bull market, the odds of picking stock winners are significantly higher than of doing so in a bear market, where the predominant direction of prices is down. Optimally, when looking to produce current income from short-term trading, it's best to trade with the trend. This means that when the market is rising, it's best to buy stocks. When the market is falling, it's best to avoid trading or, as you gain more experience, consider selling stocks short.

Being a Contrarian: Know When to Buck the Trend

A contrarian is an investor who can spot the time when it makes sense to go against the predominant price trend. For example, contrarians tend to buy near market bottoms and sell near market tops, whether in stocks, bonds, or other assets. That's because they know that a bull market usually starts when most people are expecting that stocks will never rise again. This is especially true during recessions when the economy is declining and companies are making less money. Thus, their stock prices fall as investors realize that profits and earnings will fall due to the weak economy.

Traditionally, during these weak economic periods, the Federal Reserve lowers interest rates aggressively, and stock prices eventually start to rise because lower interest rates decrease the return of savings accounts and other interest-paying instruments. At some point, the economy eventually improves, at least enough for stock prices to justify their gains, and more investors come in, fueling higher prices.

After the pandemic, this dynamic changed. As the stock market became a source of income for more people, rising stock prices greatly influenced economic activity. That means that even though the economy may be slowing, if stock prices continue to rise, the economy is more resilient. After the pandemic, the most important influence on stocks is the trend of interest rates.

This was clearly illustrated when the Federal Reserve lowered interest rates in September 2024 when there were signs of a slowing economy, but there were no overt signs of a true recession. As a result, stock prices, fueled by lower interest rates, continued to rise. Moreover, the economy, although not as strong as it was during its peak, did not fall into recession.

When liquidity dries up, you get bear markets. Bear markets reduce the amount of money that investors can put into the economy, so the economy slows and a negative cycle develops. Bear markets can last for long periods, often years. When the Federal Reserve raises interest rates, it reduces liquidity. In 2007–2008, stocks rolled over after the housing bubble burst. Prices fell throughout the year with almost no respite until finally bottoming out in 2009. This bear market was triggered by the Great Recession, and it began when too many people who bought homes on credit stopped making their mortgage payments, reducing liquidity in the financial system. The banking system froze, and the selling in stocks followed.

FACT

Bull markets are hard-charging periods when stock prices rise on a frequent basis. Traditionally, during bull markets, the economy is growing and the outlook for corporate and trading profits is positive. During bear markets, everything is negative, and the general price action takes a bite out of your portfolio and puts fear into the markets. Prices are falling, the economy is weak, and the profit outlook is uncertain. After the pandemic, the stock market's main influence became the amount of money available to trade stocks, otherwise known as liquidity. A great way to keep tabs on the liquidity in the financial system is by monitoring the Federal Reserve Bank of Chicago's Financial Conditions Index (NFCI), which you can find at www.chicagofed.org/research/data/nfci/current-data.

From October 2007 to March 2009, the S&P 500 lost nearly 57% of its value. In March 2009 when the market finally bottomed, as the Federal Reserve made it clear that interest rates would remain near zero for a very long time, stocks began a rally that gained over 300% before crashing in October 2018, as the Federal Reserve told the market interest rates were going much higher. In contrast, even during the post-pandemic period's dynamic interest rate increase (2022–2024), stocks continued to push higher. Even such a dramatic increase in rates was not sufficient to remove the amount of money the Fed had injected into the system from 2020 to 2022. Thus, liquidity was never fully drained from the system.

Before you invest, make sure the market is giving you good odds of being successful in your stock picks by keeping tabs on liquidity. Here is a three-point checklist that will keep you safe when analyzing the market:

1. Know whether stocks have been rising for a short or a long period. The longer the time that prices have been rising, the higher the odds of a significant decline—if liquidity falls significantly.
2. Know what the Federal Reserve plans to do with interest rates in the short and long term and see how the market responds. Lower interest rates should favor stocks, and higher interest rates should lead to lower stock prices, but these relationships depend on liquidity. The longer the life of the bull market, the higher the odds of a major decline should be. Between 2015 and 2018, the Federal Reserve raised interest rates from 0% to 2.25%. This increase drained liquidity from the markets. As a result, by the third week of October 2018, the stock market was nearly in free fall when huge price swings in the Dow Jones Industrial Average were happening on a nearly daily basis.
3. Understand that even though you may buy the stock of a solid company, if the market reverses its trend and falls into a bear market or a significant correction in prices, your stock will likely fall along with the markets.

Technical Analysis: Trade What You See

Technical analysis of markets is the practice of studying price charts and using your conclusions to make decisions about buying, selling, or holding assets such as stocks, bonds, or commodities. Price charts are based on the general principle that patterns tend to repeat over time and similar events tend to precede or follow similar price behavior. This can be true at important market bottoms (such as July 2024) and significant market tops (such as August 2024) where the AI stocks crashed and burned for a few weeks, as well as at some time in the future. Technical analysis works best when it is used along with fundamental analysis. There are entire and very thorough books dedicated to technical analysis that you can find through various booksellers.

And there are some great websites that are worth getting familiar with. One is *StockCharts*, which offers a great deal of free content and lets you customize charts in a way that is easy for you to understand. It also has great basic information and offers tutorials, which will help you learn how to read and analyze price charts and get comfortable with chart analysis. At *Joe Duarte's Smart Money Passport*, you'll receive a practical application of price chart analysis combined with fundamental analysis, especially interest rates and liquidity.

The most important aspect of price charts is that they can help you see the reaction to the news. For example, if there is a negative news item and stocks rise, stick with stocks. If good news makes prices fall, then act accordingly.

CHAPTER 6

Buying Stocks and Monitoring Progress

This chapter is all about making the transition from paper investor to real-life stock picker. It starts with methods that offer you support as you move toward the point where you can fly on your own. After reading this chapter, you can decide which way to go based on your own risk tolerance and personality.

Investment Clubs and Dividend Reinvestment Plans

You can transition from paper investing to real-life investing through investment clubs, where you and some friends pool money and form a partnership. This type of investment approach is part social activity and part investment, but in the present, where markets move more rapidly and where current income and building long-term wealth are the primary objectives, investment clubs aren't as useful as they used to be. They are helpful in providing a way to round out your knowledge and make some friends, but they are not likely to be a great financial boost.

ESSENTIAL

The advantage of an investment club is that you can share the work and reward while spreading the risk of any potential losses and learning from the experience of more than one person. When things don't go so well, an investment club is also a good place to commiserate with others.

You can meet weekly or monthly to talk about stocks you own and monitor any existing holdings before voting on what to do next. It's even better if you keep in touch via Zoom meetings, texts, chats, social media, and emails, as you discover new ideas and make decisions whenever something changes. You can keep it informal or move toward a more organized approach. There is a nonprofit organization called BetterInvesting.org that shows you how to set up and manage your investment club, for a subscriber's fee. BetterInvesting.org gets you going and offers instructional blogs and educational articles that continue the education process.

A great way to make the most out of an investment club is to focus on dividend reinvestment plans (DRIPS). However, the club must own at least one share of stock in the company through a broker before joining the DRIP. There may be a handling fee to the company for guarding your shares, but there is no broker commission. This works well for buying shares of stock with low costs and is tailor-made for companies that pay dividends. You build up your position over time by buying shares at regular intervals and reinvesting the dividends. Reinvested dividends buy shares, or partial shares, of stock. If your stock sells for $100 and your dividend is $25, it would buy you one-fourth of a share. You can explore DRIP investing at the DRIP Investment Resource Center (www.dripinvesting.org).

Who Will Do the Investing?

Once you've decided that you are going to be investing in stocks, ask yourself who will make your buy and sell decisions, and will you use a full commission or a discount broker to build and manage your portfolio?

Traditional Full-Service Brokers—Why DIY May Be Better

A traditional full-service broker makes sense when you have a high net worth and don't have time to research and execute your own trades. Full-service brokers double as investment advisors. They work in an office and keep a book of clients, usually using research produced by their brokerage firm to pick stocks, which they then recommend to their clients.

ALERT

Beware of a full-service broker or advisor who only markets financial instruments sold by their company. These products, such as mutual funds and annuities, can have hefty fees and may charge more if you want to exit them before a certain period. Any amount you can save on fees and other costs is money in your pocket, either for current income or future wealth building.

Traditional brokers pass licensure exams and are registered investment advisors. They usually charge large commissions and may also charge retainer fees for managing your portfolio. Traditional brokers get paid whether you make or lose money. Depending on your contractual agreement with your broker, they may have full discretion or partial discretion to trade your account.

Full-service brokers and advisors tend to market their services toward wealthy clients, so finding one who is conscientious about small accounts can be a difficult task. If you learn the ropes, you can often deliver similar or better results with a good knowledge base, a few good apps, and a discount broker with a good platform.

Discount Brokers

For the average stock investor in their twenties and thirties, discount brokers make the most sense in terms of both costs and convenience. Discount brokers usually have branch offices as well as an online presence, but most of the business, including support (often by chat), is online. The very large discount brokers, such as Fidelity Investments and Charles Schwab, have excellent and comfortable branch offices where you can conduct business when the need arises. The branch offices have computer terminals for research and trading, product brochures, and helpful representatives. The representatives can answer questions, help you fill out forms, make exchanges between mutual funds, process withdrawals and deposits from your accounts, and set up appointments with investment advisors. Discount brokers also offer managed accounts and financial planning options for additional costs. The advantage is that you can do most of these things online and via an app once you open an account.

Online discount brokers offer the following advantages:

- **Control.** You can make decisions on your own schedule based on your own experience and research. You can also trade or invest when you are ready instead of waiting for your broker to call or text back.
- **Convenience.** With an online brokerage account, you have access to your financial information at the speed of light from anywhere on your computer, tablet, or phone apps. You can even make portfolio decisions

while you are on vacation. If the market goes against you or your stock hits a sell point, you can do it in seconds from anywhere. If you need to interact with someone, discount brokers offer toll-free phone access, online chats, and branch offices.

■ **Efficiency and Economy of Scale.** Full-service brokers are expensive, but because of intense competition, online brokers are much cheaper than full-service traditional brokers. Online discount brokers usually charge less than $5 for executing your trades.

The DIY Investor

Once you decide to be a self-directed investor, you will have to put some work into it. But it's worth every penny. You must accept the fact that you're responsible for researching, making decisions, and taking responsibility for your gains and losses. So, you'll have to become a multitalented analyst. Moreover, aside from buying stock in companies that you find attractive, you must figure out the market's prevalent trend and look for strong sectors by applying your analysis system, including the five points that make a great company.

Consider a Consultant Advisor

There are times when getting a second opinion makes sense. In those cases, it's good to find an advisor who charges an hourly fee for providing an opinion on your portfolio. This may be a financial planner, your certified public accountant (CPA), a registered investment advisor, or even a broker who consults with private investors. Feel free to see if family or trusted friends can help—it's much cheaper.

Your Buy List

Once you've set up your account, it's time to put together your buy list. Here is where you put together what you've learned so far. First, consider whether you are in a bull or bear market. If stocks are generally moving higher, it's the former. If the primary trend is down, it's the latter. Either way, there is no harm in putting together a buy list and keeping tabs on the stocks on the list. Spend time each day studying their price charts and become familiar with their daily price swings.

Home In On What's Working

The best way to profit is to follow the money to the stocks or ETFs that offer the best possible odds of obtaining gains. First, review the major indexes (Dow Jones Industrial Average, S&P 500, and NASDAQ Composite). When they are rising, the trend is in your favor. Next, get to know your market sectors (via ETFs) such as broad technology (XLK), semiconductors (SMH), financials (XLF), energy (XLE), and housing (XHB).

Then, list the individual stock components of each ETF and become familiar with their price charts. Once you identify the best ETFs, you can buy into them. If you're a stock picker, concentrate on the best-looking components of each individual ETF.

Finally, you can repeat this exercise with as many sectors as you wish. Over time you'll build your list. The more you do this exercise, the better you will be at picking the sectors and sector components with the best odds of providing winners.

Know Your Symbols

Stocks trade via their symbols. The New York Stock Exchange usually tags stocks with three-letter names, while the NASDAQ traditionally uses four letters. There are exceptions. Generator manufacturer Generac Holdings (GNRC) trades on the New York Stock Exchange. Texas Instruments (TXN) trades on the NASDAQ. Online financial websites include the name of the stock and the symbol when they mention the company in articles. The references are linked to charts and news items.

Use the Stock Tables

Traditional stock tables, such as those found on online stock information sites such as *Yahoo! Finance* or Investors.com, list both the name and the symbol. Stock tables also include useful information, such as the high and low price over the past fifty-two weeks, the price/earnings ratio, dividends paid, dividend yield, the recent closing price, and the net change from the previous day's trading.

Putting Your List Together

You can start with as many stocks as you like and then pare your list down to the best of the bunch. Include the stocks of the companies whose products you use. Most consumer product companies pay reliable dividends. Consult the daily "New Highs" list that you can find on financial websites such as www.wsj.com (*The Wall Street Journal*) and Investors.com. These are usually high-growth stocks. Include some value, growth, and income stocks in your list and pick a few of each to include. Buy small numbers of shares initially. You can add larger numbers later.

ESSENTIAL

Don't be in a hurry to start investing. Even if you're trading in real time, it's good to take baby steps and to paper trade often. Give yourself a few months to a couple of years to get your footing. It's better to be patient than to become overwhelmed and discouraged by trying to do too much too soon. Learn as much as you can about where your money will be going before you take the plunge.

Don't have more stocks in your portfolio than you can keep up with. For a beginning investor, owning any more than ten stocks at any one time is probably too many. A good way to progress in your ability to pick stocks and manage a diversified portfolio is by learning the steps through participating in your investment club and via paper trading. Once you get the hang of it, you can start venturing out on your own with real money. Also, practice both long-term and short-term trades on paper. The former are vehicles for long-term wealth building, while the latter inform current income.

Think about Your Time Frame and Risk Tolerance

For most people, investing is a long-term process where they are looking for profits months or years after they buy a stock. This is how you build wealth, and it requires a different set of skills than those used to produce current income via shorter-term trades. Building wealth requires patience and allows for larger price fluctuations in stocks you own before adjusting your portfolio. A price drop in a long-term holding can be an opportunity to buy more shares at a cheaper price, as long as the company's long-term prospects remain stable.

Whether your focus is short-term trading for current income or longer-term investing for wealth building, it pays to become familiar with charting and technical analysis. For example, you may choose to buy dips in long-term holdings when the shares fall but hold above certain chart points such as the two hundred–day moving average. For shorter-term trades, it may make sense to sell a position, especially to cut losses, when shares drop below the ten- or twenty-day moving average.

Know Your Exit Point Before You Buy

Whether you are a patient long-term investor or a rapid-fire day trader, it's best to know your exit point before you buy a stock. There are two ways of doing this. Long-term investors often set targets, both in terms of price and time. You may decide that you will need the money in XYZ shares five years from the day you buy it, and you manage the position according to that strategy.

If you buy a stock with the goal of making a targeted amount for current income, such as a car payment, you must remain vigilant and set both upside targets to take profits and downside targets for cutting losses. If you follow this price-targeting strategy for a short-term income-producing trade, you may buy a stock at $50 and set a target to sell it at $52. You'd be achieving a

$200 profit while maybe limiting your loss to $100 via a sell stop at $49. If you're in a stock for the long term, you may set your target at $60 and limit your losses by using a moving average such as the fifty- or two hundred–day line to limit your potential losses. Your long-term target price may be reached in three months or two years. If the stock hits the target point in a short period, you can sell some of your shares since they hit your exit point and let the rest of the position remain open and continue to move higher.

For long-term trades, if you choose to let the partially open position ride, you can set another target and repeat the strategy. If you choose the second scenario, you should remember that your original target price was $60. If the stock rallies for a short period after it hits $60 and then rolls over and moves lower, you should stick to your target and sell it at $60 on the way back down. You can perfect your skills via paper trading.

Executing Stock Trades

When you're ready to start trading, your number one concern is how to execute your trades. If you use a full-service broker, you'll do that with a phone call. If you use an online discount broker, then you'll be using your mouse or your phone app. When you call your broker, you wait until your order is confirmed. When you trade online, you just follow the menu instructions, point and click, and your confirmation is on the screen almost immediately. Become familiar with the several types of buy and sell orders, and consider which one fits your strategy best before you start to trade actively. As a beginning investor, you may be best served by using market orders and considering the use of a sell stop. As you gain more experience, you can consider more specific order types. You can also set price alarms that alert you when your stock has reached the price where you want to enter or exit.

Market Orders

This is the most common order used by individual investors. It means you want to buy or sell stocks at the current market price, or the going rate.

Your order will be executed at the prevailing price when it hits the trading floor or the market maker. You will see two prices quoted, bid (the buy price) and ask (the sell price). The difference between the two prices is the spread. An example of Apple shares' bid price may be $225.49, while the ask price may be $225.51. The spread is 0.02.

Most trades are electronically executed by intermediaries: market makers, mostly through AI-controlled algorithms, and floor traders are the intermediaries in the transaction. They pocket a piece of the spread as commission. High-frequency traders are always there ahead of you and will also affect the price you pay for any stock, usually to their advantage. It sounds unfair, but that's life in the stock market. Stock prices are digital, and the price you pay for a stock may be different than the bid and ask, due to the interaction of all the middlemen and the often rapid flow of orders.

Less liquid stocks, which are stocks that trade less frequently, may have wider spreads. The closer the spread, the better your price is likely to be, even with all the intermediary flimflam. Low-volume stocks can be difficult to buy but are usually more difficult to sell at a price that is favorable, especially if you have a small number of shares.

Limit Orders

You use limit orders when you don't want to buy a stock for more or sell a stock for less than a predetermined price; they can be placed as day orders or good 'til canceled (GTC) orders. GTC orders have a better chance of being filled because day orders expire at the end of the trading day in which you place them.

A limit order lets you attempt to buy or sell a stock at a specific price. For example, if Apple is trading near $225 and you want to buy one hundred shares only when the price falls to $220, you place a limit order for one hundred shares of Apple at $220 per share. Your order may not get filled, as the stock may not fall to $220. It may also get filled at the first available lower price if the stock falls through $220. What you know is that your order will not get filled above $220.

If you bought one hundred shares of Apple at $220 and it climbs to $250, you might want to sell it at $255. By placing a limit sell order for one hundred shares at $255, you know that your order will fill at least at $255 if the stock hits the price point. It may sell for a higher price, but it won't sell for less than $255.

Stop Orders

Stop orders to sell, also known as stop loss orders, are used to limit losses. If you bought Microsoft at $400 but don't want to take a big loss if the stock starts to flounder, you can set a stop loss, in dollar amounts or percentage amounts, below the price. For example, your stop order may be to sell one hundred shares of Microsoft at $395. This limits your potential loss if the stock drops to $395 or below. Once your stock hits the stop point, it becomes a market order.

You can use stop orders to buy when you expect a stock to trade higher. If Microsoft is trading at $385 but is gathering steam, you may want to put in a stop order to buy one hundred shares at $390. When the price hits $390, your order becomes a market order and may be filled above or below your stop price depending on market conditions.

Managing Your Money

When managing your money, it's best to separate your goals, as short-term trades for current income require different tactics than long-term trades for wealth building. In both cases, especially when you're trading for current income, think in terms of dollar amounts, instead of number of shares. When you're trading for short-term income, your goal is to maximize your potential gain without taking a major loss and crippling your trading account. A useful rule is to only use a portion of your account for each potential income-producing trade. Thus, if your account consists of $2,000, you may decide to risk a maximum of $800 per trade and limit your exposure to one trade at a time.

For longer-term wealth-building trades, the concept is similar, although how much you risk should be based on the amount of money in your account. If you buy one hundred shares of a $10 stock, it will cost you $1,000 plus commission. If you buy ten shares of a $100 stock, it will also cost you $1,000 plus commission. If you have $10,000 in your wealth-building account and you want to own ten different company stocks, think about how you will divide the money among the ten stocks, and consider commission costs as well. If your commission is $4.95, and you buy ten different lots of stock of varying share size, your commission will be $4.95 × 10 = $49.50 to buy and an equal amount if you were to sell them all at once.

Even if you're well off and experienced, it's always a good idea to count every penny. But when you're just starting out, you should work out your costs on paper before you make a trade. This will train you for the future, especially as you progress into more complex, shorter-term trading strategies where money management is even more crucial.

Keeping Up with Your Stocks

Develop a monitoring routine based on your personality and schedule. Checking your portfolio may be as easy as logging on periodically to see how things are going. The key is to be consistent and to be consciously involved. If you decide to check your portfolio every night, then do it every night. If you decide to check your portfolio once in the morning, once at lunch, and a third time an hour before the market closes daily, then that's your routine. The key is to figure out what works for you and to be consistent.

A more casual approach may be useful for your longer-term wealth-building account. However, when you're executing short-term trades for current income, it's important to stay connected to the trade. If you can't be watching your progress live, you should set alerts to tell you when your stock has reached your target price or whether you've been stopped out. By staying connected, you're able to keep your trading account's balance healthy.

How to Pay Yourself Now

Remember, the goal of short-term trading for current income is to use your trading profits in your non-retirement account to offset some of your expenses. For example, it's a good ideal to set a goal, perhaps of making $400 to $500 extra per month via your stock trades. Set a tangible goal such as using that money for your car payment, paying down a credit card, making regular mortgage or student loan payments, or contributing to your IRA. Don't put too much pressure on yourself to achieve this level of trading at the beginning, but it's something that you can add to your list of goals for the future. And if it takes you three months to get there, that's a victory. When you achieve your goal, put that money where you initially targeted it.

ESSENTIAL

A good way to monitor your stocks throughout the day is to use the CNBC app. You can set up several watchlists with up to twenty-five stocks in each. Group them by sector or class, such as healthcare, tech, and energy. You can even have a separate watchlist for ETFs.

When evaluating your portfolio's performance, ask these questions:

- Are your long-term investments keeping up with the market trend? This is especially important in rising markets where you want to see your stocks, ETFs, and mutual funds rise along with the trend.
- Are you modeling your short-term income-producing trades after the current trend? If the market is rising, you should be buying stocks or ETFs. When the market is falling, it's best to stand aside. Once you gain experience, you may wish to target the short side of the market. As usual, because short selling is risky, you should get comfortable in the practice via paper trading.

- Are your investments keeping up with your plan and goals? Make sure to look at this during your monthly or quarterly check. Compare your portfolio to both your goals and the market trend.
- Is it time to make changes? Have your goals changed? Is your portfolio not meeting your expectations? Should you talk to an advisor or change your strategy? These are all important aspects of portfolio management that should be part of your arsenal.

The Buyer's Checklist

Here is a brief recap of successful investing habits:

- Start slowly via an investment club or a dividend reinvestment plan and paper trade.
- Decide on one of the broker styles.
- Write down your goals and develop a research routine.
- Compartmentalize your short-term skills for income production and your long-term skills for long-term wealth production.
- Put together a buy list.
- Focus on what's working in any market.
- Decide how you will sell a stock before you buy it.
- Understand the different kinds of orders to buy and sell your stocks.
- Develop a portfolio management and monitoring routine for both short-term income production and long-term wealth building.
- Review and adjust your method as needed based on goals and results.

Keeping these habits in mind will lead you to success.

CHAPTER 7

Bonds: The Glue That Holds Financial Markets Together

Talk of bonds is boring at parties, but as an investor, you should know that bonds are the glue that holds the financial markets together. Think of it this way: Bonds offer governments and companies the ability to expand for the future through borrowings, so without bonds, the global economy would be a totally different place—one of much slower growth and fewer prospects. In this chapter, you'll learn why bonds are important and how they make sense both for your portfolio and to gauge the ease of borrowing money. These investment types are quite useful to your DIY-centric investing approach, especially due to their contribution to your ability to analyze the investment climate and to know when to make critical decisions about when and how to invest.

What Is a Bond?

A bond is a loan packaged as a marketable security. When investors buy bonds, they are loaning money to a company, a municipality, or a sovereign government with the expectation that the money will be paid back at a predetermined date in the future, along with interest. Bonds usually pay interest to the bondholder, either in installments or as one lump sum when the bond matures. Most pay interest semiannually or annually. You can buy bonds directly as new issues from the issuer, or you can buy them through traders, dealers, or brokers in the secondary market. The market sets bond prices as supply and demand changes.

ESSENTIAL

Bond prices can move in the opposite direction of stock prices, especially US Treasury bonds, which are often seen as "safe" at times of market volatility or geopolitical tensions. This makes bonds an essential part of a diversified portfolio as rising bond prices can cushion any potential losses in stocks.

The major reason investors buy bonds is usually the interest portion of the bond. In exchange for the loan, the issuer agrees to pay the investor interest at regular intervals as well as return the original investment at maturity. Bonds are usually sold in discrete increments (multiples of $1,000). This is the par value or face value. Bond maturities are divided into short-, intermediate-, and long-term periods. Short-term bonds mature in less than five years. Intermediate-term bonds mature in five to ten years, while bonds with maturities above ten years are considered long-term. Bonds with maturities beyond twenty to thirty years are rare but do exist. Generally, bonds with longer maturities pay the highest interest rates due to the higher risk potential. Bond prices and yields (the current effective interest rate) fluctuate based on any current market forces and trends. Rising bond prices lead to lower yields.

Bonds have a date of final maturity. That's when your initial investment, the principal, is returned. A callable bond is a special kind of bond that can be redeemed before the final maturity. If a bond is called, you get your money before the final maturity date. You still get your whole principal if the bond is called. You just don't collect the interest for as long as you expected, so you get less than you expected when you bought the bond. However, callable bonds often pay a higher interest rate, which makes them worth the risk of early termination. The issuer must inform investors whether a bond is callable before the sale in the prospectus.

Why Do Bonds Rule the World?

While stocks get all the press and publicity, it's the hardworking bonds that pay the bills. Bonds allow the issuers to finance projects and manage expenses sooner than if they had waited until they saved enough money to do so. So next time you see a big highway project, or a new factory being built, think about bonds as providing much, if not all, of the financial support for the task.

Comparing Bonds versus Stocks

A stock is a piece of a company. Stock investors, as partial owners, participate in the fortunes of the company. A bondholder is a lender. Lenders get paid unless the issuer goes bankrupt. This is why bonds are also known as fixed-income investments. As a bondholder, you know how much you will earn unless you sell the bond before maturity. For example, if you buy a one-year maturity $1,000 bond that pays 5%, you will receive $50 of interest in that year, and you will receive your $1,000 back at maturity.

Corporate versus Treasury Bonds

A US Treasury bond is considered the safest bond in the world. That's because, even though the US government pays its bills with borrowed money, it will always pay its bills unless something very drastic happens to the economy and the world stops buying US bonds. While this is possible, it's highly unlikely. That's why, whenever there is significant trouble in the world, such as a major war or an economic crisis, investors flock to US Treasury bonds. As they buy these bonds, prices rise and market interest rates drop.

Corporate bonds differ because they usually pay higher interest rates than Treasury bonds while offering a higher risk of default. While the US government has theoretically come close to a default on its bonds, especially during government shutdowns, it has never defaulted. Corporations, on the other hand, have defaulted on their bonds. However, this is not very common, except during difficult economic periods such as the 2007–2009 economic recession.

What Makes Bonds Risky?

Bond risks are different than stock risks. The biggest risk for bonds is the possibility that you won't get paid and the issuer defaults. Other risks include inflation, the general state of the economy, credit risk, central bank interest rate risk, and income risk.

Credit Risk: Risk of Default

Defaults are somewhat rare but not impossible. When a company or government goes bankrupt, bondholders are first in line to collect on whatever is left after the legal haggling is done. But it often turns out that if there is anything to collect, it's a lot less than what you were expecting. When a government or a corporation defaults, it sets off a flurry of legal activity that can take years to resolve. During that period, there is no certainty that investors will ever recoup any of their investments. That's why, as a DIY investor, it's best to focus on the highest-quality bonds. The defaulting party would need to obtain new lines of financing and restructure the terms of the debt by extending the bond's life, reducing the interest rate it will pay, or both before the bondholders could be paid.

Inflation and Economic Risk

Inflation is the bitter enemy of fixed-income investments. If you depend solely on the income from bonds, you lose money when prices of goods and services rise since your income can't grow as fast as inflation. This occurs even if your interest rate is higher than the rate of inflation. For example, if your bond pays 5% and inflation is growing at 3%, your net return is 2%. If inflation rises to 4%, your net return is only 1%. This is why bonds are good investments during periods of slow or falling economic growth. The exception is when inflation is rising during periods of slow economic growth, known as stagflation. If the economy is growing rapidly, it may be accompanied by inflation. In this case, bond prices will fall and the purchasing power of bond-generated income will follow.

Interest Rate and Price Risk

Interest and price risk are very important if you want to sell a bond before its maturity. As a DIY bondholder, you would opt to sell only if the bond's price has appreciated significantly since you purchased it, enough for the sale to provide enough money to cover the cost of the interest payments you will miss. Otherwise, the best strategy is to hold the bond until maturity and collect the interest throughout the entire maturity. If you bought a bond at $1,000 par with a yield of 5% and the price falls to $900, the market interest rate will rise, maybe to 5.03%, but your bond would be worth less than when you bought it. Thus, if you sold your bond under these circumstances, you may lose some of your principal. If you have held the bond for a long enough period where it has paid interest, you may be able to sell it at a lower price and break even or lose barely any money. The flip side is that if the price of the bond rises, you may be able to sell it at a higher price. To make sense of this, calculate how much interest you would gain by the time the bond matures and add this figure to the current market price of the bond. If your goal is to hold the bond until maturity, your price and rate risk is usually minimal, unless the bond defaults.

Managing Income Risk

There is no substitute for planning as you structure your bond portfolio, especially when it comes to inflation risk. To diminish the potential losses from inflation, you should have the right mix of bonds in the portfolio. For example, an ultra-safe, low-maintenance bond portfolio may exclusively use US Treasury bonds or mutual funds that invest in US Treasury bonds in a mixture of 50% intermediate-term bonds, 30% short-term bonds, and the remaining 20% in inflation-protected bonds called TIPS.

A second approach is to use a technique called laddering, where you buy bonds of different maturities and stagger them so that your income stream remains stable. As one bond matures, you roll over the proceeds into the next bond. The key step in laddering a portfolio is to know the current inflation rate and to structure the portfolio so that the overall interest rate it provides remains above the inflation rate. An excellent tutorial on bond laddering can be found on the Fidelity Investments website.

Using Bond Yields As Stock Market Indicators

The US Treasury bond market isn't just an investment class; it's a marvelous indicator that you can use as a guide for choosing when to trade stocks, options, and ETFs and to find out which sectors are likely to be the most profitable currently.

That's because falling bond yields are usually bullish for stocks, while rising bond yields are usually bearish for stocks. In addition, there are sectors in the stock market that are known as "interest rate sensitives." These areas of the market tend to rally reliably when bond yields fall and tend to fall in price when bond yields rise. The three most reliable interest rate sectors are homebuilders, utilities, and real estate investment trusts (REITS).

It's a good idea to monitor these sectors and their relationships to bond yields during both bull and bear markets. Utilities and REITs operations depend on debt. Thus, lower bond yields will reduce their debt payment and increase their profit potential. Homebuilders thrive during periods when mortgage rates fall. Mortgage rates are traditionally tied to US Treasury bond yields—most of them depend on the trend for the US ten-year Treasury note (TNX). Monitoring this relationship is especially profitable if you're able to buy into these groups as bond yields are topping out or sell your holdings in these groups close to the bottom in bond yields.

Corporate Credit Check: Know the Bond Ratings

The financial analysts at Standard & Poor's, Moody's, and other agencies review and rate corporate and municipal bonds. The ratings summarize the bonds' creditworthiness—the ability of the issuer to pay. Ratings serve as a report card on the issuer, similar to how your credit rating works. Rating analysts look at the issuer's past payment record, the financial situation of the company, and the degree of risk associated with the bond. Issuers with the highest bond ratings are the most likely to make good on their debt. Sadly, the highest-rated bonds are the ones that are likely to pay the lowest interest rates.

The Bond Ratings Alphabet

The highest-rated bonds are rated AAA. The market considers AAA, AA, A, or BBB bonds rated by S&P as good quality. The equivalent good-quality ratings issued by Moody's are Aaa, Aa, A, and Baa ratings. Bonds rated BB or Ba are considered lower quality and higher risk. Bonds with ratings below B are known as junk bonds. As a self-guided investor, you should be aware of the risk/benefit ratio related to junk bonds. They pay significantly higher interest rates but also have a higher risk of default.

FACT

The best-known bond default–related crash was the stock market crash of 1987. The now-defunct financial firm Drexel Burnham Lambert underwrote and aggressively marketed junk bonds that paid such high interest rates, they were nearly irresistible. They sold these to institutions known as "savings and loans," which used the yields to attract savers to high-yielding CDs. However, the companies that issued the bonds could not make the interest payments for the entire life of the loans. As a result, the junk bond market collapsed, and the damage spread to the stock market and the banking system, especially the savings and loans sector.

Sometimes taking the risks offered by junk bonds pays off. But, in this sector of the bond universe, default is more common than in others. As a result, it's best to consider this sector of the bond market once you are experienced. An alternative is to use a "high-yield" mutual fund or ETF, as the professional management of both options reduces some of the risk.

Ratings Variability and the Tough Decisions

Bond ratings can change over time depending on the fortunes of the issuer. If a company offers BBB-rated bonds but its operations improve, its bond ratings may change to A or higher. This may increase the appeal of the company's bonds. If a company develops problems, its bond rating may fall below BBB or Baa. That's when you may have to decide to sell. Your decision depends on what your plans are for the income produced by the bond, your risk tolerance, and whether you have the time to worry about the potential for default. In other words, sometimes it's best to sell when a rating changes. The key is not to wait too long. If the company goes into bankruptcy, you could lose all your money.

Prices and Yields

Bond prices and yields fluctuate based on market circumstances and supply and demand pressures. If you want to sell a bond, you can find yesterday's price in the bond tables of *The Wall Street Journal*, *Barron's*, or *USA TODAY*. In today's real-time markets, those prices are strictly historical but can be useful. Your online broker may have more current data. Here is the basic information that you will need and that you will find in most bond listings:

Coupon: 3.125%. This is the yield that the bond carried when issued.

Maturity date: 4/30/25. This is the date on which the bond matures.

Bid: 106.875. This means that a buyer is offering to buy the bond for a price of $1,068.75 on a $1,000 bond. This bond has already delivered a profit of $68.75 (6.875%) to the bondholder on a par value of $1,000.

Ask: 106.93. This means that a seller is willing to sell the bond for $1,069.30.

ALERT

When you're mortgage hunting, keep a close eye on the TNX. It's the benchmark for the average thirty-year mortgage rate. When TNX rises or falls, mortgages follow.

Buying and Selling Bonds

For a beginner, buying and selling bonds is difficult but not impossible. Take your time, research the market, paper trade, and go live only when you feel comfortable. You may have to consider going through a full-service bond broker or work out the kinks of your online discount broker's bond quote and trading platform for a good while before you make your first real trade.

As a small investor, it makes sense to buy US Treasury bonds directly from the government by visiting *TreasuryDirect*. Here you can buy Treasury bonds and US savings bonds once you open your account. You can buy savings bonds through your bank as well. The great thing about savings bonds is that you can buy them for as low as $25 and pay no state or income taxes on the interest. Savings bonds can be bought without paying a commission.

An easy DIY trick for bond investors is to invest in bond mutual funds or ETFs. Use the same method of analysis, including monitoring the current rate of inflation, whether the economy is slow enough to keep bond yields from rising, and what the Federal Reserve's current interest rate trend is. If the timing is right, put the money to work in a mutual fund or bond ETF.

CHAPTER 8

Types of Bonds

Successful bond investors know how to structure the bonds in your portfolio to deliver the maximum return. That's what this chapter is about: providing details about different types of bonds; their risk and reward potential; and how they can fit into a well-diversified portfolio of stocks, bonds, and other investments. Knowing the types of bonds makes a DIY approach to investing much easier.

Categories of Bonds

Bonds are versatile assets and can be used for income and capital gains, and as a hedge against risk from other broad portfolio components such as stocks or commodities. You can buy US government, corporate, municipal, or foreign bonds. Each category has its own risk/reward profile, as well as particular tax implications. However, when you take it one step at a time, the DIY approach to investing in bonds is simple.

Bond investors are looking for steady income from periodic interest payments or to protect and build up their capital stores. Generally, especially during periods of low or falling inflation, bonds are more predictable than stocks. You know when you will receive your interest payments and when your principal will be returned. Thus, they are best suited for investors primarily looking for income, especially in their retirement years.

If you have a specific need for capital at a certain date in the future, such as a child entering college, zero-coupon bonds may be for you. You buy these bonds at a deep discount below the par value of the bond. At maturity, you receive the interest that has been compounded over the life of the bond and the purchase price in a lump sum. Treasury and high-grade corporate bonds are your best bet in zeros.

Before you start a bond portfolio, know what your financial needs will be, a sense of your time frame, and a plan.

FACT

The global bond market is estimated to be worth over $140 trillion. Compare that to the global stock market's capitalization, which is estimated to be worth $103 trillion.

US Treasury Securities

The US Treasury bond market is the biggest securities market in the world, with an average turnover of over $500 billion per day. That makes it a very liquid market and one in which you can raise cash rapidly if you need to. US Treasuries are considered the safest securities in the world and are thought of by many investors as cash equivalents. So, if you're a risk-averse investor and you don't mind holding on to a security for long periods, US Treasuries may be your favorite investment type. Perhaps the best attribute of US Treasuries is that once you buy them, the interest rate you receive from that bond, until maturity, is locked in. That means that your return on investment is highly predictable. There are three kinds of Treasuries. It's a good DIY practice to have a mix of each category in a bond portfolio while changing their weight due to changes in interest rates and inflation.

ALERT

While it is true that many consider US Treasury securities to be "safe" investments, this notion of safety is most applicable to bonds that are held until maturity. Treasury bonds' prices fluctuate, often in wide price ranges, in response to economic reports and geopolitical events. Thus, when you buy US Treasuries, plan accordingly.

Treasury bills (T-bills) are short-term securities. Their maturities range from four weeks to one year. You can buy T-bills in $100 increments. T-bills are sold at a discount from face value. The discount is based on the interest rate paid by the bill. These are the best bond investments for periods when interest rates are rising.

Treasury notes (T-notes) are intermediate-term securities with maturities at two, five, and ten years. As with T-bills, you can buy T-notes in $100 increments. T-notes pay interest every six months until they mature. The ten-year US Treasury note yield (TNX) is considered the benchmark for most mortgages and longer-term loans. It is also the most widely quoted bond yield in the financial press.

Treasury bonds (T-bonds) are long-term securities issued by the US government. The most traded T-bond is the thirty-year bond. The US Treasury also offers a twenty-year bond. Long-term Treasuries can be purchased at $100 increments and, like T-notes, pay interest every six months until maturity. T-bonds are the most volatile bonds issued by the Treasury. Their price will fall during periods of high inflation, but their yield will rise. So, if you buy them when yields are high and hold them to maturity, the interest you receive will be higher than if you bought them during periods of low inflation.

Municipal Bonds

These are bonds sold by cities, states, counties, and even school districts. They are also known as munis and are very popular investments because of their tax-free advantages. Municipalities sell munis to finance projects, such as building or repairing roads, bridges, schools, parks, and sports arenas. Munis are very popular because they are usually exempt from federal, and often state, taxes. As a DIY investor, you have a unique advantage—you are there. So, if you live in a well-run city that is known to pay its bills, consider buying the municipal bonds they issue.

ALERT

Not all municipal bonds are tax-free at all levels of taxation. Check the bond prospectus and your state and city tax laws. The downside is that they pay lower yields than taxable bonds.

Municipal bonds are often rated by rating analysts from Standard & Poor's and Moody's via similar ratings to those used for corporate bonds. Ratings range from the highest grades, AAA (S&P) or Aaa (Moody's), to BBB or Baa and below. When considering municipal bonds, look to own BBB-rated bonds or above. As in the case of corporate bonds, the lower the rating for a municipal bond, the higher the yield and the risk of default. With municipal bonds, you can buy bond insurance to protect against losses.

The minimum investment for municipal bonds is $5,000, and they are then offered in multiples of $5,000. The general trends for interest rates, risk ratings, and other external factors, such as the local economy for the municipality selling the bond, affect the interest rate that any muni pays investors. Prices are listed in bond tables, which are like those for Treasury bonds. You may sell your municipal bond at a higher price than what you paid for it, but you will have to pay capital gains taxes.

ALERT

After the 2008 financial crisis, many municipalities, cities, and states were in trouble as people and businesses moved away. In contrast, places where people moved often saw their finances improve as rising populations raised their tax collection. Pensions in cities with poor management and unrealistic expectations on the return of pension investments are in danger. Large cities such as San Francisco, New York, and Chicago all have voiced pension concerns. While investing, you should also pay special attention to bonds issued from cities where natural disasters have struck.

If these municipal bonds make sense for your portfolio, get to know the different types:

- **Revenue bonds.** These are bonds issued to finance specific projects such as bridges, toll roads, or airports. Interest paid to investors comes from the revenues generated by the project.
- **Moral obligation bonds.** These are special-circumstance revenue bonds issued by a state when it can't meet the bond obligation through its normal revenue stream, essentially taxes and licensing fees. In these cases, the state forms a special obligation fund that can be used to pay the bond obligation. The kicker is that the state has no legal obligation to pay bondholders from that special obligation fund, just a moral obligation. What makes this bond worth considering is that the state is

putting its good reputation on the line, so the moral obligation is often considered more powerful in the markets than the legal obligation.

- **General obligation bonds.** These bonds, also known as GOs, are backed by municipal taxes and require voter approval. The principal is backed by the full faith and credit of the issuer.
- **Taxable municipal bonds.** If paying taxes on a municipal bond sounds ridiculous, consider that these bonds, despite the taxes, can offer higher yields than comparable corporate bonds and are generally considered to have lower risks associated with them. Common uses for this kind of muni include financing underfunded pension plans or building a local sports arena.
- **Private activity bonds** are used for financing both public and private activities.
- **Put bonds** allow the investor to redeem them at par value on a specific date (or dates) prior to the stated maturity. In exchange, put bonds offer lower yields than comparable municipals because of this built-in flexibility. This early-out feature allows you to cash in your bond and exchange it for a higher-yielding bond if you can do so.
- **Floating and variable-rate municipal bonds** are good to own if you expect that interest will rise at some point in the future, as the bond will adjust. Because of this feature, the price of these bonds may be more volatile.

Municipal bond prices can fluctuate, thus it makes sense to develop a good relationship with a muni broker and to check prices with your broker on a routine basis, as well as your local newspaper and online if you use a discount broker.

Corporate Bonds

A corporate bond, also called a "corporate," is a loan agreement between a corporation and investors. And while stockholders own shares of stocks, by contrast, corporate bondholders are moneylenders to the company that issues the bond. Bondholders lend money to companies for a specific amount of time and a specified rate of interest. Corporate bonds can be riskier than Treasury or municipal bonds but, when properly chosen, have historically outperformed other bonds.

Put your DIY knowledge to work. If you own stock in a solid company, consider investing in their bonds.

ALERT

Corporate bonds are not insured and should be avoided if you are not a risk-taker. If you're more moderate in your risk acceptability, consider owning a mutual fund that invests in corporate bonds to reduce but not eliminate your risk.

Corporate bonds pay a higher interest rate because the issuing companies generally have a higher risk of default than governments and municipalities, although after the Great Recession, countries are not risk-free either. Greece and several US cities went bankrupt after the 2007–2008 financial crisis. After the 2024 hurricane season, many municipalities in the southern US may also face financial difficulties while requiring bond revenues to rebuild. After the 2025 fires, you can add California to the caution list.

Sinking-Fund Provision

A sinking-fund provision allows a company to redeem a certain number of bonds per year by using its earnings. Bonds with sinking-fund provision features must state that this is a part of the deal. The company, depending on its current circumstances, chooses bonds to be retired via this maneuver. Thus, your bond may or may not get chosen. If your bond gets chosen, you may lose money. Unless the interest rate premium is significant, it may be best to avoid bonds with this clause.

Before buying any corporate bond, check out the company's record of calling the bonds before maturity. This information isn't always easily available, but it is required to be inside any prospectus. Remember, most companies will likely call bonds early if the interest rate climate offers them an opportunity to refinance the debt at a lower rate. You can also go to the callable bond section on *FINRA* (www.finra.org/finra-data/fixed-income).

The bottom line is that corporate bonds have their positive and negative sides. Higher yields also mean higher risk. The possibility of a company bankruptcy or a quirky callable feature of the bond makes it mandatory that you read everything very carefully before investing.

Corporate Bond Checklist

Here are points to consider with corporate bonds:

- Corporate bonds are issued in multiples of $1,000 or $5,000. They are rated by S&P and Moody's using the AAA- or Aaa-based system described earlier.
- Income and capital gains associated with corporate bonds are fully taxable at federal and state levels.
- Interest is paid annually or semiannually.
- If your goal is to invest in highly rated, high-quality corporate bonds from blue chip companies, and you hold the bond until maturity, your risk of default is low but not guaranteed.

Bond Calls

When a bond is called, it means that the issuer is redeeming the bond before maturity. The most common reason for this is that by calling in the bond and reissuing it at a lower interest rate, the issuer will save money. Only bonds with a callable provision can be called early, whether they are government, municipal, or corporate bonds. The callable provision describes the details and conditions that allow the early redemption. For example, a fifteen-year bond may be called as early as eight years into its lifespan. If you reinvest in a bond issued by an entity that called your original bond, usually issued at a lower interest rate, your return will be different than that of the original bond.

Zero-Coupon Bonds

Companies, governments, government agencies, and municipalities can issue zero-coupon bonds. Zeros do not make periodic interest rate payments. You buy them at a deep discount and receive a higher-rate lump sum (both interest and principal) when the bond reaches maturity. Zeros allow you to plan for a lump sum at maturity and are ideal for retirement planning or a specific date when you know you will need that money. The downside is that even though you don't receive interest payments, you must report the amount of appreciation of the bond every year for tax purposes.

Here is how they work. If you buy a ten-year $10,000 zero-municipal bond, you may pay $5,000. In ten years, you would receive $10,000 plus all the interest accrued during your ownership as a lump sum. The longer the time to maturity, the deeper the purchase price is discounted and the greater the return based on the compounding of the interest that is not being paid until maturity. To figure out what you'll receive and when, use a zero-coupon bond calculator such as the one at Calculator.me (https://calculator.me/savings/zero-coupon-bonds.php).

High-Yield Bonds

High-yield bonds, also known as junk bonds, can provide a higher return with a higher risk of default or a rapid fall in price. That's because the companies that issue these bonds have lower credit ratings than other companies, thus their bonds get lower ratings from the ratings agencies. To attract investors, they must pay a higher interest rate.

Low credit ratings result when companies restructure or are involved in a merger that's financed by bonds. These circumstances may affect the company's stock price. Thus, the bond may lose value quickly. It may also lose its liquidity and be very difficult to sell.

When a company that issues junk bonds in its early growth stages improves its operations and its credit, it can issue higher-grade bonds in the future. The company may call the lower-grade bonds to issue higher-grade bonds that pay lower interest rates. Thus, you may receive the high rate for a shorter period than you may expect. As a new DIY investor, it's usually best to stay away from this area of the bond market until you gain experience. You can familiarize yourself with it via paper trading high-yield bond ETFs such as the iShares iBoxx High Yield Corporate Bond ETF (HYG).

No matter what you decide, understand that high-yield bonds are known as junk bonds for a reason, and that reason is that a fair amount of the time, they are just that: junk.

Mortgage-Backed Securities

Mortgage-backed securities (MBS) are bonds backed by mortgage payments. Until 2007, they were considered among the safest areas of the bond market, as it was widely believed that Americans would always pay their mortgages and that home prices would continue to rise. But this former haven in the bond market turned into a disaster area in 2007 and 2008 as the subprime mortgage became synonymous with the near collapse of the global economy. In 2023, a repeat of this event happened in the commercial real estate market. As working from home took root, office buildings lost tenants, and the landlords couldn't make their mortgage payments. Many defaulted, with the headline-grabbing debacle of coworking company WeWork leading the way. As a result, beginning investors should avoid this sector altogether.

The major reason for avoiding mortgage-backed securities, aside from their inherent high risk, is their complexity, which often involves interest rates that are collected in derivative instruments known as collateralized mortgage obligations (CMOs). In CMOs, multiple mortgages are pooled together to collect the capital to make the interest rate.

When you buy a corporate, municipal, or Treasury bond, you deal with only one issuer. Thus, you only must look to one payer—the US Treasury, a city, or a corporation—to make good on its promise to pay. Compare this to the path of a typical MBS. A bank sells the mortgage to the homeowner. Then the bank sells the mortgage to a servicing firm. Thus, for you to get paid, the homeowner must make his mortgage payment to the servicing firm that holds the mortgage. The servicing firm collects the money, then allocates the money to each pool or CMO, and then from that pool, it pays the interest to investors. Thus, there are too many steps in the chain of custody of the money, increasing the chances for something to go wrong, which is what happened in 2007 and, to a lesser but still significant degree, in 2023.

ALERT

When it comes to all bonds, the most important part of the transaction is the ability of the issuer to pay the prescribed interest. If you must invest in the MBS sector, consider doing so through a mutual fund or exchange-traded fund (ETF), which have a sound record of risk management.

Still, you can add MBS to your to-do list and make good use of your time by monitoring related ETFs such as the iShares MBS ETF (MBB). Focus on pinpointing the trend in the MBS market and related ETFs to the general interest rate trends. Find which one is more influential on the ETF at any one time in the cycle and trade the ETF along with that trend. For example, if the Fed is lowering rates but bond yields are not going along, see how the MBS ETF is responding.

The Bond Investor Checklist

Diversification is the key to success in bond investing. By owning a variety of bonds in a laddered portfolio, you can limit and, during noninflationary periods, reduce the potential volatility of your bond holdings. Adjust your bond holdings to coincide with your financial goals and your time range. Before buying bonds, consider the following:

- **Tax implications.** Do tax-free municipal bonds make sense in your portfolio? Review the potential risks of hidden taxes with your CPA, including those of triggering the AMT (alternative minimum tax) rules. And investigate the potential consequences of owning zero-coupon bonds before you invest in them.
- **Consider inflation's effect on your bonds.** If your total portfolio is well insulated from inflation, you may be able to avoid taking extra risks with your bond portfolio in search of a higher return.
- **Safety first.** A high-quality portfolio may not give the best return in dollar terms, but it will reduce your risk and offer peace of mind.
- **Remember that your bond portfolio** provides income and can add stability to investment portfolios when stocks become volatile.
- **Junk is junk, and mortgages sometimes go unpaid.** Don't chase high-yield bonds just to make more money in the short term. Avoid most junk bonds, and if you must own mortgage-backed securities, consider a GNMA (Government National Mortgage Association) mutual fund, where the mortgage securities in the fund are insured by the government.

Once you've checked this list, you should be set to invest in the bond market.

CHAPTER 9

The Mutual Fund: The Beginner's and the 401(k) Plan's Best Friend

If there were ever a financial instrument ideally suited to a beginning investor, and one who wishes to build long-term wealth via a 401(k) or IRA, it would be the mutual fund. Created in Europe in the mid-1800s, mutual funds hit the American shores when Harvard University created the first American pooled fund. Initially ridiculed, mutual funds now house trillions of dollars of money and are major contributors to market activity as well as shareholder financial reward. This chapter is all about mutual funds and how they can be a significant part of your portfolio, both when you start and throughout your time as an investor.

Mutual Funds and Retirement Accounts

A mutual fund is a registered investment company that sells shares to investors and invests the pooled assets of all shareholders in the markets on their behalf. A mutual fund share's price is the net asset value (NAV) and is the result of the mutual fund's total assets divided by the number of outstanding shares. Thus, a mutual fund with $10 million in total assets and one million shares outstanding has a NAV of $10.

Always useful, mutual funds are especially excellent investment vehicles for investors just getting started. They allow you to participate in the markets and provide a certain comfort level. Many investors who start their endeavors by using mutual funds move on to stocks, options, and futures. It's important to take your time and transition to investments with higher risk and higher work requirement investments when you're ready.

FACT

Mutual funds are managed by professionals whose job is to invest the funds' assets on behalf of their shareholders. They are well suited for long-term time horizon investing. So, they are central to IRAs and 401(k) plans.

The Secret Ingredient in Your Financial Arsenal

When you buy a mutual fund in your retirement account, your primary focus should be on building long-term wealth. But your mutual funds can pay dividends in more ways than you may appreciate at first glance.

An underappreciated value of mutual funds in your 401(k)/IRA is that during bull markets, they can increase your net worth. That means that as your funds increase in value, your net worth increases. Thus, when you apply for a mortgage, a car loan, a business line of credit, or even a favorable interest credit card, your financial health looks more attractive to the bank. Subsequently, because your mutual funds are doing well, you may gain better terms, rates, or both than you might receive otherwise.

This is a huge advantage as you progress in your investment career toward producing current income via real estate investments, which is covered in Chapter 14.

Variety Is the Spice of Life

Since there are nearly ten thousand funds available in the US, you'll have a whole lot of choices if you decide to invest in mutual funds. Nearly 50% of all funds invest solely in stocks, while some 20% invest in bonds, and some 5% are money market mutual funds. The rest are funds that combine assets such as stocks, bonds, and options.

The competition from exchange-traded funds (ETFs) has transformed the mutual fund industry. Many fund companies have cut fees while offering targeted funds where the goal is for the investor to have a specific amount of money by a certain date. These funds, called target date funds, can be useful as part of a diversified portfolio, including retirement accounts like 401(k)s and IRAs. For example, if you plan to retire in fifteen years, you could choose a fund that is targeted to wind down in fifteen years.

Knowing how much money you will have by a certain time focuses your planning. It doesn't lock you into an outcome, but it does offer a sense of security. If your plans change as the date approaches, you can retool your 401(k)/IRA to the next goal. Moreover, you can put part of your money in targeted funds while maintaining a conventional approach to the remaining portion.

The fund's asset allocation begins aggressively, with a higher percentage of growth stocks in its early stages, but it becomes more conservative as the target date approaches by increasing cash and bond allocations. When the target date is reached, the fund is designed to be 100% in cash.

Mutual Funds: Good for Your Wallet and Your IRA

Mutual funds offer investors two things: diversification and convenience. Diversification allows you to spread out your risk, while convenience makes it easier for you to invest. Both are good reasons why you should consider investing in mutual funds during your early investment career and as part of your wealth building via your 401(k) plan or IRA.

Diversification

The fund manager picks stocks and constantly adjusts the portfolio, meaning that your risk is spread beyond a handful of stocks. If a mutual fund can diversify into bonds and other asset classes as market conditions change, this can also add another layer of diversification and can protect you from excessive volatility in one asset class such as stocks. The net effect is that mutual funds can cut your costs, balance your risk, and let you participate in bull markets. The downside is that few mutual funds reduce risk aggressively during bear markets, so you can expect a decrease in your holdings during down markets. To reduce risk in mutual fund holdings, your best choice is to move some of your holdings to cash during extended down markets. By doing so, you are reducing your losses and increasing your cash reserves to deploy when conditions improve.

Built-In Convenience

Mutual funds decrease the amount of research work you do to invest in a general market trend. For example, instead of having a portfolio with fifty stocks, you can own more than one mutual fund. This helps balance the potential risk that can come with an aggressive growth stock fund by also owning shares in a conservative Treasury bond fund, especially if you are using funds from the same fund family, which lets you handle all your transactions online or with a phone call. You can also monitor hot sectors in the market and trade in and out of sector-specific funds that are acting well at any time. If international funds are acting well, you may want to own some shares there as well. A fund that specializes in real estate and a precious metals and commodity fund may also be worth considering. However, you can also overdo your fund diversification, regardless of how convenient it is to make trades. Owning more than five to seven mutual funds at any one time is likely to increase your risk as well as possibly duplicating some of your holdings. Thus, it makes sense to use different funds for separately held IRA and 401(k) plan accounts. For example, if you use diversified growth funds in your 401(k), you may focus on sector-specific funds (or ETFs) in your IRA.

Know Before You Invest

Before investing, be aware that mutual funds are not guaranteed to make money. And unless the fund manager is truly nimble and can move all the funds' holdings to a safe asset allocation in times of trouble, you will lose some money in any type of mutual fund during bad markets regardless of asset class. Yet over time, owning and adjusting a portfolio of well-diversified, well-managed mutual funds can be a pretty good deal for most investors. Above all, mutual funds are convenient, given the fact that as an investor, you only need to pick and monitor the fund as it pertains to your needs, goals, and financial plan. Thankfully, you don't have to manage the entire fund's portfolio.

ESSENTIAL

Most 401(k) plans offer mutual funds as their primary investment vehicle. If you have a twenty-plus-year time horizon, you will make the most out of your plan by maximizing your contributions to the plan every year. If your employer matches the contribution, your 401(k) plan will be double charged.

Fund Managers and Their Impact on 401(k)s

Mutual fund companies, like any other business, are always looking for ways to attract new customers. Therefore, a successful mutual fund may be marketed by associating it with a charismatic manager. Because your 401(k)/IRA is about long-term wealth, for you, it's not about the marquee value of the fund manager's name. It's about whether the famous manager can deliver the goods. Some do and some don't. Stick with the ones who do, even if they're famous.

Peter Lynch, ex-manager of the Fidelity Magellan Fund (FMAGX), became a legend in the 1980s and is considered by many to be the best mutual fund manager of all time. Under his guidance, Magellan averaged 29% yearly returns for thirteen years. Lynch was a big proponent of buying into companies that you know well and going out to "kick the tires" (looking at the business in real life) before investing. Since his departure, Magellan became an above-average, but not quite exceptional, mutual fund.

ALERT

Beware of clever marketing by mutual funds, especially when the focus of the advertising is a star fund manager. If the manager is a celebrity, make sure their results also measure up, especially during bad markets.

Lynch was an excellent manager. But he also had the best of times in which to ply his wares. As an investor, it's all about balance. You should weigh the performance of the manager but also temper your expectations based on market conditions because even managers like Peter Lynch can't beat a bear market.

Evaluating Your Fund Manager

When reviewing a fund manager's performance:

- **Look at several years of returns.** If the fund has been delivering consistent returns during the manager's tenure, look at other funds they have managed. If the performance comparison yields consistent returns, especially through good and bad markets, you've found a good manager.
- **Compare the fund's performance to the market during both up and down years.** See what the fund did during the 2020 pandemic, including how fast

it rebounded and to what degree. This will tell you a lot about what you may expect in the future, as there will be other bad markets to manage through.

- **Make sure the manager is adhering to their fund's investment strategy.** If you are looking for a conservative strategy and your review of the fund's latest report shows that there are mostly momentum stocks in the portfolio, you should consider whether the fund is what you are looking for in the long run.
- **Research whether the fund manager is a lone wolf or has a management team.** If they are a lone wolf, the fund may suffer when the manager moves on. Moreover, the next manager may not deliver the same levels of returns. If the performance of the fund is similar over time regardless of the manager, and it suits your goals, you've found a match.

Mutual Fund Families and IRAs

There are many mutual fund families, which are companies that offer a variety of mutual funds to the public. Each one comes with slight differences in the number of assets they manage. But in an industry of thousands, there are several giant firms that gobble up most of the market share: Fidelity Investments, Vanguard, PIMCO, American, Franklin Templeton, Invesco, T. Rowe Price, and BlackRock. These are not the only mutual fund companies, but these big firms offer a wide variety of funds in the growth, growth and income, sector-specific, hybrid, and asset allocation categories, which makes them an ideal place to start your search. In addition, your 401(k) plan or IRA may be managed by one of them. If you have a self-directed IRA, it's usually housed directly in a brokerage or mutual fund account with the fund company or a subsidiary acting as the custodian.

Some fund families are specialists. For example, PIMCO is primarily a bond mutual fund company, while the others offer a large variety of fund choices. Franklin Templeton specializes in international markets, while

Fidelity Investments has a very large selection of mutual funds with a specialization in industry sector–specific mutual funds.

There are also niche players that cater to a particular clientele, such as the Rydex and ProFunds families. These two families offer mutual funds to investors who like to switch/trade among mutual funds on a regular basis, often daily. These two fund families also offer mutual funds that sell the markets short or rise when the underlying assets fall in price. These funds may not be suitable for large portions of your 401(k)/IRA until you become very experienced.

When choosing a mutual fund family, consider the following:

- **Reputation:** Research whether the company has had (or currently has) any significant legal or enforcement actions against it in the past five years. If a mutual fund company turns up in the news as being investigated due to accounting problems and undergoes frequent management changes, these are major red flags.
- **Primary business:** If a mutual fund company is part of a large financial conglomerate such as a retail bank or even a big investment bank, mutual funds may or may not be its primary focus. That may make a big difference in fees, performance, and customer service.
- **Performance:** Look at mutual fund ratings in each family during good and bad markets and review how the company's funds have fared. Consistently good results are preferable to outstanding years once in a blue moon.

- **Investment approach:** Review the overall philosophy of the fund family and how it matches your own personality and risk profile. If you are a patient, conservative investor, you may find a good fit in Vanguard, a company that tends not to service investors who like to switch in and out of mutual funds frequently. If you are someone who might enjoy mutual fund switching, you may do well with Rydex or ProFunds.

FACT

There are several great sources of information on mutual funds. First is the Investment Company Institute (ICI). The ICI is the mutual fund industry group that chronicles the industry and keeps all the statistics and facts about mutual funds. The ICI offers a great deal of information, especially regarding the state of the entire mutual fund industry. If you want to gather information regarding the performance of various mutual funds, you can find all you need at Morningstar.com.

Costs of Mutual Funds and Effects on 401(k)s

Mutual funds, even the "free" ones, have expenses. Aside from trading commissions, mutual funds may pay rent for office space and may have other operational real estate and related expenses. As with any company, mutual funds also have employees who require salaries and benefits. Fund managers often travel to personally "kick the tires" of a company they are evaluating for investment purposes. And since shareholders are the major source of income for the company, they will pay for everything required to run the fund via fees.

Load or No Load?

The first fee to consider is the load, which is the fee an advisor receives from the fund company for selling you a mutual fund. A no-load mutual fund has at least an equal chance of being as good as a load fund. Some special cases of load funds sold directly to investors are sector funds. A good rule of thumb to consider when investing in sector mutual funds is that you may be better served by buying an ETF that invests in the same sector. This may not be possible in your 401(k) plan, but it is doable in a self-directed IRA.

Also, be careful when you buy no-load funds, as they may have hidden fees that could surprise you if you didn't expect them.

Digging Into Fee Details

Before investing, review the expense ratio part of the prospectus. Some companies are trickier than others, although most of the large families are straightforward in their language. If there is something you don't understand in the fee structure, it makes sense to stop and look it up or have someone help you understand it.

Here are some typical mutual fund fees:

- **Service fees:** These are fees used to pay the salaries, commissions, and consulting fees of financial planners, analysts, and brokers who help customers and provide support services to clients. Unfortunately, there is nothing you can do about the fees except choose a fund that does not use this type of marketing.
- **Administrative fees:** These fees include the cost of office space, staff salaries, office equipment, and the general cost of running the business. There's also the cost of online support, auditing, recordkeeping, and the production and printing of brochures and shareholder reports. In some cases, the funds absorb these fees into their management fees.

- **Management fees:** These fees go to the fund manager and are expressed as a percentage. Some funds have flat percentage fees, while others vary the fee based on the fund's return. Generally, the larger the fund, the lower the management fee percentage.
- **12b-1 fee:** This fee, which is usually between 0.25% and 1% on an annual basis, is used to pay for the fund's advertising. This fee can be seen as unnecessary, or you can agree with the fund company, whose point of view is that by advertising, it gets more clients and the overall costs of running the fund go down over time.

ALERT

Don't get ripped off. You don't have to pay big bucks to own a mutual fund through a financial planner or investment advisor. You can buy no-load funds with low fees directly from the fund company when you open an account. The remarkable thing is that high-load mutual funds with big expenses don't often perform any better than the no-load ones.

Total expense ratios for a mutual fund can range from 0.25% to as high as 2.5%. You should pay attention to this because it can sap your returns. If your fund has a high expense ratio and a poor return, find a new one.

Making Sense of Fund Reports for Your 401(k)/IRA

Your mutual fund's annual or semiannual reports help you measure performance. This is especially important for your 401(k)/IRA accounts, where your goal is to focus on the long-term trend to build wealth. To keep tabs on the fund's manager, pay special attention to the section that details the fund's holdings and how often the manager makes changes. A manager whose style drifts from the fund's stated objectives or who is a frequent trader, especially with poor results, could be a sign of trouble. If your fund's objective is small-cap growth, and you see large holdings of Apple, Tesla, and Amazon, your manager is showing signs of "style drifting." This is especially troubling for your 401(k)/IRA if the fund doesn't keep up with the general trend of the market.

However, you should always focus on the results. Before deciding whether this is a positive or a negative, consider why the manager may be changing the objective. Is it because the market is changing? Or is it because they are chasing performance and the large-cap stocks are acting better in the current market than the small-cap growth stocks that they are supposed to be investing in? Compare this fund's performance to other small-cap growth funds. If your fund is doing better than other small-cap funds, even with the large-cap stocks in it, it may make sense to keep it, while monitoring its activity and results closely.

Here are other things to look for:

- **Familiar names:** Look for companies that fit the bill of the fund. If there aren't many that you recognize, dig deeper. Try to get in your manager's head. If your research shows that your fund manager is heavily invested in high-risk poorly run companies, this may be a much higher-risk mutual fund than you want, especially in your 401(k)/IRA, which is the lifeblood of your long-term wealth.
- **Portfolio concentration:** If your fund is overweight in a particular sector, you should research that sector and see if its fundamentals warrant that kind of exposure. If your manager is loading up on biotech or bank stocks, research those sectors carefully. Your fund manager may be onto something or may be way off base. Regardless, what's important is the fund's return and how comfortable you are with what the manager is doing.
- **Compare your fund to the right benchmark:** The annual report should list the fund's performance in comparison to the appropriate benchmark. This is crucial for your 401(k)/IRA. There is no point in owning the fund if it's not keeping up with the market. If the report of your small-cap growth fund is comparing its performance solely to the ten-year

US Treasury note, that's inaccurate and misleading. Certainly, funds often compare their performance to that of their traditional benchmark index or sector (like the Russell 2000 Index) as well as that of Treasuries.

The report should also explain why the fund manager made the decisions reflected in their holdings, why they worked out or didn't fare well, and what the manager plans to do about it in the future. Because your 401(k)/IRA is your future, scratching your head after reading the report, especially after a period of underperformance, is a nonstarter.

Finally, you can check your fund's performance online often, as fund companies post the fund's closing price, usually after 5:00 p.m. EST, on their websites.

Approaches to Mutual Fund and 401(k) Investing

Now that you're ready to invest, it's time to consider your mutual fund share buying and style choices. As with any other form of investing, how you go about buying and selling is dictated by your personality, your risk profile, and your time frame. No matter what you decide, the most important factor is that you make money by investing in mutual funds in a way that you don't lose sleep over. If you're investing via your 401(k) plan, you'll likely be making automatic investments depending on the rules of your plan.

For many investors, mutual fund investing preludes stock investing. You buy shares in a mutual fund in hopes of selling them at a higher price or net asset value at some point in the future. If you buy shares in a fund, and it doesn't appreciate in price over a reasonable period, based on your time frame, personality, and needs, you simply sell the shares. Before you buy shares, review any restrictions or fees that may apply when you buy or sell shares. When selling mutual fund shares, you must also consider the effect of fees for redeeming shares in less than the allotted time, if applicable. These fees, if they exist in your fund, are called exit loads. Mutual funds charge these fees to reduce the effect of large numbers of redemptions on the fund's capital. Your fund will inform you, in its prospectus, if there are any such fees and how they apply. They also notify you of the sale ticket you must approve before the trade goes through. No-load funds have no up-front or back-end loads. Most mutual funds, load and no-load, limit the number of times you can sell shares per year. This number varies per fund and fund family. On average, you can switch out of funds two to four times per year.

FACT

To open a mutual fund account directly with a company, you can visit a local investor center or apply directly online. Once you fund the account, you're all set up and you can start buying and selling shares.

Dollar Cost Averaging for 401(k)s and Beyond

Dollar cost averaging is an investment method that is well suited for long-term mutual fund investing, especially for 401(k) and IRA plans. You do this by investing a fixed sum of money into a mutual fund (or shares) periodically. The fixed-sum-of-money method tends to work better due to price fluctuations in fund shares. Many investors use the dollar-cost-averaging method every month or every quarter. The net effect is that, over time, you build many shares in the fund. Sometimes you buy shares at lower prices and sometimes at higher prices, depending on the overall market. This method works well for IRAs, 401(k) plans, and other retirement plans with a twenty-plus-year time horizon. You may buy up to a specific number of shares in a particular fund, and, once you reach your share goal, you may deploy your cash into a different fund.

Dollar cost averaging, especially in your 401(k) plan or IRA, often makes the most sense at the beginning of your investment plan, although you can continue to invest this way if it suits your goals. This disciplined approach develops the habit of saving and offers the potential for building up your assets. Consider having a minimum contribution and a set schedule:

If you decide that you will buy $200 worth of shares in a mutual fund every month, then stick to it. If you have more in some months, it may be worth your while to put in a bit more. The key is to stick to the routine and build assets. You can also split the amount between your stock/bond funds and your money market fund. By putting money in your money market fund, you build a cushion for when markets fall and build up cash reserves for periods of market weakness when you decide to buy on dips.

Dollar cost averaging is the opposite of market timing, the style of investing that attempts to enter near price bottoms and exit during price tops. Market timing is difficult but can be mastered by using technical analysis. It is more suitable for short-term trading to provide short-term income. For example, market timers look to buy when markets have been falling for some time and their market timing indicators, found on price charts, are flashing signals that this may be a good moment to buy. Market timers also look to sell before a market falls. The goal of market timers is to make the most money possible when markets are trending and to sell before the trend changes. There are whole books devoted to market timing. It can be done, but it is difficult and can be a risky proposition, especially when you're just starting.

FACT

If the stock market drops 5%–10% over a short period, this may be an opportunity to buy shares at a discount, also known as buying the dip. In this case, it may be best if you move your intended allowance into the fund over a few days or weeks if the decline lingers.

Dollar cost averaging can also be emotionally difficult, as it requires putting money into fund shares even during bear markets. If you can stomach this aspect of the technique, and you have enough time for things to work out, this is a good approach to mutual fund investing. It is during bear markets when you may wish to tip the balance of your contributions to your money market fund.

CHAPTER 10

The Large Universe of Mutual Funds

In a universe where you have thousands of choices, it pays to know your stuff. And the more you know about the different types of mutual funds—stocks, bonds, hybrid, and sector-specific—the better off you'll be. Each type of fund, whether it invests in stocks, bonds, or a mixture of assets, has a potential place in your portfolio. This chapter will help you make intelligent choices. But regardless of your decisions, your return will be based on the performance of the financial class in which the fund invests, whether it's stocks, bonds, or a mixture of multiple asset classes.

Index Funds

Index funds are designed to match the performance of a specific index. To do this, the funds buy the same assets or securities in identical proportions to the index. The most common and best-known index mutual funds mimic the S&P 500. Index funds are passively managed, meaning there is little trading and asset shifting, which means lower fees for you. There are some no-fee index funds in the market via Fidelity Investments. Historically, the S&P 500 outperformed most equity funds.

Index funds are attractive because they offer:

- **Ease of investing:** You know exactly what you're getting. When you buy an S&P 500 Index fund, you expect to earn market-style results at a low cost.
- **Variety:** There are many mutual funds that track other indexes, such as small-cap and mid-cap stocks and industry sectors. For example, you can buy a mutual fund that tracks a technology index such as Vanguard Information Technology Index Fund (VITAX).
- **Diversification:** A good mix of index mutual funds may be a large-cap index fund that tracks the Dow Jones Industrial Average or the S&P 500, coupled with a mid-cap mutual fund that tracks the S&P MidCap 400 Index and an index fund that tracks the Russell 2000 Index of small-cap stocks. Add security with a Treasury bond index mutual fund and a sector mutual fund that tracks a gold stock benchmark or a commodity index.

Growth Funds versus Income Funds

There are two direct ways to make money: by growing capital gains and by receiving income. The more time you have, the more aggressive you should be with your asset allocation, meaning more growth and index funds may make sense in your twenties and thirties. A third strategy is to mix the two. Growth stocks appreciate in price, while income securities pay dividends, and there are mutual funds that specialize in either approach, separately or simultaneously. So, there's no reason to choose between these two general categories of funds. Each type has a place in your portfolio, and an appropriate blend of both tends to make for a more stable portfolio during tough markets.

ESSENTIAL

Beginning investors can benefit by owning index, growth, and income mutual funds. By combining the three categories, you can diversify your portfolio while gaining some possible protection of assets when one type of fund runs into difficulties due to market trend changes.

Growth Funds

Mutual funds that specialize in growth stocks are not as interested in the current price of a stock. Instead, they focus on stocks with the potential to appreciate in price. These funds will buy stocks at any price if they believe the price will rise, even from levels that have already risen significantly. Thus, growth funds tend to gravitate toward momentum stocks that can move significantly higher for relatively long periods, such as months or even years. Think technology stocks. The downside is that momentum stocks eventually fall, and your fund may suffer some temporary losses. These losses can be cushioned by not having all your eggs in one basket and by periodically trimming the number of shares in a fund you own as the price rises.

Growth stock mutual funds are interested in companies with extraordinary potential for gains, especially those with new products that are creating new social trends. Think of stocks that fit the profile of Apple, Amazon, Starbucks, Nvidia, and Facebook in their growth sweet spots, and you've got the commonly held type of stocks in these mutual funds. Long-term growth funds tend to focus on more mature growth companies that still have potential, while aggressive growth funds look for the "next big deal" companies earlier in the cycle.

Capital Appreciation Funds

Capital appreciation funds are the most aggressive of all mutual funds, and when they are doing well, they usually hit home runs. That's because they focus solely on the stocks that have exceptional growth potential in the short run. However, when the momentum runs out, these funds can be at the bottom of the performance lists.

Income Funds

Income funds are all about stocks that pay dividends, which are passed to the fund's shareholders. Some of these funds may also hold bonds to increase their income-producing potential. If you reinvest your dividends, you will build the number of shares you hold. Make sure to check the tax consequences of owning these funds with your CPA, as you are likely to be taxed unless you hold them in tax-deferred accounts. These funds tend to be more stable in down or volatile markets; however, remember that in the age of high-frequency trading, any stock or fund can become volatile.

Combined Growth and Income Funds

If you have a small portfolio and are looking for a one-stop shop, a combined growth and income fund may be for you. By combining growth and dividend-paying stocks, along with bonds, this type of mutual fund can deliver excellent results with less probable risk. Growth and income managers tend to be more cautious in their stock picks and are required to balance the more aggressive picks with stable dividend payers and bonds to deliver steady returns in rising stock markets and decrease the potential for losses in down markets.

Value Funds

Value mutual funds invest in shares of undervalued companies, so the companies in these funds are often struggling, or are perceived to be struggling, by the market when the value fund manager is buying their shares.

But while the appeal of a value stock may be low, the reason the stock is underperforming may be because its product cycle has hit a slow period or it's undergoing a change in management. Investors need to understand the company, its fundamentals, and the reasons why the market does not recognize its future potential.

> **ESSENTIAL**
>
> Even though value investing can sound stodgy, value funds can deliver results that are comparable to aggressive-growth funds. Even for growth investors, it's a good idea to monitor the performance of a few value funds at any time, as it may make sense to put some money in a value fund that has a hot hand.

Don't be fooled: Value mutual funds are not necessarily market laggards. A good value manager recognizes future growth potential in an undervalued stock, then buys the stock cheap so they can ride the stock's next up cycle when the growth managers start to buy it. Value funds aren't likely to be wallflowers during bull markets. Effective managers pick good-value stocks before they rally, although it could take some time before the bet pays off. As the stock rises in price and the valuation rises, the manager will sell some of the position and put the money to work in other underperforming stocks with the goal of repeating the feat. The best example of this type of investor is Warren Buffett.

Considering Sector Funds

Sector funds are ideal for investors who like to trade based on technical analysis and momentum and who have variable time frames ranging from days to weeks or weeks to months. These mutual funds buy stocks in a single sector of the market, such as healthcare, technology, or energy.

Sector funds are suitable for your 401(k) plan and your short-term income-producing trading account. There's a wide variety of sector funds, with Fidelity and Vanguard leading the way. There are specialized funds that focus on information technology, natural gas stocks, and regional banks, among many other sectors.

Generally, the narrower the focus of a sector, the greater its volatility and the higher the risk potential it offers. Still, if you are a risk-taker and like momentum, sector funds are likely for you. A simple strategy is to put together a list of sector funds. You can find them listed in the mutual fund section of *Investor's Business Daily* or *The Wall Street Journal*. Get in the habit of checking them periodically. You can chart them on *StockCharts*, see which ones are interesting, and consider whether owning shares in one or more of them makes sense.

Balanced Funds and Built-In Asset Allocation

While growth and income funds offer some asset allocation, balanced funds and asset allocation funds put together a portfolio of stocks, bonds, and cash under one roof. Balanced funds tend to gravitate toward stocks and bonds, while asset allocation funds split the portfolio into stocks, bonds, and short-term instruments like Treasury bills and short-term bonds. These are ideal for investors who want to buy a no-stress mutual fund because the manager does all the worrying.

That said, you should still check on the fund's performance occasionally by reading the annual report, watching the fund's performance (during all markets), and seeing the manager's decisions.

Here are three things to expect from a balanced or asset allocation fund:

- **Performance:** If the stock market is on a very hot streak, your balanced fund should be performing in the direction of the stock market, though perhaps not to the degree of an aggressive growth fund.
- **Safety:** The goal of a balanced portfolio is to reduce risk. That means that if the stock market is falling hard, your balanced fund should be falling less due to its bond and cash components.
- **Consistency and predictability:** Although no mutual fund can have an identical performance during any two different periods, more than growth funds, the balanced and asset allocator funds should be able to smooth out market volatility to a reasonable degree while delivering better returns than cash.

International and Global Funds

The post-pandemic geopolitical environment has made investments in non-US markets more difficult, but these funds may still have a place in diversified portfolios. Some distinctions are that global funds may include US securities in the mix, while international funds will not, and the name of the fund will describe the region(s) in which the fund invests. Consider these factors when investing in foreign-focused mutual funds:

- The risk tends to be higher in international funds, but the rewards can also be high, especially when they invest in regions where commodity booms can occur. International funds tend to follow general market trends, but they can also buck those trends depending on regional developments, such as wars and strikes. Funds that invested in South America did well in the 1990s. The early twenty-first century tended to favor Chinese investments. Europe can be volatile due to its bumpy energy transition and geopolitical issues. The key is to find the region of the world where money is flowing into. Make a list of different non-US funds and monitor their share prices periodically.

◾ Funds that invest in narrow regions, such as a single country, have wider price fluctuations than funds that invest in a region or a continent. For example, a fund that invests in Europe may be more stable than a fund that invests only in Bulgaria.

The post-pandemic changes in the global economy have made international investing more challenging. That means that a change in the trend in the US economy may or may not affect foreign markets as it once did. These funds may or may not provide any added safety if you are looking to escape from a problem in the United States.

As the war in Ukraine and the 2024 conflicts in the Middle East proved, regardless of who's in the White House, the odds favor regional and perhaps global conflicts with a higher potential for wars, which, contrary to popular belief, can be positive for the stock market. One of the best bull markets of all time was during World War II. The first Iraq War also spawned a major bull market in stocks. Beginning investors should use these funds only for diversification purposes and consider using them as only a small portion of their portfolio.

Small-Cap, Mid-Cap, and Large-Cap Funds

In the stock market and the world of mutual funds, the word *cap* means "capitalization," or the market value of the companies in which the fund invests. Large-cap mutual funds invest in the better-known large companies. Mid-cap funds invest in midsized companies. Small-cap funds invest in the small companies. Micro-cap funds invest in the tiniest of the small companies.

Large company funds are often less volatile in bull markets, while mid-cap and small-cap funds may be more volatile while offering more opportunity for capital appreciation. This is because large companies have a more stable earnings and income stream, while mid-cap and small companies are at different stages of development and have the potential for more bumps along the way. You can diversify by investing in all three areas while recognizing the risk/reward ratio and your own risk profile. As with any other stock-related investment, rising trends will favor most reasonably managed mutual funds, while falling markets will hit most funds: large-cap, mid-cap, and small-cap.

Bond Funds

Bond funds can lose money, especially when the Federal Reserve is raising interest rates or inflation is on the rise. Still, they often have lower risks (and lower returns) when compared to stock funds. Their main function is to provide monthly income via dividends. The benefit of a bond fund is that you get diversification while the fund manager does all the analysis and manages the portfolio. All you have to do is pick a good fund, keep up with how it's doing, make sure it's meeting your expectations, and gather the income.

Remember that bond fund share prices rise and fall. Longer maturity bonds are more volatile. For example, if you own a bond fund that specializes in thirty-year Treasury bonds, its net asset value (daily price) will be more volatile than a fund which holds bonds that mature in less than two years. This is especially true during times when the Federal Reserve raises interest rates, which usually leads to lower bond prices. Over time, short-term bond funds are a fairly safe place to use as a method for savings.

If you own bond funds, there is no guarantee that your principal won't fluctuate depending on bond market conditions and their effects on the investment portfolio of the fund. There are primarily three types of bond funds: treasury or government, municipal, and corporate. Corporate bond funds may invest in the high-yield or junk category of bonds, partially or exclusively.

US Government Bond Funds

This is generally the lowest-risk, and thus lowest-potential-reward, bond fund category. Even though the US government runs high deficits, the risk of default remains low. So, for now, investing in a government bond fund is still relatively safe. These funds, although not exempt from short-term periods of volatility, are excellent vehicles for stable income and provide an antidote to the potential volatility of the stock fund portion of your portfolio.

ESSENTIAL

Inflation is the bond fund's worst enemy. When consumer prices rise, the odds favor a decline in your bond fund as interest rates rise. The flip side is that your dividends are often larger. This can increase your current income.

Municipal Bond Funds

These funds invest in short-, intermediate-, or long-term municipal bonds. Cities, counties, states, and other municipal entities, including school districts, use the proceeds from these bond issuances to finance new road construction or repairs, upgrade sewer systems, or build a new high school. The incentive of most municipal bonds is that investors don't pay federal and often state taxes on the income they receive from the bonds. This extends to municipal bond funds as well. Because the income is not taxed, it tends to be lower than the income you receive from other bonds, though. Municipal bond funds can invest in national, state, or local bonds. These bond funds may be very attractive to investors in high-tax states. This advantage may only apply to bond funds that invest in the state itself, though, which is why there are many municipal bond funds that carry the state's name in their title.

Corporate Bond Funds

Corporate bond funds specialize in owning bonds primarily issued by private companies. There are multiple types of corporate bonds, and their quality is based on the kind of corporation that issues them. Generally, good-quality companies with a proven track record issue the highest-rated corporate bonds. As company fundamentals and circumstances decline, so does their credit quality, and the risk of default increases. Ratings agencies have systems to evaluate and rate corporate bonds. Corporate bond fund prospectuses detail the general quality of their holdings. The key term to look for in the prospectus and the fund's literature is *investment grade*.

> **FACT**
>
> Socially responsible funds can sometimes be controversial since there is no set definition of the term *socially responsible*. These funds tend to avoid products that involve animal testing, tobacco, defense companies, and companies that produce guns. Many avoid companies that may be involved with child labor. If you are interested in this kind of investing, you should read the fund literature carefully and match it with your own criteria.

Corporate bond funds offer a higher yield, but beware of funds that offer significantly higher yields. These will almost certainly hold large quantities of high-yield or junk bonds with a higher risk of a default.

Mutual Fund Investing Checklist

This chapter has a lot of information about mutual fund investing. Here's a useful summary:

- Mutual funds are excellent for young and new investors through which you can invest in a variety of asset classes, especially in 401(k) plans and IRAs. Sector funds are suitable for shorter-term current income via targeted trading.
- Investing in mutual funds reduces one aspect of research, that of finding stocks and bonds, while reducing the work of managing a portfolio.
- There is a large variety of mutual funds, so there is a mutual fund out there that can meet your criteria and help you to reach your goals.
- Mutual funds reflect the general trends of the assets in which they invest. If you own stocks and the stock market crashes, your fund could

register significant losses in the short and long term, depending on how the market reacts and how your fund manager adjusts to the situation.

- Bond funds can reduce the volatility of a stock portfolio, but they have their own risks, depending on interest rates, the rate of inflation, and the type of bonds in the portfolio. Generally, mutual funds that invest in US government securities are safer than funds that invest in corporate bonds. Funds investing in high-yield or junk bonds are the highest risk.
- Past performance is not a guarantee of future performance. Before buying shares in a fund, review how it performs in up markets and down markets. If possible, check to see what a fund has done in a similar environment to the present.
- Balanced funds invest in a mix of stocks and bonds. Asset allocator funds allocate their resources among different asset classes; usually a mix of stocks, bonds, and cash-equivalent securities.

Keeping these guidelines in mind, you're set to invest in mutual funds!

CHAPTER 11

Combining Funds for Performance

There is a golden rule in investing: If you can't sleep because you're worried about what you own, you shouldn't own it. At the end of the day, your mutual fund portfolio is directly related to your pocketbook, retirement plan, and income goals. This chapter is about combining your risk tolerance and your goals into a mutual fund portfolio that delivers reasonable returns over time and lets you get some sleep.

Your Risk Tolerance

Chapter 1 gave your risk tolerance profile a checkup. So, by this stage of the book, you should have a good idea as to whether you are a conservative, moderate, or aggressive investor. Use this knowledge to assemble a mutual fund portfolio that fits your risk profile and your investment goals. Remember that the primary function of mutual funds is long-term wealth building, especially via your 401(k) and IRA retirement accounts.

Once you know your risk tolerance, you can assemble a mix of funds to deliver the kinds of returns you are comfortable with to build wealth over time. Remember that although mutual funds spread out the risk of owning stocks and bonds, they still reflect the risk of the assets they own. Thus, consider how your mix will perform during difficult markets and how that aligns with your risk tolerance.

ESSENTIAL

Find the sweet spot. Remember that being conservative will reduce your returns as well as your risk, while being aggressive does the opposite. The key to success is to balance the two.

While individual stocks can make you a lot of money in the short term, a stock portfolio often requires frequent adjustments, especially when part of your investment approach features short-term trading to produce current income. In contrast, mutual funds tend to maximize their returns over the long term. This is because an individual stock can respond to earnings or other positive news immediately, while a mutual fund, even if it holds a hot stock, also has other stocks, and sometimes a mixture of assets. So, the hot stock is only a portion of a diversified portfolio and only has a partial effect on the net asset value, or share price of the fund.

It can be difficult to hold on to mutual funds during bad markets and watch your account shrink. Stay patient and realize that markets eventually turn around. By reviewing the history of how your funds (whether it is a growth, growth and income, or any other category) perform on the rebound after a bad period in the market, you may better understand what to expect. Picking the wrong fund(s) can lead to impatience when things get rocky.

A simple way to reduce risk and heartburn is to allocate your 401(k) contributions using a formula whereby the stock portion receives a larger share of the contribution during bull markets. During down markets, build cash reserves to deploy in the next bull market by increasing the cash portion of the contribution.

Diversification Is Your Friend

Diversification spreads portfolio risk around. Successful diversification means owning several different types of mutual funds and allocating them so that your risk of a major loss is decreased. In other words, when you own three different aggressive stock funds, you are not diversifying your risk and likely increasing it because you may be repeating some stocks throughout the three different funds. Ultimately, if one of the funds gets hit, all three will likely get hit, increasing your losses.

Understanding Diversification

The concept is simple: own mutual funds that invest in different assets or asset classes and spread your risk around. You need to know the ideal mix of mutual funds, how many you should own to diversify your portfolio, and how often you should change your asset allocation. With this information, you will develop a working plan to balance your goals and your risk tolerance as you develop and maintain your mutual fund portfolio.

Achieving Diversification

Diversification requires patience and an understanding of what you wish to gain with your portfolio. Here are some guidelines:

- **Be clear and detailed when setting your investment goals.** Consider your time frame, risk tolerance, and the precise purpose of your portfolio, such as long-term growth for retirement, current income, or both.
- **Choose quality over quantity.** Pick one fund at a time. Match the fund to your goal based on whether it fits your investment strategy. If one fund takes care of your goal, then choose that one fund and wait to see how things develop. Evaluate the fund over a few months and see how things are working out. Consider what kind of market is unfolding and ask yourself how your fund might do if things change. The answer to that question and how it fits into your investment goal will send you in the right direction.
- **Keep it simple.** When you've chosen a fund that meets your criteria, don't add a similar fund to the list. For example, most growth funds will trend in a similar way because they invest in similar stocks. Then, move to the next category. If the first fund doesn't work out over a couple of months or a quarter, switch it for a different fund from the same category.
- **Fewer is better.** If you find that by choosing two or three funds you've met your goals, that's great. There is no need to have more than what you need. For example, if you are a conservative investor, you may choose a good balanced or asset allocator fund as your only vehicle.
- **Evaluate your goals and your funds' performance.** Look at your funds' performance on a weekly basis and consider making changes to your portfolio on a quarterly basis, if your goals change or if the funds aren't producing the desired results.

Paying attention to these criteria will allow you to diversify successfully.

Considering Your Choices

Once you've outlined and reconciled your investment goals with your risk profile, it's time to find some mutual funds for your portfolio. And while reading a fund's prospectus is worthwhile, it makes sense to have an independent source of information. Check out Morningstar.com, which has both a free and a premium service. The free service is well worth your time. You can get useful information about mutual funds, including performance, fund holdings, and information about the management team. A premium subscription will provide the free info plus detailed analysis and recommendations for mutual funds and market trends, which may help your decision-making process. If you're unsure, you can sign up for a free trial and see if a full subscription makes sense.

Choosing a Fund Family

Big is usually, but not always, best when it comes to choosing a fund family because large, well-established fund families have money, and money tends to attract good management. However, just because a fund family is large, it doesn't guarantee outperformance. The advantage of size is that the company usually has been around for a long time and therefore has a very accessible track record.

FACT

While it's highly unlikely, online investing platforms and mutual fund company websites may have security vulnerabilities at any time. Read the security tab on the website, ask fund representatives questions about online security, and pay attention to the news regarding security problems in the financial services industry.

For example, Fidelity Investments, Vanguard, and American are huge fund families with gigantic mutual funds that usually perform in tune with the overall market or sector that they track. Plus, in a tough market, especially one in which you want to sell shares in a fund or even close an account, you can likely do so with a click of a mouse. Big fund companies usually provide better data and security for your money online than smaller firms. In a world where security breaches are common, a fund company's cybersecurity is equally important to its investment performance. Ultimately, big money fund families, although not invincible, may have better resources to protect clients from non-investment-related damage than smaller companies.

The Fund's Objective

First, match your goal to the fund's objective. If you want aggressive growth or capital appreciation, make sure the fund's objective states that clearly in its literature and verify through independent sources like *Morningstar*. If the statement in the prospectus is vague, it means that the fund manager likes to have leeway, leading them away from your objectives. Ask yourself if you can handle unpredictability before investing.

Investment Risk

The fund should state its risk profile plainly, and you should be comfortable with the level of risk in the fund if you are going to invest in it. Make sure that the fund's risk and objective match and that the combination of the two is a good match for your risk profile. If a fund is an asset allocator but the prospectus says that it's a high-risk fund, you should probably pass on it even if you are an aggressive investor. Remaining true to the fund category and how it matches your risk profile is your best bet. An easily discernible measure of risk is Beta, a measure that compares the fund's volatility to that of its benchmark index. Beta is listed in the metrics found in the prospectus. A fund with a Beta of 2 performs at twice the volatility of its benchmark index. Growth funds tend to have higher Betas than income or asset allocation funds.

Once you've made sure that the fund actually does what it claims it does, review how the fund performs in up markets, in down markets, in relation to the S&P 500 or its benchmark index, and how it stacks up to its competition. If your account is with a single mutual fund company, see if it has more than one fund that invests in the category. If it does, choose the fund that has the better performance over time and that meets your risk profile and expectations.

Breakdown of Investments

The prospectus should clearly list the limits of the fund's investment breakdown. For example, it should note if the fund's maximum exposure to stocks is 60% or a different figure, as well as its maximum bond exposure. The fund should also tell you whether it uses leverage or margin—two terms that describe the practice of investing with borrowed money—or if it sells securities short, which is the practice of borrowing securities in the hope that they fall in price to profit from the price decline. Beginning investors should avoid funds that primarily employ margin, leverage, derivatives, and short selling.

FACT

Leverage and *margin* are financial terms related to using borrowed money to invest. The goal of using leverage or margin is to own more of a security than you would own with your own capital. The downside is that if the leveraged investment falls in price, you are liable for both the loss of the investment as well as paying back the debt.

Financial History

A fund should also list its history, preferably for the life of the fund, but for no less than ten years. This information should be detailed on a per-share basis and should include year-by-year details on net asset values, dividends, and total returns so that you can gauge performance on an annual basis. This history should also include details on the fund's expenses and fees and a history of the fund's holdings.

Parsing Past Performance

The financial world's signature disclosure statement and disclaimer is "Past performance is no guarantee of future performance." The reason is that things change, and change can affect a fund's performance. Aside from the economy, other important factors include interest rates, politics, along with sector and industry trends. A confluence of influences can lead to one or two years of good performance followed by several years of mediocre growth or even a decline in the net asset value. More importantly, the reversal of any of these factors, which may have held performance down for the past three to four years, could trigger a price reversal. To best evaluate past performance, compare past and present interest rates, economic activity, and technology trends. Pay special attention to the fund's current holdings and how they compare to the holdings during similar periods in the past.

FACT

When you sell shares of mutual funds within the same family, it's called an exchange. If you do it by phone, just tell the representative that you would like to exchange shares from Fund A to Fund B. If you are making the exchange online, just follow the directions on the website. The exchange will take place at the closing price at 4:00 p.m. EST on the day you make the decision, unless you make the exchange after hours. Then it will be made at the closing price on the next business day.

Also review what the fund's category has done through any significant period of the market and compare it to the fund's performance during the same period. If a small-cap fund didn't do well when small-caps weren't doing well, such as after the pandemic, it's not the fund; it's more likely the times that held it back. By the same token, if a small-cap fund delivered stellar returns during the same periods, it may be worth looking into it, as it could be a sign of superior stock picking by the manager.

Finally, when looking at long-term performance, consider the effect of fees, operating expenses, and sales charges. Have your CPA look at the tax consequences of the fund's annual payouts. This does not apply to shares held in a 401(k) plan, IRA, or other retirement account. Also, consider the size of the fund. The larger the fund, the harder it is for the manager to deploy their cash in the markets, given the need for very large share blocks. Know how long the current manager has been running the fund. If the fund has an excellent ten-year performance record, but the current manager started six months ago, the ten-year performance record is essentially meaningless.

How Long Should You Hold Mutual Fund Shares?

Ideally, your time frame for holding a mutual fund should be one to five years; especially in retirement plans aimed at long-term wealth building. But there are some things to consider before you make your decision regarding the holding period.

Although there is no way to predict when a market trend will change, you should understand where you are in the market cycle before investing. Thus, if you buy a stock mutual fund late in a bull market cycle, you should expect that some kind of pullback or extended period of flat prices may develop after you buy your shares. In this case, you may want to wait until an opportunity for lower prices materializes or buy small numbers of shares over time as the market cycle unfolds. Bear markets tend to last shorter periods than bull markets. Thus, if stocks have been falling for the past twelve to eighteen months, the odds of some kind of rally will likely rise. This might be a good time to buy some shares and see what happens. Technical analysis of price charts can help you pinpoint excellent entry and exit points for mutual funds.

Also know what kind of fund you are investing in. If, after looking at the market cycle, you get worried about losing money in a market correction, but you still want to put some money in a fund, consider a bond fund or an asset allocator fund. These tend to move more slowly than the stock market and are more likely to cause less damage to your principal. Moreover, there is nothing wrong with putting some money in your low-risk money market fund as you wait for things to sort out in the market.

Six Fund Investment Strategies

Stay patient with your fund investing. Follow these simple rules to stay organized and profitable.

Start Now

Time is your best friend. The earlier you get started, the better, especially in your retirement account. But don't be put off because you don't think you have enough time to meet your goals. Even if you make your first investment in a few weeks or months, by starting the process now, you'll be ready sooner. The data is clear: Compounding works over time. And there is no time like now.

Go Big

Invest as much money as you possibly can as early as possible. This does not mean that you should throw your money at anything. Even if you put a sizable quantity of money in a money market fund now, you can still move the money when you come across a fund you like better in the future. Build up your cash now so you'll be prepared when you're ready to be more aggressive.

Information Is Salvation

Know as much as you can about your mutual fund and the securities, stocks, bonds, and other asset classes that it holds. As you learn, you will gain confidence and experience, which will lead to better financial decisions and cut losses.

Stay Aggressive

Aggressiveness pays off in the early stages of your investing career when tempered by the knowledge that time is on your side. This means that putting money in growth-oriented mutual funds is a must in your early years. As you get closer to retirement, you can start scaling back. Being aggressive does not mean that you should be foolhardy. Always have a well-diversified portfolio, but include growth funds, especially when you are young.

Keep the Money Working

Your investment portfolio should not be your emergency piggy bank. If you take money out of your investment portfolio every time you have a financial emergency, you are taking money away from your future. Avoid the temptation of dipping into your long-term investments to pay bills if possible. Before doing so, try every other way of taking care of any financial surprise. On the other hand, having that nest egg may come in handy when you apply for a loan, as banks love clients with fat retirement funds.

Watch the Market

External events can hit your mutual funds hard. That means that you must watch your own portfolio. Don't trust your portfolio manager to do anything other than what their job requires. If the market starts to look dicey, it makes sense to put any new money in the safety of your money market fund and wait to see what the market does before putting new money into your stock funds. Use the same basic strategy for your bond funds. Sometimes building up some extra cash makes sense, as you can put it to work later at lower prices. This applies to both your long-term wealth building and your current income short-term trading accounts.

Tracking Your Funds' Performance

Once you become an active mutual fund shareholder, it's important to keep up with your fund's activity. Review your mutual fund order on the confirmation slip that you will receive either by mail or email. Confirm that your order was put in correctly. Check the amount of money you invested and verify that you got the correct number of shares. Pay special attention to any fees that were deducted when you bought the shares, especially if the fund is advertised as a no-load fund, and inquire about any discrepancies as soon as you notice them. If you buy the fund online, you should see a confirmation page before putting the order through. If you are buying the fund over the phone, your mutual fund company representative should confirm the order to you before putting it through.

Check your funds' performances weekly, no less than on a quarterly basis. In the age of high-frequency trading, a politically volatile world, and an economy where interest rates often fluctuate, somewhat frequent checks are a must. Compare your fund to its benchmark index and other funds in its category. Check on the fees charged by competing funds and fund families and make changes if they make sense.

When to Sell

Deciding when to sell is difficult. But with a good plan, you should have decided when to sell before you buy. Generally, you should sell a fund when it no longer fits with your long-term plans. Good reasons for selling are poor performance, a change in the fund's management, market conditions, or even bad service from the fund's family. Also consider selling if your fund isn't meeting your expectations or keeping up with the market or its category. If you see that most funds in the category aren't doing well, you should consider avoiding the entire category of funds and rethink your strategy and goals.

Mostly, you should sell your fund if holding it is making you uncomfortable. Maybe it's too volatile and you're starting to get nervous. If you're reaching for the antacids, that's a sure sign that you need to look elsewhere.

Always use technical analysis as a tool. A simple metric is the two hundred–day moving average. When a fund drops below that long-term benchmark, it can be a sign that it's time to sell at least a portion of your holdings.

The Fund Monitoring Checklist

Here are nine tips that will keep you from losing sleep over your mutual funds:

- Inspect and carefully verify every document you receive regarding your investments. If you find errors, address them immediately and record responses and corrections in writing.
- Keep notes of all conversations with investment professionals, ranging from your CPA and financial advisor to mutual fund or brokerage company reps, regarding your portfolio.
- Check that all investment-related correspondence is addressed to you. Your advisor, if you use one, should get copies. You should get the first copy.
- Keep up with your paperwork. If you make a trade and you don't get confirmation by email, text, on the fund's website, or by regular mail within a reasonable amount of time, find out why.
- If something unfamiliar or unexpected shows up in your account, contact your fund company or broker immediately.
- Never make your investment deposit checks or bank transfers to an individual. Always make them to the company and list your account number. Brokerage companies and mutual fund companies always provide investment slips with critical ID information that you should include with your check.
- If you decide to use a broker, make sure you meet them in their office before putting down any money.
- Know your investments. Don't rely on someone else's research or sales pitch. Get used to working with reliable independent websites like *Yahoo! Finance*, where you can find useful information free of charge.
- When in doubt, review your portfolio. There is no reason that just because you have mutual funds, you shouldn't keep up with what's going on. *The Wall Street Journal*, Investors.com, MarketWatch.com, and CNBC.com are great sources of information.

Remember, mutual funds are great investment vehicles for beginners and experienced investors. But just because the fund manager is making the buy and sell decisions doesn't mean you shouldn't still be informed and involved.

CHAPTER 12

Exchange-Traded Funds—
Made for Trading

Exchange-traded funds (ETFs) are securities that resemble mutual funds because they are composed of groups of assets, such as stocks or bonds. However, unlike mutual funds (which are priced after the market closes), ETFs trade like stocks throughout the day. They've been around since the 1990s and have revolutionized the way both individual and professional investors trade and invest. This chapter is all about how you can make ETFs work for you and how to avoid the potential errors that can cost you money.

What Are ETFs?

ETFs are hybrid securities that behave both as a stock and a mutual fund. They resemble stocks because they trade like stocks on an open exchange, through a brokerage account that charges a commission. They are like mutual funds because they are a portfolio of securities chosen by a manager. So, when you buy an ETF, you are buying shares in a portfolio, but because it trades like a stock, you don't have to wait until the market closes to buy or sell the shares. ETFs may also offer you better tax treatment and fee structures than mutual funds.

ETFs are your best vehicles for short-term and intermediate-term trending trades through which you can achieve current income to pay bills. They are also useful in 401(k) plans and IRAs, especially sector ETFs, which offer the opportunity to stay in long-term sector trends. One of these sector trends occurred when AI took off in 2024, and technology-focused ETFs outperformed many other sectors.

There are thousands of ETFs with trillions of dollars in assets, most of which are invested in equity-related funds with the rest in bonds or other types of funds. About 1% of assets reside in hybrid funds, which hold multiple kinds of securities, much like a balanced mutual fund.

ETFs are best suited for short- to intermediate-term trading, although they can be used for long-term investing as well. And while you may not be interested in trading when you are a beginner, trading may become attractive as you develop skills toward gaining current income from trading. Like mutual funds, with ETFs, you don't have to pick stocks. You are picking a portfolio that matches a market trend.

Moreover, there are no trading limits on ETFs. While mutual fund companies limit the number of times you can exchange in and out of a fund, you can trade ETFs like you trade stocks. And you can use margin, which expands your ability for short-term trading opportunities for current income.

In addition, some ETFs offer you the opportunity to sell the market, or specific sectors, short. Short selling is an investment method where you borrow and sell shares of a stock from your broker in hopes that they fall in price. If they do, you buy them back at the lower price, and your profit is the difference between the price at which you borrowed them and the price at which you bought them back. For example, if you think XYZ is going to fall, you may decide to short it at $100. You borrow one hundred shares from your broker and sell them, gaining you $10,000. However, you still owe your broker one hundred shares of XYZ. If XYZ falls to $80, you may wish to cover your short. This means you would buy one hundred shares of the stock back at $80 per share and pocket the $20 per share profit. When you buy the stock back, it goes back to your broker since you owed them one hundred shares. If the stock price goes up instead of down, however, you could lose money and still owe your broker one hundred shares.

While this is risky and is not advisable for beginners, short selling is a useful skill when you want to hedge your risk to protect your portfolio in a falling or volatile market, or when you see a weakness in a specific area of the market. Inverse ETFs, a special category of ETFs, do the short selling for you, so all you have to do is pick the ETF. The use of inverse ETFs requires a special agreement with your broker.

ETFs offer built-in leverage. As with short selling, using leverage is dangerous even for experienced investors. Yet, as with other advanced trading techniques, the use of leverage may have a place in your strategy at some point when you become more experienced. By using leverage, some ETFs move at two or three times the rate of their underlying index. This kind of investing is to be avoided by beginners and is only designed for short-term trading.

ETFs versus Mutual Funds

There are several important differences between mutual funds and ETFs. Since ETFs trade on an exchange like stocks, you can trade them at any time during the trading day; there is no minimum or limit on the number of ETF shares you can buy; and each time you buy ETF shares, you will have to pay a brokerage commission. ETF management fees tend to be lower than mutual fund fees, always review this before you trade any ETF shares.

ETFs don't make capital gains distributions like mutual funds. ETFs, especially ETFs that invest in bonds, do pay possibly taxable dividends. Remember, a capital gains distribution, in the context of mutual funds, is a different entity than a dividend because capital gains are incurred by mutual funds when they sell assets on which they have a profit. A dividend, in the context of a mutual fund, is a pass-through of dividend income that the fund has received. Also, ETF shares, outside retirement accounts, will incur applicable capital gains taxes when you sell them.

Finally, ETFs update their holdings daily on their company websites. This is a better deal than what you get with mutual funds, which are only required to report their holdings twice a year. This is important because knowing what you're buying in real time may influence your decision and could save you money in the long run as you avoid investing in something you may not want.

What Kinds of Investments Can You Make Through ETFs?

Like mutual funds, ETFs come in a wide variety of choices. Historically, stock index ETFs that focused on the popular indexes, such as the S&P 500 and the Dow Jones Industrial Average, were popular. This is still the most popular category given their low cost and ability to track their respective indexes. But as the market has expanded, so has the number of offerings. Now you can buy and sell ETFs that only invest in indexes that focus on aggressive-growth or dividend stocks, small stocks, large-cap stocks, or blue chips.

ALERT

Actively managed mutual funds can have higher fees than index ETFs and some mutual funds. And the return isn't guaranteed to be better since managers can have hot and cold streaks. Be aware that mutual fund companies offer these actively managed ETFs to broaden their investor base and to increase their fees. In fact, some of the time, actively managed ETFs are basically clones of their traditional mutual fund counterparts, often having the identical name. Why pay more for the same assets and sometimes worse performance?

You can also invest in municipal, government, and corporate bond ETFs that hold bonds with maturities from short term to twenty years. ETFs that specialize in real estate investment trusts and preferred stocks are easy to find. You can trade ETFs that invest in foreign currencies or the US dollar, while some offer you the opportunity to sell the bond or stock market short, and profit when prices fall. After 2014, actively managed ETFs have emerged. These funds, unlike index-based ETFs, use a portfolio manager to make changes in the portfolio based on the manager's indicators and trading philosophy.

Spiders, Vipers, Diamonds, Cubes, and Single-Stock Choices

ETFs often have great nicknames. But don't let the fun and games distract you, for these are all serious investments, and a wrong choice could cost you money.

- **Spiders** is the market's nickname for the first family of ETFs, the S&P 500 SPDR ETF (NYSE: SPY) and related funds. SPDR stands for S&P 500 Depository Receipts, which means these ETFs invest in stocks listed in the S&P 500. SPY was created by State Street Global Advisors and spawned the Select Sector SPDRs, a series of sector-specific ETFs such as the Technology Select Sector SPDR Fund (NYSE: XLK) and the Health Care Select Sector SPDR Fund (NYSE: XLV).
- **Diamonds** are another set of ETFs that let you own the stocks of the Dow Jones Industrial Average, while **VIPERs** (Vanguard Index Participation Equity Receipts) are Vanguard-issued ETFs. VIPERs, depending on which one(s) you choose, offer investment opportunities in stocks, bonds, and international markets.
- **The Cubes** (NYSE: QQQ), run by PowerShares, is the ETF that tracks the NASDAQ-100 Index (which houses the largest capitalization shares in the NASDAQ). By investing in the Cubes, you buy into shares of companies like Alphabet, Microsoft, Apple, Netflix, Amazon, and Intel, among others. PowerShares uses a method called dynamic indexing, which allows them to focus on the best performers in the underlying index.
- **Single-stock ETFs** (singles) were introduced in Europe in 2018, and in July 2022 in the US. Now you can trade a single stock through an ETF, often for a fraction of the price of the underlying shares. These ETFs are usually leveraged and closely mirror the general trend of the underlying stock. You can trade Amazon.com's single stock ETF (AMZU), Apple's (AAPB) and Nvidia's (NVDL) among others. These ETFs are especially

useful for short-term trades to produce current income. For example, if you recognize that shares of Apple are rising ahead of an upcoming earnings report, you may wish to buy AAPB for a few days, if the trend remains up. You can set a target for your return, such as $200.

FACT

Terms such as *Spiders* and *Diamonds* can be confusing, but they are commonly used and part of the market's jargon. By becoming familiar with them early in your investment education, you will be better informed in the future when doing research or when market news hits the wires.

Choosing Wisely

Aside from being excellent short-term trading vehicles, ETFs can be used to diversify your wealth-building portfolio via your 401(k) plan or IRA or even as the sole asset class of a well-structured portfolio. Sector Selector Service (https://buymeacoffee.com/wsdetectivx) offers a diversified ETF portfolio that is adjusted for market conditions as they evolve.

ESSENTIAL

Put together a list of reliable ETFs before you trade. Review their price charts regularly to see how they trend and respond to market conditions. Paper trade the ones you like before putting real money into them. Set up entry and exit price alerts on your brokerage account and track your paper trades based on your setups. Be specific by using technical indicators for both entry and exit limits and compile your results.

Because of the broad ETF options out there, your portfolio can participate in a piece of just about every asset category that's available. Perhaps the largest advantage is the fact that you can do this for a lot less than what it would cost you if you bought individual stocks, especially if you use single-stock ETFs. For example, you could own a large-cap, a mid-cap, and a small-cap index ETF. You can add one, two, or more bond ETFs, coupled with a diversified-commodity ETF, a gold ETF, a real estate investment trust ETF, an international equity, and bond funds. You can mix actively managed mutual funds and ETFs into your portfolio as well, further diversifying your holdings.

ALERT

ETFs are ideal for trend-following trading strategies based on technical analysis. This is because, as a more experienced investor, you will likely develop a better sense of the overall market's trend, and ETFs, by design, are trend-following investment vehicles. By using ETFs, you can focus on trading the trend instead of individual stocks.

Diversification can be overdone, so it's often best to stick with simple strategies and asset classes. If you decide to try out a popular new strategy, please study it and paper trade it before putting money into it. In 2018, a previously little-used strategy known as the selling short of market volatility gained popularity. This strategy was exercised via an exchange-traded note—basically an ETF with a finite life and lots of small print associated with it—known as the VelocityShares Daily VIX Short-Term ETN (VXX). When you owned shares in this exchange-traded note, you were betting on the market's volatility remaining low for the foreseeable future as based on readings of the Cboe Volatility Index, which measures the volatility of the S&P 500. However, on February 5, 2018, VXX lost 80% of its value in the after-hours trading session and triggered a provision in its bylaws that said if the NAV fell below a certain point, the ETN would liquidate. When it did, many investors lost most or all the money they had put into VXX in a few hours. Additionally, when Bitcoin ETFs hit the market in 2024, they were all the rage. Unfortunately, their introduction coincided with rising volatility of the cryptocurrency markets.

These are common investment pitfalls for investors who don't do their homework. To avoid these mishaps, whether you are a beginner or more experienced, stick to what you understand. Knowing the basics of using stocks, bonds, mutual funds, and ETFs that use straightforward strategies will serve you well in the long run. Furthermore, if, during your research, you find that you don't understand how something works, it's a sign that this is not an investment for you.

When choosing ETFs, you should compare expenses and performances between ETFs and similar mutual funds. Index ETFs and traditional funds that invest in similar holdings should perform similarly. But if one is more expensive than the other, your overall returns, especially over the long term, could be affected. Remember that a no-load mutual fund won't charge you a commission when you trade, while adding shares to an ETF will carry commission costs every time you buy. In other words, if you find a no-load mutual fund with equal or better performance compared to an ETF, choose the mutual fund. Also important is the cost per share. A mutual fund may cost less on a per-share basis than an ETF.

Competition between ETF families could save you money. For example, if Vanguard's S&P 500 ETF has lower fees than the SPDR fund, it might make sense to buy the Vanguard fund, given that it is investing in the same equities, and that performance should be nearly identical.

Avoid thinly traded ETFs. Before buying shares, make sure that any ETF has enough capital invested in it and that it is actively traded. If an ETF has assets of more than $10 million and has a robust trading volume, it makes sense to consider it. If the ETF has less than $10 million and trading volume is less than a few million shares per day, it means that it is not very liquid. And that means you may have a difficult time trying to sell shares.

ETFs and Time Frames

Short-term income and long-term wealth require different goals, skill sets, and time frames. For your short-term income goals, focus on technical trading and target your trades toward that goal. If your goal is retirement in thirty years, and you are just getting started, stay patient. Focus on your risk profile, your overall goal, and your time frame. Does this mean that you don't make changes or improve your asset allocation or trading techniques? Of course not; flexibility and the ability to recognize important changes in market dynamics are paramount for your long-term success as an investor, in both your short-term income goals and your long-term wealth building.

A great way to trade specific stocks with high share prices for short-term income is via single-stock ETFs. A commonly traded one is the Granite-Shares 2X Long NVDA Daily ETF (NVDL), where the ETF rises and falls at twice the rate of NVDA shares. This ETF normally trades for half the price of NVDA shares. Single-stock ETFs are best traded once you become comfortable with technical analysis. If you get the trade right and stay disciplined, you can produce reliable profits in short periods.

ALERT

Sector-specific ETFs may be useful in special market situations. For example, if there is a great deal of money being invested in energy-related stocks, it may make sense to evaluate and consider investing in an energy-specific-sector ETF. This strategy is suited for both long-term wealth building and short-term income.

ETFs let you carve out special niches inside your long-term wealth-building portfolio for special situations that can enhance your results. Work this out on paper before you put your money down.

Let's say your 401(k) plan's core asset allocation has a large-cap, a mid-cap, and a small-cap equity ETF along with a diversified bond ETF. You notice the technology stocks are on a momentum run. Thus, it might make sense to add a technology ETF. Remember, tech stocks won't go up forever, so you'll have to keep a close eye on this ETF. Technical analysis will help. You can use a moving average as a potential selling area for this fund.

Buying and Selling ETFs in Your 401(k) and Beyond

If you can trade stocks, you can trade ETFs. The difference is—excluding single-stock ETFs—with an ETF, you get a diversified portfolio instead of an individual stock. You still need a broker. You will pay a commission. And before you make the transaction, you need to do your homework and go down your strategic checklist. Consider when you will sell the shares. And understand the tax implications outside your retirement accounts. With ETFs, you can use limit orders and sell stops. The big difference between ETFs and mutual funds is that if you decide that you made a mistake, you can sell all the shares at any time without getting a notice from your mutual fund company because you sold your shares too soon and they don't want a "day trader" using their funds. No matter what, remember your 401(k) is for long-term wealth building, not short-term income. You can choose short-term opportunities as they arise. But short-term trades should not be your major focus in these accounts.

Technical Trading with ETFs in Your 401(k) Plan

Timing entry and exit points are important, although difficult. ETF trading can juice up the potential gains in your 401(k). This is best accomplished by setting aside a portion of the money in the plan for shorter-term technical-based trend trading. Indeed, ETFs are the perfect vehicle for this kind of trading, in which, based on your time frame, it is possible to profit over a few days, a few weeks, or a few months, depending on how long any market trend lasts and how good your timing strategies and attention to detail are.

These trend-based strategies require a working knowledge of technical analysis, as these tools are critical in finding optimal entry and exit points for trades. The simplest methods use moving average crossovers. For example, you would buy an ETF when it rises above its forty-day moving average and use the average as a sell stop. You remain in the position during the period the ETF stays above the average, but you can trim your position size as the ETF rises, thus increasing your chance of profiting. This is the perfect type of strategy to achieve short-term income via trading. You should also review any restrictions regarding frequent trades in your 401(k) plan. A self-directed IRA in a standard brokerage account has no frequent trade restrictions.

It's a Risky Business

Technical trading, also known as trend trading, involves risk and risk management. This trading is not investing, although it is a tactical portion of a long-term investing plan, such as when it serves to deliver the short-term income in non-retirement accounts. And it is not something that should be done by investors who are just starting out. As a beginner, focus on maximizing your 401(k) and IRA to build long-term wealth through mutual funds. But as you work on your long-term wealth, take the time to learn the steps required for successful technical trading and practice via paper trading.

ESSENTIAL

Index-specific ETFs are ideal for technical trading in your retirement accounts. If you know that the largest money flows are going into the S&P 500, your best bet, as a technical trader, is to invest in the S&P SPDR (SPY) or a similar ETF. Your final trading decision should be based on a technical assessment of the market's trend and requires a good working knowledge and a high level of experience in trend analysis and risk management, such as the judicious use of specific entry and exit points and profit targets.

ETFs are great vehicles for technical trading because your only focus is the direction of prices. The only thing that matters in technical trading is whether a market or sector is primarily rising or falling. When you buy stocks, you should pay attention to valuations, company management, the company's product cycle, and a host of other parameters that are detailed in Chapters 4–6. Technical trading is all about putting your money into an asset based solely on the direction of prices.

Tools of Trend Trading with ETFs

It's best to make ETF buy and sell decisions based on technical analysis, the study of price charts and trends, as it increases the accuracy of entry and exit points into positions. For example, when the stock market is rising, trend traders often buy an index ETF such as the S&P 500 SPDR ETF. The goal of trend trading is to remain in any position, such as an ETF, as long as the direction of prices remains intact. Keep positions open as they stay above moving averages. Sell them when they fall below. Remember, investing is a marathon. So, when you sell shares, you're raising the cash in your 401(k) plan's money market fund, which gives you capital for the next up leg in the market.

While long-term investors have time on their side, trend traders are looking to make money over shorter periods, though not necessarily as day traders. That means that they make buy and sell decisions more frequently, sometimes as often as every few days, although most trend traders are hoping to be in position for at least a few weeks, to maximize profits. This is a trading strategy best suited to your trading account, not your 401(k). In other words, trend trading in your 401(k) should be guided by an intermediate or long-term indicator such as the 50- or 200-day moving average. By using price charts and related indicators, timers take away the emotion associated with buying and selling.

Specifically, trend traders use indicators such as moving averages and oscillators, which help them to pick precise exit and entry points when the market is "oversold," meaning the selling has been exhausted and prices will likely rise, or "overbought," meaning the market has risen far enough that prices are likely to fall in the not-too-distant future. You can learn all about these useful tools at StockCharts.com.

Leveraged ETFs and Market Timing

Aggressive traders and market timers often buy a leveraged, or single-stock, ETF, which may move at two or three times the underlying price of the real S&P 500 or single stock. When they use leverage, trend traders can make or lose more money in shorter periods. Because technical traders hope to turn a sizable profit in less time than short-term investors, and because they tend to be experienced traders, they can afford to take the added risk of using a leveraged ETF. If a trend trader concludes that the stock market is about to fall, they may buy shares in an ETF that sells the S&P 500 short. These specialized ETFs, also known as inverse ETFs, rise in price when the S&P 500 falls. These types of ETFs are not best suited for your 401(k) because of their volatility.

Because there are ETFs for all markets, trend traders can use ETFs to time bonds and other investment classes. For example, you can use ETFs to trade commodities, including gold, oil, and agricultural commodities such as coffee, wheat, corn, and even cattle. There are specialized ETFs that offer the opportunity to trade in these areas either as part of a commodity index or as separate commodities. You can also use trend-based techniques to trade currencies such as the euro, the Japanese yen, the British pound, the Swiss franc, the US dollar, and the Canadian and Australian currencies. And yes, there are leveraged and inverse ETFs available for timing markets beyond stocks.

ETFs As Hedging Instruments

Hedging is used to limit the risk of falling prices in a diversified portfolio. A common hedge is the use of bonds or bond funds to limit the risk in a stock portfolio. Experienced traders and investors use ETFs as hedging instruments. Aside from using bond ETFs, traders also use inverse ETFs to hedge risk. For example, let's say that the stock market has risen 10%–15% in a few weeks. History shows that this kind of advance is likely unsustainable. During these periods, rather than selling a portfolio, an experienced trader may buy shares in an inverse S&P 500 ETF with the hopes that if the stock market corrects, the losses will be less, as the inverse fund shares will rise in price. This trading technique, as with other market timing techniques, is not without risk, but it could become useful as you gain experience, especially in your trading account to deliver short-term income.

You can protect your 401(k) or IRA with hedges during moderate pullbacks in the markets (a few weeks), but it makes more sense to go to cash when the markets enter longer-term down trends, such as a prolonged bear market.

Tracking Your ETFs

Tracking your ETFs is just like tracking your stocks. You can find daily prices and instant quotes on financial websites such as *The Wall Street Journal, Investor's Business Daily, Yahoo! Finance*, and many other sources, which will give you tick-by-tick prices if you like that kind of real-time information. You can also set up alerts with your broker that will let you know when your ETF reaches your profit goal or has fallen to your sell stop.

CHAPTER 13

ESG Investing

If you're socially or environmentally conscious, there are ways for you to invest profitably and stay true to your beliefs. And, contrary to popular belief, socially conscious ESG (environmental, social, and governance) investing, through the right vehicles, can be just as rewarding as mainstream investments. The key is to find the right vehicle to invest in and to follow sound investment principles. That said, ESG fell on hard times after the pandemic and after the 2024 election.

What Are ESG Investments?

Socially responsible investments can be a touchy subject since everyone's definition of social responsibility might be slightly different. Moreover, during political seasons, volatility in this sector may increase.

Vicky Vegan might be opposed to eating animals and might not want to invest in a restaurant chain that serves animal products, while Gary Green might not care about animal products but wants to protect the environment. Nevertheless, ESG investments are part of the investment landscape, albeit with ups and downs and variable profit potential. In the end, investments are about making money, and political causes are about bringing about change. ESG investing is no different in this regard. Still, there is a happy medium that can be profitable. That's what this chapter is about: finding the areas where ESG and capital gains meet.

Truly socially conscious companies put their money behind helping the world and avoiding business decisions in areas that are ethically wrong or include subjectively questionable practices. A socially conscious company actively pursues helping not just their bottom line but the entire world through their actions. As a result, Wall Street and Main Street focused on this area of investing in the pre-pandemic period.

After the pandemic, due to geopolitical changes and inflation, certain socially conscious sectors such as solar and wind energy fell on hard times. Many mutual funds and ETFs that invest in these companies struggled after 2020. This spread to municipalities and corporations that sold bonds to finance environmentally friendly projects. The key is to carefully research the general trends in the sector and then to become acquainted with further details as you prepare to make investment decisions.

ESG Stocks

ESG stocks let you become part owner of a company whose efforts, in delivering its goods and services, are positive for the environment or other causes. This may be achieved by its use of cleaner fuels; development of new methods that produce less, or cleaner, waste products; or avoidance of doing business with known abusers of ESG concepts. Sometimes these companies are donors of capital or volunteer their employees for ESG-positive causes. Unfortunately, both the science and the finances required to deliver on the promise of green investments struggled after the pandemic. This became most evident in the solar, wind power, and hydrogen fuel sectors, which fell out of favor due to the expense of implementation in many cases.

FACT

Keep it simple. Use your common sense. Starbucks is a green company that is well integrated into the mainstream. It makes money while using solar power to fuel stores, buys products from local organic farmers, and gives portions of its profits to green causes such as clean water initiatives. Microsoft and Alphabet (Google) are investing in nuclear power to power their AI centers as they move away from fossil fuels.

The potential for fraud is always present. Before investing, consider the following:

- Does the corporation that you might invest in have products, or are things still in the development stage?
- Is there a reasonable time frame to test the products and market them?
- What is the market the company is targeting? Is there a real need for the product?
- Is the company realistic in its expectations?
- Does the company describe how it expects its products to evolve and how it will expand its market share over time?
- How do this corporation's ideas, technology and business models, management team, and practices compare to others that are leaders in the sector?

If you can't get good, solid answers to these questions, especially when you are looking through company-produced documents, look somewhere else for a place to put your hard-earned green. Generally speaking, bonds of all socially conscious companies qualify for investment by those who wish to follow this particular direction. As with the equity side, this category of bonds also ran into difficult times after the pandemic. Yet there are still some opportunities.

Green (ESG) Bonds

A green bond is issued by a corporation or municipality where the proceeds will be used to finance an environmentally related project. Unlike traditional loans, where a borrower asks for money from a bank, bonds are loans that spread the risk by using money borrowed from the public, investors, and other entities, including banks. For you, as an investor, bonds produce income.

If the issuer is a corporation, consider the default risk along with your green meter, using the six questions outlined in the previous section. These bonds all operate in the same way as normal bonds, including the same ratings and risk/reward decisions as nongreen bonds.

Official green bonds (Qualified Green Building and Sustainable Design Project Bonds) are tax-exempt bonds issued both by corporations and municipalities. The federal government designates them for the purpose of developing underdeveloped, underutilized land parcels or old abandoned buildings. Often, the land where the work is to be done is polluted and contaminated, and the bond proceeds are used to clean up the environmental problems.

Green and Socially Responsible Funds

You can find traditional mutual funds or exchange-traded funds (ETFs) that specialize in green and socially responsible companies. ETFs may be a better deal because you can look at their component stocks in real time and apply your own personal socially responsible meter to the companies in the ETF before investing. Some funds bend the rules. If the prospectus tells you that the fund may invest its money "as much as 50%" or something along those lines, in green companies, it may not be for you.

Green funds are a subset of the socially conscious investing universe and come in three basic varieties: eco-friendly, alternative-energy, and sustainable-resource funds.

Eco-Friendly ESG Funds

This is the broadest category of ESG funds, where the fund can invest in companies that strive to improve the environment, produce and design environmentally friendly products, or work to actively reduce their negative impact on the environment.

The Calvert family of mutual funds specializes in green mutual funds and has a variety of offerings. The Calvert US Core Responsible Large-Cap Index fund may strike a good balance for you while their bond funds also offer the opportunity for diversification. The large-cap fund specializes in corporations that are socially responsible but have also found the sweet spot in delivering profits to their shareholders. A sampling of the stocks they hold may surprise you, as they include Microsoft, Alphabet, Visa, and JPMorgan Chase.

Beware of false claims or mushy language in fund prospectuses and other information. Look at the holdings of the fund before buying shares. If you are truly committed to socially responsible investing, you don't want to put your money in the wrong place.

Alternative-Energy ESG Funds

These funds invest in companies that develop or produce alternative or renewable energy sources, such as solar and wind power, biofuels, or hydroelectric power, and the companies that are involved in the infrastructure and manufacturing of the components used to make the final products for alternative fuel production. An example of such a fund is the First Trust ISE Global Wind Energy ETF (NYSE: FAN). This fund is often overweighted in global utilities (solar and wind) and utility infrastructure. Always research before you invest.

FACT

Looking inside the holdings of an ETF should lead you to do research on individual companies whose stock may be worth owning, on their own or along with the ETF. For example, the largest holding of any ETF could provide you with clues as to what kind of new trends may be unfolding. Jot these companies down and do more research on them later.

Sustainable-Resource ESG Funds

Sustainable-resource funds invest in companies that share the double goal of maximizing profits without depleting natural resources. This is where the water funds fit. These funds invest in the entire gamut of the water industry, including water distribution, water consumption, and other subsectors of the water industry such as pipelines, storage, measuring devices, flow controls, disinfectants, and so on. The water industry is widely tracked by multiple indexes, and, in turn, there are several ETFs and mutual funds that also track individual indexes. A diversified global water ETF is the Invesco S&P Global Water Index ETF (CGW). Non-exchange-traded water funds are available, too, such as the actively managed Calvert Global Water Fund (CFWAX).

Looking Beyond the Green

Even though socially conscious investing is appealing, it can be just as dangerous as mainstream investing, and often for the same reasons. As with any investment, when the premise, the investment vehicle, and the execution of the management team at a company or a mutual fund are what they say they are, and everyone does what they say they will, the odds are in your favor, while interest rates and the economic fundamentals cooperate. Just remember that scam artists are everywhere—even in these good causes.

Because social responsibility is partially an emotional decision, big Madison Avenue advertising firms craft socially responsible "messaging" statements and "narratives" for their clients, to brand companies that aren't green or socially responsible as such to increase sales. This "greenwashing" is well embedded into the corporate culture. Companies, much like politicians, try to spin their products and practices to make them look green, when in fact, scrutiny often reveals that there is more effort on the spin than on the green practices advertised.

FACT

An example of "greenwashing" is when a cable company paints itself as green but uses tons of paper in its direct mail advertising campaigns. Another example is when a water bottler pitches its larger bottles as helping the environment, but the bottles end up in landfills just the same.

Research what companies do to appear green and socially responsible. Ask tough questions. Is a biofuel company using twice the amount of oil for input to create clean fuels? Do agricultural companies burn land, creating smoke pollution, to plant biofuel stock? Do biofuels pollute the air more than gasoline as some forms of ethanol do? What happens to a riverbed and a fish population if you remove that niche algae to craft synthetic motor oil? If you look hard enough, you may find that in many cases, the "green" outcome is achieved at the price of significant environmental destruction and that the long-term implications may be worse than what's advertised. Consider where a company makes its products, who its workers are, and how the workers are treated. And remain balanced. The green and socially responsible activists are not exempt from their own spin and may be looking to just take your money.

As an investor, you need to become an investigative reporter and do your homework before putting your money into a moral commitment potentially not aligned with your morals.

Your ESG Portfolio

ESG investing has changed since the start of the twentieth century. Companies that are sincere and well managed are flourishing as they find a balance between environmental consciousness and profit. From a price-performance standpoint, big-money players are the ones that move stocks and bonds. So, when a nongreen mutual fund sees something in a green company, it is quite likely that the stock of the company is going to move higher. As an investor, be aware of this and prepare to act on it. Also, note that some regions are against ESG investing because it is seen as harming their natural resources. Oil-producing states in the US and countries around the world have pushed back.

To avoid getting burned, adapt the basic rules of investing with ESGs. Know your risk profile. Stick to leading companies with top management teams. Keep up with the general news and trends and monitor how a company responds to the news. Develop a watchlist of ETFs and mutual funds and monitor their performance. Change your allocation as needed. A quick glance at a stock or ETF's price chart will tell you a lot in a short period. Don't put all your eggs in one basket.

Finally, ESG investments may be a part of your portfolio, but they should not be your entire portfolio. There is no substitute for careful analysis, diversification, risk management, and weighing your long-term goals.

CHAPTER 14

Real Estate Investing: Always Be Prepared

Once you've gotten on track with your long-term wealth building and short-term income generation via the stock market, it's time to add real estate to the plan. You may have heard that real estate never loses its value, especially as a hedge against inflation. Between the housing crisis in 2008 and the pandemic, the housing market actually *is* unstable, with opportunities for buyers' and sellers' markets. Thus, having your finances in order and a thorough knowledge of the business will get you ready when opportunity knocks.

The Basics of the Real Estate Game

Real estate investing can become a full-time job. But don't be discouraged. Start small, solidify your finances, be patient, and learn the craft.

As a DIY real estate investor, you're responsible for making sure everything develops along the right lines. And the more you know, the better off you'll be. Although it's not necessary for everyone, you may consider taking some courses or look into getting a Realtor's license.

No matter what, before you make your first hands-on real estate purchase, you should have a sound financial situation. A well-positioned 401(k) or IRA that you can use as collateral for mortgages will help. Lenders see well-funded retirement as a sign that you're a good lending risk. Additionally, prior to your first purchase, decide whether you want to flip the property or use it as a rental. Either way, once you've made the purchase, your priority is to be cash flow–positive on your first property before expanding your holdings.

Because it's harder to get out of real estate investments than to sell a stock, you should be well versed in the local market. Indeed, to be a landlord, you must learn a whole new language, including the definition of closing costs, resale value, liquidity, inspections, and more. You will also need a good attorney in case relationships with renters, prospective buyers, business partners, and contractors sour.

Supply and Demand

Real estate is driven by supply and demand. When there are too many options (rentals or homes for sale) prices fall. When there are too few, prices go up. Supply and demand are also influenced by location. Supply and demand can be magnified during periods when supplies are tight throughout all markets.

Balance your strategies between buying at the lowest price possible or sometimes paying up a bit to catch a premium location. In either case, it helps to be well financed. For example, if you buy too early in the cycle, before a meaningful turnaround appears in the market, you may be forced to pay taxes and upkeep costs while the property remains empty. The flip side is that you may wish to sell a property sooner than you originally planned during periods when prices are rising rapidly.

ALERT

Keep your finger on the market's pulse. In 2022, the post-pandemic housing market hit a fever pitch. The combination of shifting demographics, low housing supplies, and nearly record-low interest rates created a bubble environment. Had you owned property during this period, it might have been a good idea to sell, likely at record prices. By 2023, prices began to fall and anyone who bought during the bubble was likely underwater.

Watch how markets respond to mortgage rates. The best transactions are those made when there are few buyers competing for assets. This is usually when mortgage rates are close to topping out and prices are low.

The Post-Pandemic Environment

The pandemic shook up real estate, directly affecting supply and demand. On the commercial side, office vacancies soared and rents dropped, leading to large numbers of loan defaults. On the residential side, city-anchored properties suffered as renters and owners moved to suburbs, rural communities, and other states.

ESSENTIAL

Be willing to go against the grain. If you are well financed and have a long-term time horizon, it's worth considering purchasing properties during the bust periods that follow every bubble. Do your homework and focus on getting the best deal possible for both the property and the mortgage rate, especially when the latter has bottomed out.

These changes created potential opportunities. If you lived where people were moving to, and you were an active investor, you might have been able to buy at low prices and sell for higher prices. However, if you're starting your real estate career after the pandemic, you face a different set of challenges: tight supplies, higher home prices, and populations that are still in flux. This makes things difficult. Stay focused on the basic principles of real estate: supply, demand, and location. Patience will pay off.

Leverage, Method, and Attention to Detail

Real estate investing, in any period, requires money and time. Sometimes, it makes sense to borrow that money, otherwise known as leverage. Leverage is useful when applied prudently. In stocks, leverage is called margin. In real estate, it's a business loan, a mortgage, or tapping into a line of credit. However, leverage is a double-edged sword. When used properly, it lets you own more property than you would with just cash on hand. But even when you use leverage properly, it still increases your risk. Throughout the loan's life, you must pay it back, and these payments can eat into your profits. As a DIY investor, you should be well versed in how loans are structured and how to manage the risk. You may consider getting some coaching or having a thorough discussion with a banking friend or family member who knows the inside workings before taking the plunge.

Successful real estate investing requires the right mix of properties and leverage and keeping your cash flow on the positive side. If you own rental property and it's unoccupied, or you have unexpected costs such as repairs or legal problems, your cash flow could suffer. Thus, you must make enough money to at least make your monthly loan payment and cover your costs such as taxes and repairs. That's where stock investing and trading come in handy.

A great way to learn the real estate ropes is by first investing through homebuilder stocks and real estate investment trusts (REITs). First, real estate investing can generate income and over time build wealth that can be put to work elsewhere. Second, this investing allows you to learn how the sector works through careful study of how the pros run their business. You can then put your knowledge to work in your own physical real estate business.

Using Leverage to Your Advantage

Before soliciting a business loan (or mortgage) to buy a property to rent or flip, make sure you are well financed and know all the details of the type of loan you're getting. The bank will focus on your credit score, credit history, and current debt while reviewing your assets. Aside from having ample cash on hand, this is where having a well-funded 401(k) plan or IRA can make the difference between approval or denial.

ALERT

If interest rates rise before your adjustable-rate mortgages mature, you may have a higher rate when you refinance. Thus, the best time to use leverage is when interest rates are falling or have been low for a while. So, while a line of credit, or a short-term (five- to fifteen-year mortgage) may be useful, you should make every effort to pay off your real estate loans ahead of maturity. Work it out on paper. If it doesn't add up, don't use leverage.

A great DIY way to fund your down payment is with any money left over from your stock trades that doesn't go into paying bills or contributing to your retirement/long-term wealth-building fund. In addition, although it shouldn't be your first choice, you can borrow from your 401(k) plan to help fund the down payment.

Your Action Plan—Cash Flow, Cash Flow, Cash Flow

As a DIY real estate investor, positive cash flow—having money left over after paying all your bills—is the key to success. It's most critical in real estate because positive cash flow offers opportunities. When you have money left over at the end of the month, you can give yourself a bonus, pay down mortgages faster, or use the cushion provided by the cash flow to borrow money and expand your holdings through the prudent use of leverage.

A sensible way to use leverage is when you have a set of properties that are producing stable and reliable cash flow, and a new property opportunity comes along that aligns with your long-term business plan. It then makes sense to use an existing line of credit or to apply for a loan to finance the new purchase if the interest rate climate is appropriate and the real estate market is stable. A perfect example of this type of market is when interest rates are falling and your listings all have multiple offers.

ESSENTIAL

Keeping an eye on the bond market is just as important as keeping an eye on the Federal Reserve's interest rate moves. If you must choose between the two, go with what the bond market is telling you. The US ten-year Treasury note yield (TNX) sets the rate for the average thirty-year mortgage and influences all other rates. Thus, if the Fed is lowering rates but TNX is not falling, wait for TNX to confirm the Fed's moves before searching for a loan.

When you use leverage, never borrow more than you can pay back. Read your loan contract carefully and make sure there are no hidden clauses, especially if you want to restructure the loan to a lower interest rate in the future or to expand the time for repayment. You should also ensure there's no penalty for early payment of the loan. Banks like to hide little surprises in loans, especially the loans they make to young entrepreneurs. DIYers sometimes need help. If the loan doesn't make sense, get a CPA or advisor to look at it, or don't take it.

While you use borrowed money, invest your own money wisely to improve cash flow. Work toward finding opportunities that will create profits in short periods and give you predictable income, like flipping a house or getting tenants who pay their rent reliably. If you make enough money in a short period, use some of it to pay your loan down or off altogether.

Choosing the Most Profitable Real Estate

Once you're ready to move into real estate, you must decide what kind of properties make the most sense based on your long-term goals as it takes a long time for properties to develop and provide a good return on your initial investment. The choice is whether you will hold a property for an extended period as a rental or try to flip it for a quick profit. Each method requires a distinctly different approach and will lead you to a different marketplace.

The artful challenge is finding a suitable location and then deciding if that location makes sense for your business plan. As a DIYer, you may wish to partner or consult with a Realtor who has access to solid leads. A good place to look for properties is in an area that is being revitalized; you'll then have some flexibility. A good review and a thorough analysis of the current area and what's likely to happen there commercially and politically are vital. Is this an area where people are flocking? If it is, then what's the attraction? Once you understand the dynamic, then you can tap into it in the most cost-effective and potentially profitable manner.

Considering Commercial versus Residential Property

After the pandemic, the commercial property market, especially office buildings, collapsed as more people worked from home. However, if you were a bargain hunter with a long-term time frame, this collapse offered some opportunities.

The bottom line is that markets rise and fall. Thus, if you decide to invest in commercial properties, put on your small business owner hat and look for areas where large companies are moving their headquarters—you may have some long-term success. Consider whether you would own a business in this area and why. Look for other businesses that are coming to the area, such as restaurants or other retail establishments that could make your real estate location attractive. You can buy an empty building, refurbish it, and lease it for businesses. Try to find out what no one is doing there and then fill that niche. Is there a dry cleaner in the area? Does it make sense to consider offering medical office space? Anything is possible if you take the time to study the needs of an up-and-coming area.

For residential properties, focus on the needs of your renter or buyer. Families want access to shopping, good schools, restaurants, and entertainment. They also want good roads or easy access to public transportation and low crime rates. Put yourself in the potential renter's or buyer's place. Would you move into this area? The key to success in both commercial and residential real estate is that you can put together the best possible package for your customer.

In addition, during inflationary periods, consumers are price-conscious. So, once you own a space, see what rent is doing in the neighborhood. It may be worthwhile to offer a slightly lower price with some incentives in exchange for a longer-term lease agreement.

Consider offering a rent-to-own arrangement where the client signs a long-term lease with the intent of purchasing the property and having part of the monthly rent go toward the purchase price. This approach has some fine points to consider, so fully research this option first. It may make the difference between a "Yes" or a "No" with a potential client.

The Fix and Flip Business Model

House flipping became a popular business model because of trendy TV shows that featured the practice. But don't be fooled, real estate, especially house flipping, is risky even in good markets. Much depends on your ability to stay well financed, organized, and budget conscious. Before investing, investigate any real estate properties thoroughly: learn the current state of the market, interest rates, and potential issues.

Understand the difference between an investor and a speculator. An investor is in for the long haul, while a speculator is looking to flip a quick profit and move on to the next house. Investors are patient and look for properties that are within their means, while remaining flexible, including changing plans from flipping to renting the space. Speculators are willing to use leverage and take higher risks. As a new real estate investor, it's a good idea to start small and learn the ropes over time. A good advisor, an experienced investor who is willing to share their wisdom or make you a partner as they teach you the basics, is often helpful. Consider hiring a coach or subscribing to a great real estate coaching service provided by Dr. Axel Meierhoefer via Substack at https://idealwealthgrower.substack.com.

> **FACT**
>
> Manage your time wisely. Painting your own properties may take too long and not save as much money as you think. You can use that time to look for another property, especially one that is inexpensive and that you may be able to sell or rent quickly. If you turn a $30,000 profit in 100 hours of work with the new property, you just paid yourself $300 per hour, more than enough to pay for painters.

Start with small rental properties. You can look at a fixer-upper house. Usually, the easiest properties to get started with are single-family homes due to how easy they are to buy and sell compared to other types of units. Townhomes and duplexes may work, as they may offer more manageable expenses and may be easier to rent, especially during periods of high inflation where potential homebuyers may be focused on the cost of a monthly payment rather than on building equity through buying a home.

The Fixer-Upper Dilemma

A flipper's dream is to buy an inexpensive older home, fixing it up, and selling it for a big profit. This is plausible and, in the right market, can be done. Yet it's not without risk. When buying a fixer-upper, consider the following factors:

- **Expertise.** To know your financial exposure and risk, check into the building design and construction style. This will help in figuring how much work, money, and time you'll have to put into the project. Figure out what you can do and how much you'll have to pay contractors to do. Add in building material costs and factor in the unexpected and inevitable problems you'll encounter, especially plumbing and electrical surprises.

- **Patience.** Even if you are looking for short-term profits, things happen. Expect surprises once you start remodeling and develop patience and a sense of purpose. Remember that even though you turned a trash bin into a diamond, market pressures will affect your ability to sell a property. Be prepared to hang on to it for a while and factor in the cost.
- **Inspection.** Don't buy a house without getting a professional home inspector to do a comprehensive inspection. Always check out the inspector's references. And be prepared, as even the most thorough inspector won't find everything that's wrong.
- **Location.** Location is as important as interest rates. Study the neighborhood, the shopping around it, the roads, the access to highways and mass transit, the schools, and the recreational opportunities. If the neighbors don't take care of their homes, you'll likely encounter trouble selling it even after fixing it.

ESSENTIAL

To protect your rental property investment, you will need rental insurance and property insurance, in addition to your homeowner's policy because your homeowner's policy won't cover any liability for alleged damages that your renters may cause.

Keep It Simple

Whether you're flipping or working with rental properties, commercial or residential, avoid unconventional or niche properties. Stick to properties in good locations, which offer a better chance of paying off over the long run. Pay special attention to any possible structural damages or defects in the property before you buy it. Anything that shows up after the closing will cost you money. Think about the potential demand for a property in five or ten years. And always keep your eyes open for special features in a property, such as a state-of-the-art kitchen, truly remarkable bathrooms, or great closet space.

In the end, the state of the market will depend on interest rates and the status of supply and demand. If interest rates are rising, save your money and wait.

Common Sense Is Key

When flipping or investing in rental property, use your common sense. If you bought a house in a vibrant area and suddenly you learn that the largest employer in the community is about to close its plant, expect trouble unless you move quickly. Remember, aside from interest rates, sales value is only as good as the property and the local economy.

Building Wealth and Producing Current Income Through Rental Properties

Rental properties can provide current income through rent and build long-term wealth via accruing value over time. But before you start, you should be in an excellent financial position. If you're not, then your risk rises and no one will lend you money.

It may not be wise to borrow money because that loan payment could squeeze your cash flow, especially if you're not able to get tenants or if you lose tenants without quickly replacing them. At the end of the day, tenants or not, you still must pay the bills.

Do Your Homework

Beware of what you don't know. Ask your Realtor friends if they have important information as sellers may hide critical information, or something beyond your control may happen, such as a bad economic event. There's also always the chance that something more closely related to the property may crop up, like a new freeway overpass that is going to be built across the street from your potential rental place. Thus, be prepared and always consider:

- **Location:** Always check the location's past and present while also considering the future.
- **Rental history:** Get as much detail as possible, especially the length of any rental engagement and related circumstances.
- **The property's age:** Older properties will require a detailed inspection and a potentially substantial repair budget.
- **The coding status:** Rely on your inspector to find out if your plumbing, electricity, foundation, and roof meet local ordinance requirements.
- **Repair work:** Your inspection will tell you how much work the property needs. Detail the expenses and plan to spend twice as much or more than the highest estimate as your worst-case scenario. Remember older homes and office spaces may not be wired for high-speed Internet and multiple phone lines. Landscaping, painting, and repair work will also cost you money and time.
- **Maintenance costs:** Commercial properties will require custodian and security budgets.
- **Zoning details:** If you plan to rent the property as office space, make sure the city has designated your area as commercial. Check out the ins and outs of owning the property as your own business by making sure the zoning allows for it.
- **Accessibility:** A business property needs to be well located, easy to access, and visible, while a summer cottage is better if it's well hidden and private.
- **Local future projects:** If a new mall is coming, how will it affect your business property? Do you want to own a rental property just when a year-long road construction project begins across the street?
- **Insurance costs:** Canvas several agents and figure the costs into the overall costs of your property.

- **Property taxes:** How will they affect your cash flow and your profit margin? Think about the breakdown of their tax deductibility—personal and business.

If the checklist and the numbers don't add up, regroup, and consider another property.

The Management Challenge

The next step is to consider what it takes to manage your properties for maximum efficiency and income. That requires brushing up on your management skills and having an eye for detail, while balancing customer satisfaction with fiscal reality.

Think of it like this: Once you own rental property, you are the landlord, the opposite of the renter's experience. Remember that a good landlord tends to keep tenants, while a not-so-good one has trouble renting the house and loses money. As a landlord, you're not protecting your own home. You are managing a source of income. That means you must be aware of what it takes to keep the place going. Think about the time and money it requires and measure that against your return. Do the right thing, but make sure your efforts are paying off.

Maintenance

Time and cash management are everything. If you are handy, you can do some of your maintenance, although it may make more sense to hire someone so you can handle other things required by the property or your stock trading for current income. If you hire someone to do the maintenance, factor in their costs, experience, and reliability. Remember that contractors may have multiple jobs at any one time. They can be hard to find and pin down, affecting their reliability. Thus, you may have to manage angry tenants or wait with an empty house during times when repairs are pending. And unlike with owning stocks, you are the one who will be getting the complaint calls.

Landlord-Tenant Communication

Yes, you can be a good landlord and still make money, especially if you communicate well with your tenants. Make them aware of your expectations, rules, and regulations in advance. Don't sign a lease unless these points are addressed and agreed upon by the tenants. Any changes in the terms should be communicated in a timely fashion in writing, and you should have proof that the tenant received the information and agrees to the changes.

Other Important Considerations

It will take some time from the moment you buy the rental property to when you will find tenants. The monthly checks won't just appear in your bank account. If you don't have the time to manage the property, hiring a professional management firm may make sense. They do take care of things for you, but they charge fees, which can cut into your cash flow and profit margin.

Real Estate Investment Trusts

As you wait for your physical real estate investments to develop, investing in real estate via real estate investment trusts (REITs, pronounced "reets") is a great idea. A REIT is an investment company, in many ways similar to an exchange-traded fund (ETF), that allows you to participate in real estate without being on the front lines. You can buy REIT shares on a stock exchange, or you can buy a mutual fund or an ETF that invests in REITs.

REITs have been around for decades and are a convenient and safe way to invest in real estate. You make money in a REIT as you do with stocks, by collecting dividends and selling shares when prices rise. REITs are pass-through securities, where the business isn't taxed but shareholders are.

What's in a REIT?

REITS buy or manage real estate usually in the form of properties or mortgages. Property REITs profit from the cash generated by the property. Mortgage REITs invest in mortgages used to finance the purchase of properties and profit from mortgage payments. Hybrid REITs invest in both. Mortgage REITs lend money to real estate investors and may pay a higher dividend than property REITs, but they often have a higher risk of losses because they only make money if the investors make their monthly payments.

One advantage of owning REITs is that they can provide current income and help with wealth building in your 401(k) and IRA. They can also deliver capital gains without the potential hassle of real estate directly. A great benefit of REIT investing is that as a DIYer, you can learn a lot about real estate by reading REIT earnings reports and literature. You can get a great deal of information about REITs through the National Association of Real Estate Investment Trusts, also referred to as Nareit (www.reit.com or its toll-free number, 1-800-3-NAREIT).

Comparing REITs

Here is a list to help you pick the right REIT:

- **Dividend yield.** Compare the dividend yield of your REIT to that of US Treasury bonds. For example, in November 2024, the top ten REIT yields ranged from 4.9% to 14.4%, while the US ten-year Treasury note was yielding 4.36%. Remember to do your research before investing, especially as to why a REIT may pay a much higher yield than Treasury bonds.
- **Earnings growth.** Look at the funds from operations (FFO) category to see the earnings history of your REIT. The FFO trend tells you how well things are going. FFO is the net income, excluding gains or losses from property sales and debt restructuring, and including real estate depreciation.

- **REIT's holdings.** Holdings can be anything from shopping centers to office or apartment buildings, resorts, healthcare facilities, or other forms of real estate such as farmland or empty land awaiting development. Many REITs have pivoted to single-home rentals. Reviewing their earnings can tell you a lot about the current rental market.
- **Location is everything.** Make sure you know where your REIT invests: regionally, nationally, or internationally.
- **Diversification.** Consider a diversified REIT that owns different kinds of properties in different locations.
- **Management.** The management company of your REIT is as important as that of a mutual fund or as a company CEO and their team. Check out their experience and track record in different types of markets.

ALERT

REITs are sensitive to interest rates. During periods of falling real estate prices and higher interest rates, REITs fall in price and can deliver losses even if their dividend yields rise. They may cut dividends during tough times.

REIT Mutual Funds and ETFs

You can own REITs through traditional mutual funds and ETFs. These are especially useful in your 401(k) and IRA but are even better as current income vehicles because you can buy them before their ex-dividend date, capture the dividend, and sell them after the ex-dividend date. Morningstar .com has great data on REIT funds, and most of the major mutual fund companies offer REIT mutual funds. Many of them are no-load funds and offer quarterly dividends. Nareit offers great tools, including up-to-date news on the industry, a directory of REITs with phone numbers and websites, a list of REIT ETFs, and a portfolio optimizer tool.

Tracking Your REITs

You can track your REITs, funds, and ETFs online via your CNBC app or through your brokerage account. Just type the REIT symbol as you would with a stock.

Even though real estate investment is not for everyone, it can still be profitable via REITs.

Owning Homebuilder Stocks

A second and often profitable way to piggyback into real estate indirectly is by trading homebuilder stocks of companies like D.R. Horton (DHI) and Lennar (LEN). Homebuilder stocks rise and fall in response to the supply and demand of homes in the market and interest rates, especially bond yields, which in turn set mortgage rates. You should apply the same analytical methods to homebuilder stocks as you would for any stock. Start with your "Is This a Great Company?" checklist (Chapter 5), check out the price chart, review recent earnings calls transcripts, and see where interest rates are at any time.

CHAPTER 15

Taking More Risks

Risk is best defined as the odds of losing in any task. When it comes to investing, risk is best managed when chosen wisely and backed with investment experience and knowledge. A balanced approach is based on your risk profile (found in Chapter 1) balanced with the results of your current approach. In the end, if what you're doing now is working, then you're likely taking as much risk as you need to. This chapter is all about the ins and outs, the good and the bad, of risky investments, and risky investment techniques inside and outside of the financial markets.

The Two Faces of Risk

Risk is the balance between your willingness to chance losing large amounts of money in exchange for big gains. Risk-taking behavior is influenced by the notion that you can make a lot of money in a hurry by taking big chances.

In stocks and related markets, you increase risk by using alternative or derivative securities, such as options, or by using risky maneuvers, usually involving leverage. The combination increases the level of unpredictability. Riskier market alternatives can include initial public offerings (IPOs), commodities, options, futures, leveraged ETFs, penny stocks, cryptocurrencies, using margin, and short selling. When you add risky securities, you increase your portfolio's volatility, and you may lose money rapidly. Because investing should not be like a trip to Vegas, this chapter is about developing an understanding of higher-risk investments, inside and outside the financial markets; how to use them appropriately; and when it's best to avoid them altogether.

Selling Short and Using Margin

Short selling is the opposite of going long. "Going long" is Wall Street jargon for buying stocks, bonds, or other assets. Long investors are hoping their assets rise in price. "Going short," or short selling, is the opposite. Short sellers are hoping that prices drop.

Selling Short

Short sellers borrow stock, usually from their brokers, and sell it. If the stock drops in price, the short seller buys it back at the lower price, profiting from the difference in the price at which they borrowed it and the price at which they bought it back. Short selling is not for new investors. On the other hand, you can use inverse ETFs to short the stock market or individual stocks via single-stock ETFs (discussed in Chapter 12). Short selling may be useful after the underlying asset for the ETF, such as the S&P 500 or a stock (like Nvidia), has had a lengthy gain and is due for a correction.

For example, if Nvidia has risen for an extended period and is showing signs of weakness, you may wish to consider the Tradr 1.5X Short NVDA ETF to speculate on a drop in shares of Nvidia. This ETF rises at 1.5 times the rate of a drop in NVDA shares. It also falls when NVDA rises. Inverse ETFs can reduce the risk of an actual short sale of a stock.

If NVDA falls, you make money if you sell the ETF before the stock reverses. If NVDA rises, you're likely to lose money. If NVDA shares don't fall, you can just sell the ETF for as close to even as when you bought it.

Margin Trading

Margin involves borrowing money from your broker to buy stocks or to sell them short. It requires a margin account from which you can trade with leverage or margin. It requires a signed agreement with your broker after they vet your finances and trading experience. A margin account lets you buy more assets than with a cash account by borrowing some from your broker. Usually, the money in the account is about a 50-50 split between yours and your broker's. A margin account with $10,000 allows you to trade with $20,000.

FACT

Experienced traders, such as hedge fund managers and day traders who use sophisticated and often technical analysis–based techniques, use margin. Short-term volatility and big drops in the stock market can trigger margin calls.

If your stock goes up, you're okay. If the price drops, you may have some problems, as according to federal law, your margin account must have at least 25% of the value of the stock you borrowed. Your broker may have a higher margin requirement. Thus, read your margin agreement carefully before signing it. When your balance drops below the maintenance margin set by your broker, you will get a "margin call," which is Wall Street lingo for "you need to put up more money." You do this either by transferring money into the account or selling the stock at a loss and hoping that it covers your debt.

Let's say that Jane wants to buy one hundred shares of social media stock ABC. ABC stock costs $50 per share, and she only has $2,500, so she borrows $2,500 from her broker in her margin account and buys one hundred shares: $2,500 worth of equity in the stock plus a $2,500 debt to her broker. If the price of ABC drops to $34, the total value of her one hundred shares is $3,400. Because of her margin debt, her equity drops to $900 because she still owes the broker $2,500 plus the interest accrued on the margin loan. Jane's choices are: put up another $1,600 or sell her shares at a loss and pay off the loan.

Initial Public Offerings

Initial public offerings, or IPOs, can be risky. An IPO is what happens on the day when a company's shares debut on the stock exchange. On that first day, the gains or losses on the price can be extreme. IPOs raise money for companies without adding debt. It can be an opportunity for early investors to cash in some of their shares and be rewarded for their initial risk.

FACT

A secondary offering raises money, after an IPO, for some purpose, such as buying back debt or financing an acquisition. They are usually not as big a news item as an IPO and can bring the stock's price down.

You may have a knack for picking IPOs. Still, it may be best to start via an IPO ETF. You can read more about them at www.etf.com/topics/ipo.

ETFs Can Solve the IPO Risk Problem

Because IPOs are risky, it's sometimes best to delegate tasks by investing in an ETF focusing on specific areas of the market. This is a great way to participate in the IPO sector. Because ETFs are run by well-informed portfolio managers, they have access to better information than the rest of us, which means they are more likely to pick winners.

The Renaissance IPO ETF (IPO) owns shares in recently issued IPOs. It has an excellent record of picking winners. Moreover, because it is a diversified, professionally managed portfolio, it also sells stocks that do not meet their investment criteria. This is an excellent alternative to investing in individual, recently issued company shares.

Investor's Business Daily offers excellent information on IPOs that have been public for some time and whose shares are doing well.

Balancing Risk Through Sector Investing

At first glance, sector investing may seem risky. After all, when you put your money in one area of the stock market, you're literally putting your eggs in one basket; this seems to go against the principles of portfolio diversification. However, sector investing, especially through sector-specific ETFs, is often very profitable. That's because when a sector gathers momentum, many of the stocks that make it up move up simultaneously, compounding the gains. The key to success is to remain watchful of the action in the sector, know which stocks are the leaders, and monitor their activity.

The Best Sectors

Any sector can trend higher for an extended period, but there are four that historically fit the bill best: technology, healthcare/biotech, energy, and utilities. Each one responds to its own set of influences, therefore keeping up with news and developments.

Technology offers the most reliable trends because there are frequent new developments in the field, such as AI, that bring in money and make the stocks profitable. The healthcare sector is similar, as pharmaceutical advances (like weight-loss drugs) can lead to long-term advances. Energy is a bit more difficult to predict because of the vagaries of oil and natural gas. Yet new trends in renewable energy continue to emerge, and that subsector can trend for long periods. Utilities are interest rate–sensitive while central to technology.

How to Trade Sector ETFs

Your best bet to invest in sectors is through ETFs. You can invest in them for both short-term income and long-term wealth building in your 401(k) or IRA. Here are some simple steps to get you started:

- Make a list of sector ETFs. Here are some symbols: XLK (technology), XLV (healthcare), XLE (oil and gas), and XLU (utilities).
- Make a list of sector ETFs and watch their price charts regularly.
- Keep up with sector-related news. If a new type of drug is increasing in popularity, check XLV. Do the same for other ETFs on your list.
- Paper trade these ETFs based on technical analysis. For example, when one moves above its fifty-day moving average, buy some shares. When it drops below the average, it's time to sell.

Commodities and Precious Metals

Commodities are raw materials ranging from food to raw materials for high-tech gadgets. The major influence on commodity prices is supply. Even fears of limited supplies can send commodity prices higher. Real supply crunches, such as in the post-pandemic period, are usually inflationary. When investing in commodities, it helps to monitor supply and demand. Commodities, especially those owned through a mutual fund or ETF, can be an important component of a diversified portfolio.

Commodities

Investing in commodities requires dedication and a good understanding of technical analysis. Aside from investing directly in commodities, keeping up with the price activity in this area of the markets may provide useful information about other sectors and the industrial and market sectors where a commodity plays a vital role. Here are some examples of everyday commodities that may be worth considering for investment:

- **Lumber and housing.** A housing boom is bullish for lumber prices. High lumber prices often precede higher prices in homebuilder and related stocks.
- **Oil** remains central to the global economy. Its price also influences gasoline, heating oil, natural gas and derivative chemicals, and other industries.
- **Cotton** is important, as it is used in clothing and many other products such as coffee filters.
- **Wheat** is a central global commodity.
- **Corn and soybeans** are among the most widely traded commodities in the world.
- **Gold, silver, and platinum** are widely used in jewelry. Silver and platinum are central to the automobile industry. Gold and silver are widely seen as inflation hedges.
- **Coffee, cocoa, and sugar** are important commodities. Booms and busts are common in these markets.

It is best to participate in these markets through a mutual fund or an ETF.

ESSENTIAL

The Invesco DB Commodity Index Tracking Fund (DBC) is an ETF based on oil and gold and a batch of agricultural commodities. Track this ETF on paper before investing.

Gold

Gold differs from other commodities since you can invest in it directly via physical gold bars (you can buy these at Costco) and through mutual funds or ETFs.

Gold bars may be the most difficult way to own gold as an individual investor. Gold bars must be made of at least 99.5% gold bullion and weigh a uniform 400 troy ounces (the standard weight measure of gold). Gold bullion coins are legal tender. Their worth may be more than their face value, depending on their weight and the market price of gold at any one time. Gold coins are popular investments, especially among collectors and during periods of inflation or political uncertainty.

Trading Currencies

For new investors, it can be difficult to see how you can make money by trading money. But currencies, although not the best market for a newbie, can still be lucrative. The simplest currency trade is what anyone does when they visit a foreign exchange booth while traveling abroad. In fact, currency trading, known as FX for "foreign exchange," is a huge market, with over $2 trillion exchanging hands daily. Although it's an important market, it's best suited for day trading and requires your full attention. Thus, if you have an aptitude for currency trading, it could fit well into your short-term income trading plan. My book *Day Trading 101, 2nd Edition* offers the full details on this topic.

FACT

You may enjoy currency trading if you're a night owl. This trading goes on twenty-four hours per day, starting at 5:00 p.m. EST on Sunday and going on continuously all week until 4:00 p.m. EST on Friday. It's also helpful that most currency-trading platforms offer paper trading accounts, which let you work out your strategies ahead of time.

Derivatives and Options

Derivative investments get their value from another investment. Without the underlying asset—as the related investment is called—a derivative is worthless.

Derivatives are contractual agreements between two parties, such as options, futures, swaps, and forward contracts. Derivatives can be based on stocks, stock indexes, bonds, currencies, and commodities, as well as weather data, the size of crops, or even more esoteric things, such as the derivatives that nearly crashed the world economy in 2008 (bets on whether people would actually make their mortgage payments).

The most traded derivatives are options based on stocks. In fact, the volume in options trading is larger than that in stock trading. Options give the holder the right, but not the obligation, to buy or sell the underlying security at a specific price by a specific date. Thus, the option trader bets that the price of a security will move in both direction and amount. Success in options is built on both the direction and the magnitude of the move before the option expires.

FACT

The largest options exchange in the United States is the Chicago Board Options Exchange (www.cboe.com). This company's website offers useful information, including options symbols and other data that can be helpful in analyzing the stock and bond market.

Stock Options

Options trading requires knowledge of basic facts and terms:

- **Call option.** This option lets you buy one hundred shares of XYZ stock at the specified price.
- **Put option.** Put options let you sell one hundred shares of XYZ stock at the specified price.
- **Expiration date.** This is the date on which the option becomes worthless.
- **Strike price.** This is the specified price of the stock on which the option is based.

Option buyers are buyers. Option sellers are known as writers. When you write an option, you sell the buyer the opportunity to buy or sell the underlying security at the underlying price.

For example: Buying an October (of the current year) $35 call option on XYZ stock offers the option of buying one hundred shares of XYZ stock at $35 on or before the expiration date. If you buy the $35 call option when the stock is at $35 and it rises to $55, you could exercise the option and buy a stock that is selling at $55 for only $35. You could then turn around and sell it for $55, pocketing the nice profit. If the stock falls below the strike price, you would let the option expire worthless. A call option has unlimited upside potential. Your maximum risk is what you paid for the option if it expires worthless. A put option, however, can be a risky proposition if the stock rises in price.

FACT

Options allow you to participate in the price trend of the underlying asset for a fraction of the price you would pay for owning the asset. For example, a call option on a $50 stock may be purchased for $2. Thus, options trading can provide huge percentage returns while limiting your losses to less than if you owned the underlying asset.

The value of an option is influenced by four different factors: the underlying price of the stock, the strike price, the cost of holding a position in the underlying stock, and an estimate of the future volatility of the stock.

Selling Options to Generate Income

Selling (writing) options can deliver current short-term income and is a worthwhile trading technique to learn and incorporate into your DIY system. When you write an option, you collect a premium. You can sell an option without owning the stock (naked write) or you can own a stock and sell an option (covered write). Selling options is a great way to make money when stocks move sideways for extended periods. A great place to learn about selling options is Edward Corona's *The Options Oracle* (https://optionsoracle.substack.com).

LEAPS

LEAPS (Long-Term Equity Anticipation Securities) are widely available long-term options. Use them to bet on the direction of a stock over a period of several months or perhaps years. Otherwise, LEAPS resemble regular options.

Employee Stock Options

Employee stock options differ from publicly traded options because, unlike listed options, there is no third party involved. Instead, employee stock options are a direct contract between the employer and the employee. Here are a few important facts:

- Employers use them as incentives and rewards for employees.
- Always research the tax angles associated with these options, as they may be useful sources of deferred income.
- Employee options have mandatory holding periods before the employee can exercise them and can be as long as one to ten years.

Employee options are often used by start-up companies or companies in rapid periods of growth. Often these companies have plans for going public at some point in the future and use these options to entice, recruit, and retain employees. The downside is that if the company goes bust or underperforms, it could be difficult to cash these options in.

Cryptocurrencies As an Investment Opportunity

Everyone has now heard of cryptocurrencies, such as Bitcoin or Ethereum. These are digital currencies traded on various exchanges all over the world.

You can even trade futures and options on cryptos on the Cboe or invest directly or through multiple ETFs. Cryptos are suitable for both short-term income (requiring technical trading skills) and long-term wealth building (buy and hold).

If you buy Bitcoin directly, you'll have to open an account at an exchange, such as Coinbase. There you can buy fragments of coins (known as satoshis) or entire coins. In January 2025, a full Bitcoin was trading at nearly $100,000. Cryptos are widely accepted and are now considered a major asset class.

FACT

You can find excellent crypto information and trading websites on Substack. Two such sites are *Ecoinometrics* (https://ecoinometrics.substack.com) and *CryptoSlate* (https://cryptoslate.substack.com).

Bitcoin has become a popular "flight to safety" asset to which investors often flock when uncertainty arises in the world. Bitcoin is legal tender in many countries, including the US, Jamaica, and Brazil. Other countries have some limits on its legality.

Thinking Outside the Box—Private Equity, Collectibles, and Farmland

Other options more suited for long-term investing include the use of private equity and collectibles. These are niche investment sectors that often require larger sums than those used in stock trading.

Private Equity

A private equity firm is a partnership that buys mature—sometimes distressed—companies. The firm then takes those companies private, retools them, and sells them for a profit, either privately or as an initial public offering. Entry into these partnerships often requires large sums of money and involves detailed vetting of your financial status. They traditionally require ten to twelve years of holding your money without the ability to withdraw it. After that time, they usually begin profit distributions to investors.

On the other hand, you can trade the stocks of the largest private equity groups, Blackstone Inc. (BX), KKR & Co. Inc. (KKR), Carlyle Group Inc. (CG), and Apollo Global Management (APO).

Collectibles

Collectibles are a popular alternative investment offering a wide world of possibilities ranging from baseball cards, Pokémon-related memorabilia, antique toys, and more traditional categories such as rare paintings. As with any investment, you should develop a working knowledge of the underlying markets, their fundamentals, reliable information sources, and the effect of outside influences on the markets, especially interest rates and inflation.

The most popular categories remain trading cards—sports or otherwise —artwork, and fine wines. You can invest in the latter online through platforms such as Vint (vint.co).

Other categories include classic cars, traditional antiques, figurines, and toys. Who knows? Rummage through your attic and see what you may find.

Farmland

If you're an outdoor enthusiast, you may consider owning farmland. This is still a viable investment alternative, especially after the pandemic. The downside is that prices in some locations rose after the pandemic due to population migration. However, prices may start coming down as people move back to the city. As with any other real estate investment, the important factors affecting price are supply, demand, and location.

An indirect way to invest in farmland is through a REIT. A popular one to consider is Gladstone Land Corp. (LAND). Because REITs are highly interest rate–sensitive, LAND is best owned during periods of falling rates.

In conclusion, alternative investments are not for the novice investor. Over time, as you gain experience, you may slowly move into these areas. Most professionals will tell you that alternative investments are fickle and should not be your primary sources of income or the foundation of your long-term wealth-building plan.

CHAPTER 16

Working with a Financial Advisor

In the early stages of your investing career, an advisor may come in handy, just as an experienced second opinion can come in handy. This chapter is about finding the right advisor and how to best put one to use.

What Kind of Advice Do You Need?

Because you are about to put real money on the line, it makes sense to get all the help you can get, even if you are a natural. Much depends on how quickly you grasp the organizational and analytical aspects of investing. But if you can't decide whether you want to own growth stocks or whether bonds make sense, you may need an advisor.

The Personal Survey

Take a personal financial survey. Consider whether the thought of managing your own portfolio makes you uncomfortable. Do you always carefully monitor and think through your decisions? Do you know what to do when stocks are crashing? Do you have time to analyze market trends, look for the best-performing sectors, and crunch numbers to evaluate mutual funds, stocks, or ETFs?

Are you resilient when you make mistakes? Is your favorite TV channel CNBC? Is your first morning read a financial information site? If you answered yes to many of these questions, you're likely a self-directed DIY individual investor.

ESSENTIAL

A good financial advisor should be a consultant and teacher working with you to develop a long-term investment plan and help you with budgeting, taxes, and estate planning.

If you agonize over which mutual fund to own, you hate keeping tabs on financial news, or you just don't have the time, consider hiring a professional.

The Time Trade

Time will affect whether you use a financial advisor, especially when you balance your input with what you are getting in return and how it affects time with family or work. In the beginning, you'll take longer to make even simple decisions, thus getting some advice makes sense. Still, if you eventually want to make your own decisions, you might use an advisor as you develop a knowledge base. Advisors can be an excellent source of learning materials, such as books or websites, where you can gain insight and experience before slowly weaning yourself away.

What Can You Expect from a Financial Advisor?

Different kinds of advisors provide different services. Look to find one that fits your needs. Here are some different types:

- **A money manager** is someone to whom you delegate decisions after a thorough consultation about the style and purpose of your investing. Some money managers will only do a certain kind of investing, such as aggressive or income-related securities. Once you choose your money manager, you will leave all the decisions to this person and check the progress on statements or when you have conferences.
- **Financial planners** help you map out your long-term strategies and offer investment advice. With a financial planner, you make the final call about pulling the trigger.
- **Analysts and advisors** focus on giving you information but are not involved in planning. They give you advice, but you do everything else on your own.

All financial professional should send you quarterly reports with details about your accounts. You should also have direct online access to the accounts and meet with your advisor more often than quarterly to discuss the results in person. This helps to develop your relationship and education. Remember: Your financial professional has other clients, and they may not be able to keep up with everything. Only work with professionals who are available and willing to spend time discussing details with you. If you can't get face time with your advisor or they never return your calls on time, move on.

The Advisor's Roles

Your advisor monitors and reviews your portfolio, discussing changes in allocation or investment choices that make sense, while monitoring the markets and communicating potential concerns or significant events that may affect your account's balance and performance. Most of all, your advisor should keep you calm and focused on your long-term goals if the markets turn volatile while providing the tools you need to succeed.

Good advisors shine in a down market. Their job is to keep you from losing big money and to preserve your wealth. The best advisors minimize your losses and manage your emotions. Good portfolio managers, regardless of the size of your account, should have great market timing and the ability to make changes in your asset allocation as needed. This might be a simple thing, such as not investing your newly deposited cash as they wait for a better opportunity, or advising you to take some profits after a mutual fund has had a good run. More importantly, the advisor should be able to communicate these strategies and changes to you and make sure that you are comfortable with what they did and understand why they did it.

Shopping for the Right Financial Advisor

Aside from reviewing their long-term record, consider whether this person who will be managing your money is someone you can get along with. Check out their credentials and details about the services provided. Review monthly or quarterly statements and fully understand their content. If they work for a big company, make sure they aren't or haven't been under investigation for fraudulent practices. Look into their customer service, whether the company is insured against fraud, and if the advisor attends continuing education courses. Most important, ask them about their successes and failures and what they tend to do in down markets.

Choose wisely. You wouldn't want a radiology technician to take out your appendix; that's a surgeon's job. The same thing applies to your money. You want the right person for the right job. If you want a high-level, aggressive stock trader for your advisor, you may not be well served by the same person who handles your car insurance.

> **ALERT**
>
> Before you sign any agreement or pay for any services from a financial advisor, find out how they get paid for taking care of your account. Sometimes advisors are paid bonuses and extra fees for selling you specific high-fee products that may or may not fit your needs.

Certified Financial Planner (CFP)

An advisor who has earned the CFP certification has put in their time and has experience in financial planning, from the study of the stock market and individual stocks to the intricacies of estate planning. CFPs are certified through a rigorous, standardized curriculum that requires passing a certification examination, work experience that meets certification requirements, and passing the CFP board's fitness standards for conduct, a stringent set of ethics guidelines. The criteria and requirements for certification are created, monitored, and enforced by the Certified Financial Planner Board of Standards (www.cfp.net). CFPs specialize in creating long-term financial plans and providing the strategies required to meet goals.

Chartered Life Underwriter (CLU)

These are insurance professionals, certified by The American College, who pass through rigorous training and licensure programs in the insurance field. They must pass eight courses, meet minimum experience standards, and follow a strict code of ethics to become licensed. They are also required to undergo high-level continuing education.

A CLU's expertise goes beyond life insurance and includes training in estate and retirement planning. A CLU may make sense for your longer-term strategies, another financial professional may better serve you when it comes to stocks, bonds, mutual funds, and real estate investment trusts.

Chartered Financial Consultant (ChFC)

These professionals are also accredited by The American College and are often CLUs as well, but with added benefits. To earn the extra letters, they delve into every area of financial planning from the client's perspective. Their goal is to customize a plan based on your financial know-how, position, and goals; put the plan in motion; and keep it on track. After they complete the program, they must pass the requisite exams and have three years of experience in the industry before they can call themselves ChFCs. They can become a one-stop shop for you, as they are well versed in tax planning, investments, insurance, retirement, and estate planning.

Personal Financial Specialist (PFS)

A certified public accountant (CPA) with additional financial planning qualifications is known as a personal financial specialist. This type of professional may be worth considering given their knowledge of the tax code. This aspect of financial planning could help reduce the tax burden of your investment portfolio.

QUESTION

What else are CPAs known for?

CPAs complete additional educational requirements as demanded by the American Institute of Certified Public Accountants (AICPA) to become a PFS. Another way to achieve this certification is to have a CFP or ChFC designation and accreditation.

Keeping both the CPA and PFS designations requires continuing education and adherence to strict ethical guidelines. A PFS can be very helpful in determining your net worth, assisting with your retirement needs, and developing strategies for your long-term goals.

Registered Investment Advisor (RIA)

Most pure money managers are RIAs. To become an RIA, you must pass a state certification test. Some RIAs are also brokers, while others are CFPs or CPAs. RIAs manage active client accounts. Any professional who passes the test, follows the continuing education and ethical directives of their state, and runs a clean shop can become an RIA. The state securities board or the Securities and Exchange Commission regulates RIAs.

How Much Will It Cost?

Costs depend on what type of advisor you choose. Generally, financial advice is not cheap. Advisors are required to give you their costs up front along with a detailed list of what your money will be buying. Each advisor has a different cost scale. By the end of the interview, you should have a good idea as to what you are paying for and whether it's worth it.

> **ESSENTIAL**
>
> You may be put off by advisor fees. And you may have good reason to not hire someone, especially if they are expensive and not all that good. Consider negotiating with them or discussing a different fee structure.

The three most common fee structures are commissions, flat fees, and fees based on a percentage of your assets under management. There may also be some transaction fees, below-minimum-balance fees, and account maintenance fees. Some advisors, especially money managers, charge a combination of fees, such as a flat fee for office and materials expenses and a separate fee based on a percentage of assets under management. In addition to the advisory fee, you will incur trading commission fees.

Commissions

Advisors who get paid via commissions, separate from trading commissions, make money by selling you something, like a mutual fund or an annuity, or by trading your account, in the case of stockbrokers. Most commission-based advisors are ethical and scrupulous. Some are not, and they prey on novice investors. Thus, it may make more sense for you to use a fee-based advisor.

Flat Fees

Fee-only advisors get paid an annual fee. You are their source of income, and their fee is not based on your assets or how well your account does. Sometimes, these advisors get fees from mutual fund companies and brokerage houses for having certain kinds of securities in your portfolio. They need to tell you that they do this. If they don't and you find out later, you should fire them. Period.

Percent of Assets

This is the way money managers get paid. A money manager, or an RIA, usually charges 1% to 3% of your total assets under management annually to manage your account. You usually pay the fee on a quarterly basis (0.25% to 0.75%), whether the advisor makes money or loses money for you during the quarter. Smaller accounts are sometimes charged larger fees, which fall if the account grows. Money managers tend to focus on larger accounts and are often active traders.

What's Best for You?

Be realistic. If you have a small account but you need advice, try a consultant. Financial planners can help you put together a plan and schedule a quarterly or biannual conference with you or remain available when you have a question. For estate planning, a CLU may make sense. If you come into a large sum of money from an inheritance, bonus, or promotion, consider an RIA and retain a good PFS. Above all, make sure you know what you are paying for, keep up with your portfolio, participate in the decision-making process, and don't hesitate to move your money if you're not getting the service you're being charged for.

How to Find an Advisor

Finding an advisor who is both qualified and a good communicator may take some time. Stay patient and get it right. Reliable referrals from someone you trust, a friend or a family member, are helpful. You can also get good recommendations from the National Association of Personal Financial Advisors, the American Institute of Certified Public Accountants, the Society of Financial Service Professionals, and the International Association of Registered Financial Consultants.

CHAPTER 17

Doing It Yourself

Because investing is a personal thing, you may be your best bet. If you are an independent, thoughtful, patient, and adventurous person, you're in luck because this is the golden age of DIY investing. Online trading, the wealth of information available on the Internet, and the rise of investing apps can make it all possible. This chapter is all about helping you make the decision to do it yourself and setting you on the right path to current income and future wealth.

How Much Work Are You Willing to Do?

Ask yourself how hard you are willing to work to grow your nest eggs (for current wealth and long-term wealth). Certainly, almost anyone can randomly pick stocks and mutual funds. But portfolio management is different, as much of the work includes study, analysis, position adjustments, and monitoring of your overall return.

Questions to Ponder

It's important to compartmentalize your two goals: current income and building long-term wealth. To set yourself up for DIY success, you'll need to know some basic parameters about your money-making goals. Thus, here are some important questions:

- **How much time should I spend becoming an investor?** If you're looking for investments to lightly supplement your income and lifestyle, you may wish to devote a few hours per week to the endeavor. If you wish to derive a larger portion of your income and build long-term wealth faster, you will have to consider investing as your second career and give ample time to it.
- **Is this investment decision for current income or building long-term wealth?** Getting this right will focus you on the right time frame for your exposure to the investment.
- **How long should I allow for this investment to flourish?** Depending on your answer and what nest egg you're focusing on, you may have different game plans. If you're looking to make $200 to pay your electric bill, you may wish to trade a single-stock ETF in a short-term trade. In contrast, a growth mutual fund is better suited for your 401(k).

Keeping these questions, and their answers, at the front of your mind will help you succeed.

Developing a Routine

Regardless of your financial timeline, you'll need to develop a routine that works for both current income and long-term wealth. Because you're a money manager, even if you don't work for Fidelity, your routine can start with your morning coffee and a review of the action in the overnight markets. And money managers spend a lot of time worrying about their portfolio and making sure that things are headed in the right direction.

Online Investing

The greatest advance in the history of the financial markets for the individual investor is online investing. Now you have access to real-time information and the ability to manage your investments yourself with instant feedback.

FACT

You're only as good as your "trading rig" (jargon for your computer setup used in online investing). Use and update the latest operating system for your PC or laptop. To reduce the odds of a hack, don't scrimp on security to keep your computer clear of malware and viruses. You can find excellent reviews and links to trial versions of great computer security programs at www.cnet.com.

The Ups and the Downs of Online Investing

Online investing gives you control of your current income and long-term wealth accounts, vast access to excellent and timely information, and the ability to make decisions rapidly. Moreover, 24/7 access to your accounts and the low prices of commissions make online investing ideal. The downside is that you are on your own when it comes to making decisions. You can learn to manage the potential negatives by being disciplined, thinking things through, and continuing to improve.

Over time, you will hone your technical analysis proficiency. Make sure that your computer, Wi-Fi, and phone can handle the data associated with stock charts. Slow downloads can kill a good buying or selling opportunity. Here are some practices that will help:

Are You Well Connected?

If you don't have a good Internet connection at home, at work, or through your smartphone, you will be in trouble. If you are not connected and a negative event in the markets happens, you may have a tough day.

Setting Up Your Online Account

Choose the right type of online trading account. With some online brokers, you will set up a mutual fund account that only allows you to make exchanges between their own funds. If that's all you need, that's fine. If you want to trade stocks, ETFs, or mutual funds from different fund families, you will need a brokerage account. You'll need a margin account for short selling and trading options.

Go slow. It makes sense to set up your brokerage account after you've gained some experience with mutual fund switching and investing. Options trading is best for very experienced traders, but it's a worthy goal.

Preparing Before Trading

Before you make any trade, put your money in the broker's money market account linked to your trading account. This account is a storage place for investing capital. Deposit any new money to this account too.

If you must put some money to work right away, use small amounts and see how things go before making bigger bets. Paper trade bigger trades in both your current income and long-term wealth accounts. Do your homework and find the mutual funds or stocks that best match your long-term plans before allocating. Read the prospectus and online information at *Morningstar* and *Yahoo! Finance*. Don't be afraid to call the fund family or broker and ask their phone reps questions. Don't make a move until you're sure that this is what you want to do. If you're not confident, make sure to paper trade first.

Checking the Market

Get into the habit of checking the general trends of interest rates, the stock market, and the general financial and economic themes of the present. Pros do this daily. You can start once or twice per week. Instead of checking your *Facebook*, *X*, or *Instagram* with your morning coffee, go to *CNBC* or *Yahoo! Finance* and make sure that there are no surprises lurking.

What Moves Your Money?

Always know what events mean to both your portfolios (current income and long-term wealth). See how your mutual funds and stocks respond to what the market is doing. Match which market sector influences the price of your mutual funds by checking the closing price of the index regularly and comparing the price change in your mutual fund to the activity in the index.

Most growth funds rise and fall in tandem with the NASDAQ Composite Index (NASDAQ). If your growth fund falls when NASDAQ rises, it may not be a good growth fund. Do this for all your funds. The more you perform these tasks, the easier it will become.

Develop Contingency Plans Before Problems Arise

Aside from deciding how much money you will put into the markets and how often, also consider what you will do if markets become volatile or prices start to drop aggressively.

Assume the Worst

So many things can go wrong when you trade. What will you do with your asset allocation if the Federal Reserve raises interest rates? What if the economy starts to shrink? How will you change what financial assets you own? Will you set limits on your losses? How much are you willing to lose before you cash in your chips? Will you buy on the price dips? If so, how often will you buy these dips? What will you do if your Internet connection goes down and you know that the market is going to be volatile?

Knowing the answers to these questions is crucial to your financial success. You can discuss emergency plans with your financial planner or consultant. You can also read blogs and articles online about these many topics. The important thing is to be prepared for difficult times.

The Dangers of Online Investing

Because online investing is so easy, you can spend all your time monitoring your portfolio. When you're starting, because of the amount of data you may receive, you may end up making too many trades, and many of these trades may not work out because of inexperience or market conditions.

Indecision and mental clutter can hit you when you have too many things on your plate, leading to anxiety and trading failures. To avoid such developments, stay patient and settle on the most accurate sources and methods that fit with your personality. Meanwhile, hone your analysis of markets and companies, technical analysis, and risk management skills. You may be an excellent short-term or momentum trader. No matter what, stick with your strengths.

Also, remember to watch out for scams. Some websites are dishonest and only interested in taking your money. Some may even be criminal.

Others may only be interested in selling you subscriptions without caring about the results. This is especially true of penny stocks websites, which specialize in "pump and dump" schemes. Since they are stuck with owning losing stocks, they "pump" them up to gullible investors and often "dump" the loser shares as you buy them. So, if it sounds too good to be true, it probably is.

Avoiding the Scammers

A great way to avoid scammers is to visit the SEC's website (www.sec .gov). Under the "Latest News" section, you'll find the agency's latest actions against scammers. The website's enforcement link provides information about companies that are in violation of their required reporting to the SEC but are still actively traded. These companies may dump stock of companies with no businesses or earnings.

What to Do If You Get Caught

If you get caught in a fraudulent scheme or stumble onto a website that looks suspicious, contact your state's securities board or go to the SEC website's EDGAR section to see if the security is currently registered. Your state securities board can help if a person who has contacted you is not licensed in your state and let you know if there are any open complaints against them.

Investing with Apps

Apps are great tools to keep tabs on your stocks. The best two free apps for stock investing are the CNBC and Investing.com apps. Both apps function separately from the associated websites. Both offer information on all markets, but CNBC's app is best for stocks, and Investing.com's app is quite useful to keep track of futures, Crypto, and currency markets. Investing .com's 24/7 real-time quote section lets you review overnight futures trading in stock indexes and other asset classes around the world.

The CNBC app offers CNBC financial news and updates as events happen. The best feature of the CNBC app is the watchlists you can set up for your stocks and exchange-traded mutual funds. Both apps offer basic stock charting and alert services.

Portfolio Management Apps

There are other apps available to help you invest. Here are four good ones:

Empower is free and lets you track your holdings. It is scalable, as it offers three portfolio tiers based on your net worth: $100,000, $250,000, and $1 million. The app figures out your tier after you plug in your info. It also offers a robo-advisor option.

Quicken offers two low-cost apps—Simplifi ($2.99/month) and Classic Premiere ($4/month). Simplifi is for budgeting and personal finance. Classic Premiere is best used as a comprehensive tool for experienced investors.

Zigma costs $9.90/month ($89.88/year) and is best for aggressive investors. This may be worth your while as an optimizer for short-term trading activity for current income.

Online Investing versus Apps

Online brokers also offer excellent apps through which you track account balances; do research; and trade stocks, ETFs, and mutual funds on any mobile device or PC.

Two very popular broker apps are thinkorswim from Charles Schwab, and the Fidelity Investments mobile app. Fidelity also offers Active Trader Pro, a more sophisticated trading platform for PCs. These apps are professional-grade trading suites that are free of charge if your trading volume is high enough. Both apps feature high-grade charting; research; access to news and analysis services for stocks, bonds, ETFs, and options; and high-speed trading execution. They also have excellent technical support.

What to Look For in an Investment Website

When investing online, look for sound information that provides actionable recommendations about what to buy and sell and how to allocate your portfolio. Big portals like MarketWatch.com offer reliable but basic information; brokerage websites that house your accounts offer more detail; and subscription websites should provide detailed analysis, such as charts and editorial commentary, as well as buy and sell recommendations. Plus, a good investment website should meet some basic requirements.

The Big Portals and Subscription Websites

Here are some important characteristics to look for in an information website:

- **Ease of use.** If it's not easy to navigate, it's useless.
- **Actionable news and thoughtful commentary.** Personalities and celebrities won't help you make money. Information will, especially if it improves your efficiency and enhances your profits.
- **Reliable free features.** Any large portal should have free real-time quotes and timely useful articles about events such as changes in interest rates as they happen.
- **Useful insights and easy-to-understand buy and sell recommendations for subscriber websites.** If the site provides recommendations and model portfolios, make sure they list their results. If you have to pay a subscription fee, you should be getting good information for your money.

Your Account Website

Your broker's website should have these important features:

- **Security.** An easy-to-access, password-activated, hacker-proof site with high-level security.
- **Ease of use.** An accessible and intuitive trading screen that's easy to move through and warns you when your order has errors.
- **Real-time quotes.** Don't trade stocks without real-time quotes. Old data can be costly.
- **Versatility.** You should be able to trade stocks, mutual funds, ETFs, and bonds on the same website.

- **Immediate confirmations.** You should always be able to confirm your intended trades before hitting the "Buy" or "Sell" button.
- **Real-time updates for your accounts.** Always know how much money you have every time you click that icon to refresh the page.
- **Customer service.** Access to 24/7 instant customer service, online, by chat, by phone, or all the above is a must.
- **Low minimum balance requirement.** This is a must for someone who is just getting started.
- **Access to specific buy and sell orders.** These, such as limit orders and sell stops, should be standard on your basic trading menu.
- **Moving money into a money market fund.** An automatic daily sweep of any money that you don't have invested in the markets into a money market fund is essential.

ALERT

Beware social media sites such as *Reddit* or *4chan* along with other online chat rooms. You may find useful information there, but they can also house scam artists. Always check out what you hear in chat rooms on your own.

Useful Investment Websites

There are hundreds of investment websites. But there are only a few that offer something special that makes them stand out from the rest. Here is a list of very useful sites and what makes them different from the rest of the pack. This is not a ranking list, but it is meant to provide a cross section of sites and give you a variety of ideas as to what is out there.

MarketWatch.com (www.marketwatch.com). This is one of the original portals of online investing. Thus, it has stood the test of time. Aside from providing access to great information, such as company financials and real-time quotes, the editorial content, especially the analysis, opinion, and news reporting, is top-notch.

Investors.com (www.investors.com). This site is all about trading and investing. You get clear and actionable information about the stock market, individual stocks, futures, options, ETFs, and mutual funds.

Yahoo! Finance (https://finance.yahoo.com) is a big portal like *Market-Watch*. The major difference is that much of the editorial content is linked from outside sources, although these are high-level sources. Real-time quotes, great financial research on companies, and general news are also available.

CNBC.com (www.cnbc.com). Although CNBC has changed its format over the years, it's still the leader in business TV. Its website has interesting editorial content, which is more topic-focused and newsy than other financial websites. The CNBC app is a great way to keep track of your portfolio.

The Motley Fool (www.fool.com). The "Fool" specializes in making financial analysis and recommendations easy to understand. It's a good place to get comfortable with analysis and the markets overall and a great resource for company earnings call transcripts.

Morningstar (www.morningstar.com). This is a premier financial information site with a special emphasis on mutual fund ratings and performance data. It's a great place to do your homework.

Substack (https://substack.com). This is a platform which hosts a wide variety of content. Many are financial websites including *Joe Duarte's Smart Money Passport*, which offers market analysis, interest rate commentary, and buy and sell recommendations for stocks and options.

CHAPTER 18

Investment Taxes

Investment taxes are part of the investment landscape. Yet, unlike other taxes, they can be managed with some flexibility. It's crucial to find a good CPA or tax expert to help you make the best possible choices in this area. And while no one likes to pay taxes, the other side of the coin is that in investing, if you pay taxes, it's a sign that you are making money.

General Changes in Current Tax Law

Before diving into investment taxes, it's important to recognize that the 2024 tax changes may affect all your taxable income and thus affect your ability to invest. Because everyone is different, you should check with your CPA for full details, while always preparing for future changes.

In 2024, the IRS made changes in standard deductions, while leaving the tax rates intact. Future administrations may look to lower taxes. Keep abreast of capital gains and personal income rates. There are also some changes in healthcare-related taxes, which may change over time too.

How Taxes Affect Your Portfolio

When it comes to investment taxes, investors are caught between Wall Street and Washington. Wall Street wants low taxes. Uncle Sam wants as much as possible. Your political preferences make no difference because if you invest in a non-retirement account, you will pay taxes now. For your IRA, 401(k) plan, or a similar retirement vehicle, you will pay taxes later.

You can't fight the IRS. Instead, focus on how to legally pay the least amount possible. Know the two ways the IRS will take its share from you: capital gains taxes and investment income taxes. Then talk to your accountant and see how you can make the best of the situation.

Although any investment may be taxed at some point, most often you will have to deal with taxes on your American stocks, bonds, and mutual funds, as well as the effect of your tax-deferred strategies, such as your IRA, 401(k), and other retirement plans.

Types of Investment Taxes

The government taxes investment through capital gains, investment interest, and dividends. Company profits are, at least partially, passed through to shareholders, who choose to receive them either as a dividend payment or decide to have them reinvested in company shares through a dividend reinvestment plan (DRIP).

Capital Gains

You capture a capital gain when you sell a security or any asset for a profit. Capital gains taxes differ based on your investment income, your tax bracket, and how long you held the asset outside of a retirement account. Short-term capital gains are applied to investments held less than a year, while long-term capital gains are applied to investments held more than a year.

ESSENTIAL

Keep accurate tax records. Carefully document your investment confirmations, dividends, and related expenses to save yourself a bundle every tax year. Your broker also produces a 1099-DIV form at the end of the year that summarizes all the details.

In 2024, individuals pay no capital gains taxes if their filing income is below $47,025. Joint filers pay no capital gains up to a filing income of $94,050. Single filers with long-term capital gains with income between $47,026 and $518,900 and joint filers between $94,051 and $583,750 pay a 15% tax, while any income above either $518,901 for single filers or $583,751 for joint filers is taxed at a rate of 20%.

Interest and Dividend Income

Interest income, which you receive from your bank account, bond holdings, or money market fund, is taxed at your ordinary income tax rate. If you own municipal bonds, this may vary, so you should double-check this with your accountant.

Mortgage deductions are capped at $750,000 until 2025. Margin interest, which is the interest you pay on loans from your broker to buy stock, is still deductible on Schedule A, a special section of your tax return. Check with your CPA for more details.

Dividend income is taxed based on how long you own a stock and whether the dividend is *qualified* or *ordinary*, based on the IRS's definition of both terms, which is complicated. The longer you hold the stock, the more likely you are to pay a lower tax rate on dividends.

You can get the full details at the IRS website (www.irs.gov).

Crafting Your Investment Tax Strategy

Your goals are to keep as much money as possible and to do it legally. Thus, avoiding taxes within legal means is acceptable; evading taxes is illegal and can get you in big trouble. Get all the details from your tax and investment advisors.

FACT

The 2018 tax cuts are set to expire by 2025 unless Congress adjusts the law.

Consider legal tax shelters, although the IRS and Congress are reducing them. Fortunately, in many cases, some tax shelters that have been in place for some time may be exempt or phased out over time. Enforcement action is increasing, especially when it comes to offshore accounts and similar vehicles. Consider your mortgage and business expenses, and if you're feeling a bit more sophisticated, you may want to look at oil and gas limited partnerships.

How to Measure Gains and Losses

The only positive of a losing year is that it may reduce your tax bill. If you had big gains, get ready to pay some taxes unless you've done some planning ahead of time. Start your tax planning in October. If you have some losing stock or mutual fund investments, you may wish to sell them then to reduce your taxes.

In addition, if you've had a big loss, consider selling some of your winners because you are locking in more of your big gains, as the losses essentially hide your gain from the IRS. By offsetting your gains, your losses reduce the amount of taxes you would pay for the winners.

ALERT

If you use current income gained from trading stocks to pay off business-related expenses, the trading income is deductible. Check with your CPA for details.

Taxes are an integral part of investing, so doing them carefully is essential. You will keep more of your money if you make the rules work for you. Finally, remember that your goals are short-term income and long-term growth, not tax planning. Indeed, your best tax plan won't do you a bit of good without good investments that make you money.

Make the Most of Your Deductions

Investment expenses can be tax deductible. These can be legal fees or any other expenses related to communication with investment professionals. Here is a list of some of them:

- Trading account management fees.
- Books, subscriptions to websites, apps, investment newsletters, or investment courses, including real estate courses, that you read or participate in to improve your financial management skills.
- If you trade on your phone, your phone bill may be partially deductible, as may be your home Internet bill. Your CPA will let you know.
- Travel expenses to meet your financial advisor or for an investment course.
- Fees related to recordkeeping of your investments, account setup fees for your IRA, or custodial fees.

Methods for Reducing Your Tax Liability

If you make money, the government makes money. But planning can reduce your bill. The key is to focus on the details of your tax strategy. The following section provides some excellent guidelines to get you on the right side of the dreaded tax issue.

Stocks

Keep good records of your stock trades, especially if you've bought shares of the same company at different times. When you sell the stock, determine whether you have a gain or a loss by subtracting the cost basis of your stock (the amount you paid plus commission) from the sale price. Also note the holding period—the length of time you held the stock—as it will sort the long-term or the short-term capital gains rate to the sale.

Here is an example:

Let's say you bought one hundred shares of the fictitious Walla-Walla Corporation (WW) for $1,000 in January 2021, including the commission costs. Your basis is $10 per share.

In March 2021, you bought another hundred shares of WW worth $2,000, including commission costs. This time, your basis is $20 per share.

You like Walla-Walla, and it continues to shine, so in February 2022, you buy another hundred shares for $3,000, including commission. Your basis for this one is $30 per share.

Walla-Walla continues to do well, but in October 2024, it hits $50 and you think it's time to take some money off the table. So, you sell one hundred shares.

Without further instructions, your broker will follow the IRS guidelines of selling the first-in, first-out shares. Thus, your shares from February 2021 will go. If you want to sell a particular set of shares with a better tax advantage, pick which lot you wish to sell. No matter which shares you sell, you will receive $5,000.

The difference between your profit margin and your tax rate would come from the holding period. If you sell the January 2021 shares, your tax rate would be less since you held them longer (January 2021 to October 2024). That would give you a $4,000 long-term gain. The March 2021 shares would have a $3,000 long-term gain, while the February 2021 shares would bring you a $2,000 short-term gain.

Remember, your tax decisions should focus on paying the smallest amount possible. Look for short-term losses to offset short-term gains. If you don't have any transactions to offset, you can just use the long-term shares to pay the smallest amount of tax on this profitable trade. Think the strategy through before making the sale.

Mutual Funds

Mutual funds have three different potential tax implications: dividend distributions, capital gains distributions, and gains or losses from the selling of shares. If you sell shares for more than you paid for them, expect a tax bill. If you lose money at the sale, you can use the loss to potentially offset a gain. Time factors for short-term or long-term holding periods are applicable as normal.

> **FACT**
>
> Dividends from a municipal tax bond fund are usually not taxable. Also consider that if you are holding mutual funds, stocks, or any other investment that pays dividends or offers any other kind of distribution in your retirement funds, these are tax-deferred, so you don't pay taxes at the current rates. In that case, the distributions are best taken as shares of the mutual fund to increase your fund holdings.

Dividend distributions and capital gains distributions are different. Usually in the May-June and/or the November-December time frames, mutual funds pay dividends (monthly or quarterly for bond funds). Stock funds will pass on capital gains and dividend distributions during this time as well.

Dividend distributions, per share, result from the dividends that the mutual fund collects on its holdings. Capital gains distributions are the proceeds from the funds' profitable asset sales. You are required to report them on your tax bill even if you receive the distribution in more shares of your fund holdings rather than cash.

Municipal Bonds

The interest income earned from municipal bonds, issued by municipalities or states, is exempt from federal income taxes, just as the interest from federal securities is exempt from local and state taxation. As a result, municipal bonds pay lower interest rates than bonds that are fully taxable, such as corporate bonds.

Still, municipal bonds are not 100% tax-free securities because even though the interest is lower, any capital gains or losses that you receive when you sell them are taxed based on the same rules for other assets. That means that if you sell munis for more than you paid for them, you will pay capital gains taxes. On the other hand, if you sell them for less, you will have a reportable tax loss and can use that to your advantage.

Life Insurance

Term life insurance is a good thing to have, yet it has little benefit other than at the holder's death. However, there are other special types of life insurance policies that may be useful as investment and tax advantage vehicles for you. That's because by choosing a whole life, universal life, or single premium policy:

- You can save for retirement. Instead of paying only for insurance, part of your premium builds cash value. The IRS does not tax these investment premiums.
- You can borrow from your policy. Once your policy builds cash value, you can borrow from it, and you don't have to pay it back. If there are

loans outstanding at the time of death, they are deducted from the insurance payoff to your beneficiaries. Interest due on the loan may also be paid via the policy's investment income.

■ Although this is not advisable for routine expenses, if you have a financial emergency, you can use the cash value of your whole life, universal life, or single premium insurance policy to cover it. If you are faced with this significant choice, check with your insurance professional and your financial advisor for full details.

Annuities

Annuities are another popular insurance-investment hybrid with big tax advantages. Annuities are structured so that your heirs will inherit the amount of money that you have put into the policy, even if it has lost money. In fact, annuities are like IRAs and 401(k) plans, as they allow you to save tax-deferred until you withdraw funds.

ALERT

Beware the penalties. If you cash out your annuity before retirement age, you are likely to run into steep penalties, a.k.a. surrender charges. Look into the details before you buy. Some annuities in the same categories will have different charges and structures depending on the company that issues them. Furthermore, if you withdraw from the annuity before age fifty-nine and a half, the IRS will tack on a 10% penalty.

Think of an annuity as a tax-deferred mutual fund or CD. It rises in value, but you don't pay the taxes until you retire. At that time, you can take out a lump sum or receive payments periodically. And while you can deduct your contributions into an IRA or other retirement plan, you can't deduct money you put into an annuity. Annuities are usually expensive to buy and have large surrender and maintenance fees, along with expense and mortality risks (risk based on your risk profile, age, health, and so on).

Understanding Legal Tax Shelters

To shelter your income from the tax collector, you can either defer the tax bill by contributing to your retirement fund or avoid paying taxes completely via tax shelters. You can shelter taxable income in many vehicles, including investments and special investment accounts, and by using planning strategies that lower your current taxable income or offer favorable tax treatments.

Real estate is a great tax shelter because of the depreciation deduction you get on investment properties, especially rental properties. Depreciation is a calculation on paper that determines the loss of value in assets, such as real estate due to wear and tear, allowing the owner to write off the cost of an expense over time. Because you can write off the cost over time, this deduction increases your net income by spreading out the tax deduction over the life of the property.

ALERT

The IRS is always on the lookout for tax evaders, so choose your shelters wisely and legally. If the rules change at some point in the future, you may be liable for both past and current taxes. Always cut your tax bill legally and avoid breaking the rules, as the penalties and consequences could be very significant.

Also consider oil and gas investments, such as limited partnerships. They offer big deductions for drilling and exploration costs. The downside is that if the partnership does not find oil or gas, you can expect some losses. This could leave you with some deductions but no income to offset them. Similar shelters include equipment leasing—and cattle breeding—related partnerships. You will have to go through a specialist investment advisor to find these in most cases.

The simplest ways to shelter your money from taxes are to:

■ Hold your investments for longer than one year to reduce the capital gains tax rate.

- Maximize your contributions to tax-deferred investments, such as IRAs, 401(k) plans, and college savings accounts.
- Fully use your itemized deductions by including your investment-related expenses.
- Above all, work closely with your tax professional to shelter the maximum without breaking the law.

To keep more money legally, be aware of the tax consequences of your investments, keep good records, and know the rules ahead of time.

CHAPTER 19

Investing for Education

You don't want your kids saddled with over $100,000 in student loan debt, as high education prices aren't likely to fall anytime soon. However, it's never too early to start saving so that your kids will have a chance at a good career or a trade (and maybe eventually following the steps in this book to build their own wealth). There are several investment options that will help you to do this without sacrificing your retirement. You can invest in state-sponsored 529 plans, set up your own plan like an IRA, or both. It's important to explore your options and get started as early as possible, once you've established your short-term income and long-term wealth-building plan.

The Evolution of the Educational System

Rising costs and changes in the supply and demand for workers both require some creative problem-solving. Not only does tuition continue to rise (requiring more effort to send children to secondary school); these secondary educations are losing value as well, as the job space is more and more crowded. Battle the tuition rates by saving earlier or looking into a different (and potentially more lucrative) type of schooling.

Look Into Trade School

In some fields, there are too many candidates and limited numbers of positions. Thus, noncollege-trained occupations, such as the trades—plumbing, carpentry, welding, and other machine-sophisticated technical professions—may be the way to go. Many offer over $100,000 annual salaries with opportunities for advancement, and if your child is entrepreneurial, a trade can develop into a self-owned business.

Plan Now

You can't go wrong by saving for your kids' school tuitions now. But education costs money, so early planning is important because of the power of compounding. Don't fret; there are some great tools that can help you start.

Tax-Sheltered Education Savings Plans

In 2017 and 2019, Congress expanded the scope of higher education savings plans, making them both tax deductible and applicable to apprenticeships, while allowing funds to be used for both student debt payment and Roth IRA contributions.

These plans let you grow your post–high school nest egg in a tax-deferred format and save more, and they also offer better choices when it's time to spend the money. Treat these plans as if saving for retirement, even though you need the money sooner and are expecting to spend it faster.

The rules vary by state, so checking with a tax professional is important. The money is tax-free when you withdraw it to pay for approved college expenses. The IRS website is a good place to start your review.

The 529 Plans

Qualified tuition plans, known as 529 plans, offer significant tax advantages. Since 2018, the money housed in them can be used to pay tuition at elementary, secondary, private, or religious schools along with apprenticeships. Some states allow personal tax deductions for donations to these plans. Contributions are not federally deductible. There are two categories: savings plans (the most popular and commonly used type) and prepaid tuition plans.

ALERT

The tax laws limit the amount of money from a 529 plan that can be used for elementary, middle, or high school expenses to $10,000. There is no limit for college expenses.

The account holder, usually a parent or grandparent, sets up the account on behalf of the future student, the beneficiary, and makes the investment decisions for the plan, including investment choices, asset allocation, and risk management. There may be some limits on one or more of these functions depending on the specific state laws. When the need arises, you can withdraw the money to pay for education-related expenses: fees, books, and other needs that conform with state and federal laws. If you follow the rules and spend the money on what the plan allows, you won't have to pay federal income taxes. Often you won't have to pay state taxes either.

Check your state contribution levels. There are usually no income limitations to who can start a 529. The 529 plans are not federally tax deductible, but earnings grow tax-free. Some states offer other breaks. The per-year 2025 contribution limits are $19,000 for individuals and $38,000 per year for couples to claim the federal gift tax exemption. Get more details at www.savingforcollege.com.

Investment choices in 529 plans may be limited, and the lifetime contribution limits vary by state. Some states may offer only one or two mutual funds, while others may offer as many as thirty choices. Also, you can only switch investment choices once per year. Finally, a 529 plan reduces the amounts you can qualify for in other forms of financial aid.

ALERT

Read the fine print. If you use 529 plan money for unallowed expenses, you could receive a tax penalty on top of any other tax liabilities.

Coverdell Education Savings Accounts

Coverdell Education Savings Accounts (ESA) are set up as trusts. They offer tax advantages and flexibility. The money can be used for any education-related expenses, including primary, secondary, and college educations. The contributions are not tax deductible, but the earnings on the account are tax-free when you use them for allowable expenses.

You can open one account per child at your local bank, brokerage, or other financial institution. One child can have more than one ESA to their name, such as when different family members wish to contribute separately. Check IRS.gov for more details.

Contributions are limited to $2,000 per child. So, if your child has three accounts, the $2,000 annual contribution must be split among the three accounts. Contributions over $2,000 will trigger a tax penalty. You can't contribute to ESAs after the child turns eighteen, except when you contribute in the same year and use the funds to pay for tuition.

ESAs can limit or eliminate your child's ability to qualify for other financial aid because an ESA account is considered your child's asset.

Other limitations include contribution limits based on your income. Check with the IRS for full details. Finally, the benefits must be completely used by the time the beneficiary turns thirty.

The major advantages of ESAs are:

- Proceeds are eligible for any level of education: primary, secondary, or college.
- You can open the account anywhere you want; invest the ESA in any type of investment, stocks, or mutual funds; and control it in any way you wish.
- You can contribute to both 529 plans and ESAs if you follow the rules, keep good records, and plan for the tax consequences.

Prepaid Tuition Plans: Are They Worth It?

You can contribute to a child's education now via a prepaid tuition plan, through which you pay now for future tuitions. These are covered under 529 rules. Each state has different rules.

QUESTION

Where can I get detailed help on the specifics of my state plans?
Look at the College Savings Plans Network (www.collegesavings.org) for both general and specific information about all the major college savings plans, including detailed information about individual college savings plans for each state.

The money you put in the plan today buys college tuition at today's public college rates and guarantees that price when it's time for the child to go to college, no matter what the cost is at that time. Also, because of demographic changes, tuitions may be close to topping out. Thus, you may wish to wait before plunging into this option. Some states offer a transfer value that qualifies private college costs if they have agreements with the state. To qualify for the guaranteed price, sign up by the yearly deadline set by the state and buy however many tuition units you want. So, if your state charges $100 per tuition unit and you buy twenty units, you have purchased $2,000 worth of tuition in the future at today's prices. Always check your college institution options, including both private and public. Unused money can be transferred to another relative or saved for grandchildren. Sometimes you can get a full or partial refund. These plans reduce your child's eligibility for financial aid, dollar for dollar. That means that if your child decides to go to a more expensive private school, you probably won't qualify for financial aid.

Plans vary widely from state to state. All states offer full prepaid four-year college tuition plans, while many states let you pay for room and board costs through the same plan. Always check the individual state plan rules. Consider choosing a prepaid tuition college savings plan if:

- You don't like uncertainty.
- You lose sleep worrying about the future.
- Your tax bracket and circumstances will disqualify your family from financial aid.
- The school your child wants to attend is covered by a prepaid plan.

If your prepaid plan doesn't cover all your costs, you can also set up an ESA. With this combination, you might be in a better situation, without suffering tax consequences.

Education Bonds and CDs

Mutual fund–based 529 plans have had huge appeal during times in which the stock market has delivered high returns. But educational CDs and bonds also make sense if you are a risk-averse saver or during periods of uncertainty. These vehicles offer the opportunity for safety and portfolio diversification.

Education Bonds

Education bonds are issued by the US Treasury and are like savings bonds. Specifically, education bonds must be issued after 1989 and are series

EE or I bonds. These bonds are different in their tax treatment from regular savings bonds, as your interest earnings will usually be completely exempt from federal income tax. Here are the rules:

- You must use the bond proceeds, interest, and principal to pay for the qualified educational expenses in the same year that you redeem the bond.
- You can't buy these bonds unless you are at least twenty-four years of age.
- You must register the bonds in your name if you plan on using them for your own educational expenses.
- If you plan on using them for your children's education, you must register them in your name or your spouse's name.
- If you're married, you won't get the tax benefit unless you file a joint return.
- Your child can only be registered as a beneficiary, not as a co-owner of the bond.

Always check with your CPA or check online to see if there have been any changes in the rules. The US Treasury website (www.treasurydirect.gov) is also a good place to look for the latest information.

College Certificates of Deposits

A certificate of deposit is a long-term bank deposit that pays you interest over its life. Once you buy the CD, you can't withdraw it early without a penalty, and you give up the interest payments that remain over the life of the deposit. In the case of a college certificate of deposit, the idea is similar, with some wrinkles. You still deposit a lump sum of money for a specified period. There is still a penalty for early withdrawal. The difference is that the interest rate paid is a college-oriented rate based on the Independent College 500 Index (IC 500), an index created by the College Board, the same people who put the SAT together.

This is the big picture. The IC 500 rate is considered the benchmark for the inflation rate of college expenses. Banks then link the return on the education certificates of deposit to reflect the annual figure of the IC 500. Although there are some standards to govern these instruments, always check before you sign on the dotted line to make sure you understand how your bank "links" the rate of return on the CD to the IC 500.

FACT

The Independent College 500 Index is compiled from the costs of full-time tuition, room and board, and fees from the nation's most expensive not-for-profit colleges. The index is published once per year and is a measure of the change in costs on a year-over-year basis with information compiled from the schools that make up the index. It's not a bad idea to check this out on a yearly basis at professionals.collegeboard.org.

These CDs are simple to use. Once you've made sure you've read the fine print and have all the details ironed out, you buy units. Each unit is the cost of one year's education. The minimum account to fund a unit is $500. You can buy the whole year at once or build it up over time, such as by using an automatic monthly savings plan. The beauty of the CD is that the money you deposit will grow at the same rate, or better, than the IC 500's year-over-year rate of change.

CHAPTER 20

Retirement Planning

This book is all about simultaneously investing for current income and building long-term wealth. And this chapter is where the long-term wealth aspects come together. Although it's never too late, the earlier you start planning for retirement, the better. So, keep in mind that the longer you save and invest, the more time your money has to grow based on its own gains, especially during inflationary periods. This chapter is about retirement planning skills and building long-term wealth through 401(k) plans and IRAs.

Don't Worry If You're Behind

Stop worrying about your retirement; get started, especially if you're in your twenties or thirties. That's because the system is in your favor. Here's a secret: The government doesn't want to be your only retirement option because it's not sure if there will be enough to go around when you turn sixty-five and start dipping into Social Security.

Time Is on Your Side

If you're employed, pay down your bills, get into a positive cash flow situation, and start maximizing your 401(k) plan, time will continue to be your ally. This will take care of a nice chunk of your long-term wealth building.

If you're self-employed, start that IRA or even a SEP IRA, which offers you the ability to sock away even more than in a regular IRA. Consider a SEP when you are a self-employed individual or contractor.

FACT

A SEP IRA is a Simplified Employee Pension Arrangement. A company establishing this type of plan can only offer it to employees if they have worked there for five years, received at least $650 in compensation, and are age twenty-one. The employer can contribute up to 25% of the employee's income to the plan.

The Genius of Tax-Deferred Investing

Congress often gets a bad rap. But it certainly got it right when it comes to tax-deferred investing. Normally, if you have a savings account that pays interest, at the end of every year, you give the government some of the interest as part of your tax bill. With a tax-deferred account, you pay taxes at a later predetermined time. That deferment lets your money build up faster because you don't pay taxes until you withdraw it from the tax-deferred account.

The IRS will tax the income and capital gains in your nontax-deferred investments in the present. This applies to stocks, bonds, mutual funds, and real estate. Even businesses and niche investments, such as collectibles, outside of tax-deferred accounts pay taxes.

FACT

A tax-deferred account differs from a tax-exempt account. The latter is an account in which you never pay taxes, such as with the interest on a municipal bond.

Tax-deferred investments let you delay paying taxes, as long as you don't withdraw the money from the account. Another advantage is that most contributions to tax-deferred investments are either partially or completely tax deductible. There are exceptions, such as Roth IRAs or deductions that are phased out for higher-income taxpayers.

Early withdrawal from these accounts comes with hefty penalties that reduce the amount of your withdrawal. If possible, avoid early withdrawal from a tax-deferred account.

ALERT

Keep tabs on your retirement. Often, people contribute to their IRA or 401(k) plans and don't bother to monitor their progress. Just because it's a long time until you will need the money, and despite the long-term uptrend for stocks, you should always pay attention to your asset allocation. Also monitor how you're doing compared to the markets and make sure the accounting and fees are correct and fair.

The money you put into tax-deferred accounts, such as 401(k) plans and non-Roth IRAs, is pretax money. That means that the money is deducted from your taxable income. Thus, you don't pay taxes on the money you put into the account, and your overall taxable income is reduced.

It's Never Too Early to Start

It's a fact; the earlier you start investing, the more time you will have to maximize the amount available for retirement. Give your money the most time possible to become as large a sum as possible. There will be economic booms and busts. There will be periods of dramatic changes in technology, wars, climate events, and periods of personal difficulties. By starting early, you give your money more time to ride the ups and downs and recover from any significant surprises.

Let's compare two twenty-five-year-olds in similar jobs with similar earnings and similar access to a 401(k) plan. Ellie starts right away and socks $2,000 per year into her plan for ten years. She stops at age thirty-five and then never invests again. Rory waits until he's thirty-four before starting. He puts $2,000 in his plan for thirty years and saves three times as much as Ellie. If they both earn 10% per year on average until they retire, Ellie ends up with $556,197, while Rory ends up with $328,988. And that's why you should start early.

To see how compounding may work for you, visit www.investor.gov and search for the investment compounding calculator.

The 401(k) Plan

These hybrid DIY retirements have stood the test of time. Set up by employers, they've largely replaced traditional pension plans, shifting the burden of retirement, at least partially, to employees. If you use them correctly by investing in them early and staying connected to their progress, you can do quite well by your retirement age.

Here's why you should take all opportunities to contribute to your 401(k):

- The money you save in the plan is earmarked for your retirement and is deducted from your pretax dollars.

- You get a tax deduction, and you don't pay taxes on the money in the plan until you take it out in the future.
- Employers often match your contribution—as much as 10%, 25%, or even 50% of what you contribute. By contributing, you trigger free money into your account. Thus, your employer's matching contribution is helping the growth rate of your investment at no charge to you.
- Because the money is in a retirement account, you won't get at it easily before it's time, and neither will the IRS. That means that it will have the best chance to grow and be there when you need it.

The downside is that if you take the money out before a set date, usually age fifty-nine and a half, the IRS penalizes you.

ALERT

Check with your employer or the IRS (www.irs.gov) every tax year to see proposed changes for 401(k) plans, especially when you reach age fifty-nine.

Your 401(k) Investing Strategy

Retirement investing has a long-term focus. Thus, it's not as important to worry about weekly or monthly changes in the stock or bond market as it is to put money into the plan's money market fund from which you can make allocation decisions later. There is no excuse for neglecting your nest egg. Always prioritize putting money into your account at regular intervals. Dollar cost averaging, putting the same amount of money into some of the mutual funds or ETFs in the plan regularly, is ideal for 401(k)s.

When you become proficient at trading, you can stack money into sector-specific ETFs or available sector mutual funds in your plan to pad your returns (more on this in Chapter 12).

Always know how each of the investment choices in the plan is working at any one time. Don't be afraid to make changes from one class of investment to another over time to get better returns or reduce risk. In other words, a 401(k) is no different than other investments when it comes to your responsibilities.

Be careful of 401(k) plans where the employing company's own stock is the major investment vehicle for the plan. The plan's returns are only as good as the company's stock at any one time. If your company is faring well, your retirement is likely to do well during the period. But if things go south, your retirement may be in jeopardy. It's not necessarily a bad thing to have some company stock in your 401(k), especially if that's how your employer contributes its portion to your plan. Just make sure that company stock is not the major portion of your investment or the only asset in your 401(k).

You Can Take It with You

You can't take your money when you die. But you can, and should, take your 401(k) plan with you when you change companies or become self-employed. If your new employer has a 401(k), you can have your current plan transferred or rolled over to a new account. Rolling it over, or having it directly transferred from one trustee to another, will save you 20% that would be levied on the money if you take possession of the money in the plan yourself. If you take possession of the money but don't reestablish it as a retirement plan with your new employer, you'll get hit with more taxes and penalties. If you take possession and then restart the 401(k) elsewhere, you need to come up with the 20% that your old employer took out from your pocket. If you become self-employed, turn your 401(k) into an IRA. No matter what you do, make sure you avoid taking possession of the money yourself and make all the rollovers, transfers, and establishing of new accounts within sixty days of changing jobs.

Taking Money Out of a 401(k) Plan

You may be tempted to borrow from your 401(k) or to use it as a piggy bank to fund down payments for a new home or maybe to buy a sports car. But you're just asking for trouble when you take out money tagged for retirement for short-term uses. Of course, if you are facing a life-or-death situation, such as your house is near foreclosure or you're hit with some unforeseen medical expenses, and you have no other means of getting through, your 401(k) is fair game. So, while it's okay to use the 401(k) as part of your net worth for loans, you should avoid borrowing from it unless it's a true emergency.

If you borrow from your 401(k) plan under certain circumstances, you may not incur penalties or tax consequences if you follow the rules. You must pay back the loan in full before you stop working for the employer who maintains the plan.

Finally, you can take distributions (withdraw money) from your plan without penalties starting at age fifty-nine and a half, whether you are retired or not. By the time you turn seventy and a half, you must take out the minimum required distribution.

Individual Retirement Accounts (IRAs)

IRAs are immensely popular because they allow you to save for retirement while deferring taxes, are very flexible in what you can use for investment vehicles, and come in two basic types: traditional and Roth. In 2005, the Supreme Court ruled that IRAs are fully protected from creditors if you need to file for personal bankruptcy.

Traditional IRAs

The good thing about IRAs is that Congress, in its quest to make the Social Security fund last longer, periodically changes the rules to make it more advantageous to save for retirement through IRAs. For example, in 2008, your maximum contribution was $5,000. In the 1990s, the maximum that you could put in a traditional IRA was $2,000. For 2025, you can contribute $7,000 to your IRA or $8,000 if you are over fifty. Married spouses can contribute to individual IRAs if they file jointly, even if only one spouse works. Contributions may be tax deductible depending on the situation and the current state of the rules, which do change from time to time. Your contribution can't exceed your taxable compensation for the year. You can find easy-to-use IRA contribution information at IRS.gov by searching for IRA information.

As with 401(k) plans, you can start withdrawing your money at age fifty-nine and a half, and you must start withdrawing the minimum from the account by the time you reach seventy and a half. You will pay taxes at the current tax rate when you make your withdrawal, but only on the amount that you withdraw. And here is a bonus: Your income level, even if you work part-time, is likely to drop when you retire. That will likely put you into a lower tax bracket.

You can start your IRA through a bank, a brokerage house, or a mutual fund family. Because there is stiff competition for your business, you should look for a no-fee IRA. Those are easy to find through the big mutual fund families and brokerages. Banks tend to offer fewer options and may have higher fees. And with a mutual fund or brokerage firm, you will have a greater opportunity to tweak your asset allocation and manage your portfolio according to market conditions and your risk profile. Don't be too passive with this money. Consider taking some risks if it suits your risk profile. But always be aware that with unmanaged risk, you could incur big losses. Generally, keeping an eye on your IRA on a weekly, monthly, or quarterly basis makes more sense than minding the store every five years. There is no substitute for knowing what you need to know when you need to know it.

Roth IRAs

These IRAs have been around since 1998, and they offer a different approach to retirement savings. Because you pay the taxes on the contributions as you add the money to the account, you don't pay taxes when you make withdrawals. Your contributions are also not tax deductible as with traditional IRAs. The benefits of the Roth accounts are simple:

- You don't have to pay taxes when you withdraw the money.
- There is no minimum distribution requirement.

- If you are a young part-time worker or college student, the Roth may make the most sense since your tax bracket will only go up as you get older. With a Roth, you can sock more away with less worry about paying taxes later.
- If you don't withdraw the money, you can pass the account to your heirs tax-free when you die.

Generally, the contribution limits are similar to those for traditional IRAs. However, they are subject to income levels, and they are subject to change. It's a good idea to get advice from your CPA or visit the IRS website for the latest information.

You can roll over money from a traditional IRA to a Roth account, but you should check with your tax advisor and make sure it's a good idea to do so based on your current financial situation. If you can't deduct your current contributions but still have money available to save for retirement, you may want to use the Roth option, if you are eligible. Roth IRAs also make sense if you expect higher tax rates upon your retirement or if you think you might need that money before you retire. If you are uncertain about the future of tax rates, or if the unknown keeps you from getting sleep, a Roth IRA may make sense for you.

If you decide to make the switch to a Roth, you can start by asking your current IRA custodian about your next step. They will provide you with a good analysis of your situation and send you the correct forms. Your CPA will also help. Make sure you are well informed and comfortable before making the switch.

To Roth or Not to Roth: Which Makes the Most Sense?

The answer to the proverbial Roth IRA question depends on whether paying taxes now or later makes the most sense for you. And, as with everything else financial, what you do depends on your individual financial situation and expectations for the future. Your CPA is also likely to generate some fees based on your query, while likely making the most sense as a source of assistance.

But here is the real answer: No one knows what lies ahead over the next thirty years. Politics, your health, and the general chaotic nature of the universe will influence what happens, no matter what you do. So, keep it simple: Whether you choose a traditional or Roth IRA, you are making a good decision because you have decided to save for your retirement.

Health Savings Accounts (HSAs)

The general trend in healthcare is for higher deductibles and out-of-pocket expenses along with higher healthcare costs. You should also consider the fact that Medicare benefits, disability requirements, and other forms of assistance, such as Medicaid, are also likely to change, probably toward the side of being less generous and more expensive. That's why it makes sense to consider a health savings account.

Here are the basic facts:

- With an HSA, you can save money for your health expenses—as much as you would save for retirement via an IRA or 401(k) plan.
- You must have a high deductible healthcare plan, with no other health coverage.
- Generally, the higher the deductible, the more you can save in an HSA.
- For 2025, the maximum individual contribution is $4,300, and $8,550 for family coverage.
- You can manage your HSA in a similar fashion to your IRA, and the money and compounded earnings that you don't use will be there until your death.
- You can no longer contribute to your HSA once you enroll in Medicare.
- If you die, your beneficiary receives the money in your HSA. If the beneficiary is your spouse, the HSA becomes your spouse's HSA. If your beneficiary is someone else, that person will pay taxes on the money in the HSA for the current tax year.
- You must not be listed as a dependent on someone else's tax return.

There are some different rules for employers, employees, and the self-employed regarding HSAs. And there are likely to be some changes to these general requirements in the future as the healthcare system dynamics change. Always check with IRS.gov before making HSA decisions.

How to Catch Up on Your Retirement

If you're behind, you can catch up by maximizing your retirement plan contributions every year and then add additional funds after age fifty-nine by following the current IRS rules.

Pay Down Your Debt and Maximize Your Cash Flow

Pay yourself dividends by paying down your debt and using those funds to contribute to your retirement fund. This requires patience and planning, but over time, it will pay off handsomely.

Maximize Your Contributions

You can catch up by using your current income from stock trading or real estate to pad your IRA or 401(k) contributions. Moreover, once you maximize your contribution to the 401(k), your employee's matching contribution will also increase.

> **ESSENTIAL**
>
> If you receive a large sum of money from an inheritance or an insurance settlement, consider putting as large an amount as possible in your retirement fund.

If you have a SEP and you haven't been putting in the maximum amount, you can change your allocation contribution to catch up.

Time and Focus Are Your Best Allies

Your youth, especially when it comes to retirement planning, is a blessing and an opportunity. That's because time is on your side and, if you stay focused, you can learn from your mistakes and have the time to show that you have learned from them.

Here are some things you can do that will serve you well over time. Take advantage of all your tax-deferred opportunities. If you can invest in an IRA and a 401(k) simultaneously, do it. Even if you can't deduct both of your contributions, they will still grow tax-deferred. Plan for the worst-case scenario. Plan your retirement as if Social Security will not exist when you turn sixty-five. It will probably still be there. But if you've planned for the worst, you will make a better effort and be in a better position.

Online and Discount Brokers

Included are the largest, most accessible discount and online brokers in the United States. The list is meant to get you started quickly in your DIY investing. The list is purposely tilted toward the largest brokers because they tend to have the best online platforms, 24/7 support, easy-to-read tutorials, and well-trained reps who can help you get started or answer questions as you progress.

Charles Schwab

www.schwab.com

800-435-4000

High volume and low prices from one of the biggest of the brokerage houses. Local branches located throughout the United States.

E*TRADE

https://us.etrade.com

800-387-2331

High volume, very popular site with low prices. Walk-in branches in several states.

Fidelity Investments

www.fidelity.com

800-343-3548 or 800-972-2155

Fidelity Investments is an excellent hub for financial services. It offers brokerage services, mutual funds, annuities, retirement planning, and advisory services. It has top-notch customer service and even offers weekend phone reps to answer questions and manage issues. Many investor centers are located throughout the United States.

USAA

www.usaa.com

800-531-8722

A full slate of financial services, including insurance, mutual funds, and retirement programs, is offered to current and former military personnel and their families.

Vanguard Brokerage Services

https://investor.vanguard.com

800-531-8722

Vanguard Brokerage Services, unlike Vanguard mutual funds, doesn't mind if you trade in and out of securities. Otherwise, it is a standard discount broker offering a wide variety of services.

Investment Publications

The Internet is full of excellent information, yet some websites will waste your time and money. When choosing sources of information, consider your risk profile, your long-term goals, and your willingness to spend time tending to your investing program before you make any buy or sell decisions. Most of the websites listed have apps, mobile sites with excellent execution, or both. Some of the sites listed offer subscriptions but are worth the money if you take advantage of the information offered. To decide which publications are the most useful before you shell out the money for a long-term subscription, check out the free sections of the websites or take advantage of the free trials. When actively investing, consider the following:

The Wall Street Journal

The Wall Street Journal is the leading global newspaper with a focus on business. Founded in 1889, the newspaper has grown to a worldwide daily circulation of more than two million readers. Plus, *The Wall Street Journal Special Editions* are special sections written in local languages and featured in more than thirty leading national newspapers worldwide. *The Wall Street Journal Americas*, published in Spanish and Portuguese, is included in approximately twenty leading Latin American newspapers. *The Wall Street Journal* offers digital-only subscriptions for less than $30 per month. **www.wsj.com**

Barron's

Barron's is also known as the *Dow Jones Business and Financial Weekly*. With its first edition published in 1921, *Barron's* offers its readers news reports and analyses on financial markets worldwide. Investors will also find a wealth of tips regarding investment techniques and in-depth information. You can often get combined subscriptions to *The Wall Street Journal* and *Barron's* via special offers. **www.barrons.com**

Investor's Business Daily

Founded in 1984, *Investor's Business Daily* is a newspaper focusing on business, financial, economic, and national news. The publication places a strong emphasis on offering its readers timely information on the stock market and stock market–related issues. The online edition can be purchased individually or as a package which includes, MarketWatch.com, WSJ.com, Investors.com, and Barrons.com. It offers specialized publications emphasizing short-term trading and investment styles. The IBD app features real-time stock charts and news, similar in format to the website.

www.investors.com

MarketWatch

MarketWatch offers news, financial market analysis, and personal finance information via well-written, easy-to-understand articles, blogs, and alerts. If it has to do with money, it will get covered here. The site even discusses mortgages and the housing market, interest rates, travel deals, seasonal shopping guides, credit card finances, retirement planning, and automobile ratings. There is also a mobile app with comparable content.

www.marketwatch.com

Yahoo! Finance

Yahoo! Finance is a data-driven site with articles covering daily stock market activity, in-depth stock and mutual fund quotes, and information on listed options and commodities. It also covers more traditional financial topics via articles and blogs. *Yahoo! Finance* has an app that is similar in content to the website.

https://finance.yahoo.com

CNBC

CNBC.com is the traditional home of financial news. The website has ongoing news coverage and discussions along with after-market stock market discussion and trading shows such as Jim Cramer's *Mad Money*. You can get a quick overview of the markets here, and their programs will often have thoughtful analysis of key stocks and earnings reports.

The CNBC app offers superb features, with similar coverage to the channel via articles and blogs as well as market graphics for stocks, bonds, commodities, and currencies. Its best feature is the watchlists where you can follow individual stocks and ETFs in real time.

www.cnbc.com

Value Line

This website offers in-depth ratings, reports, opinions, and analysis on stocks and specific sectors of the stock market, based on the activity in the Value Line Composite Index. The Value Line Composite Index is an index of seventeen hundred stocks compiled by *Value Line*, which is considered a reliable and broad index of the market. The Value Line Composite Index offers a look at a very broad selection of stocks and can be useful in gauging the health of the market beyond the S&P 500. *Value Line* has a wide pricing range for digital subscriptions, from its basic Wealth Newsletter ($49/year) to its Value Line Investment Survey ($598/year).

www.valueline.com

Ecoinometrics

This website is all about cryptocurrencies and blockchain. It provides excellent insight and news about cryptocurrencies. It updates frequently and should be a bookmark for crypto fans. Perhaps its best feature is the in-depth articles about insider activities such as emerging platforms, the interactions among different factions of the crypto world, and the moves governments make as they adapt to cryptos.

https://ecoinometrics.substack.com

Joe Duarte's Smart Money Passport

This is a great place for stock trading ideas. Joe Duarte writes frequent columns about the stock, bond, commodity, and crypto markets. Premium subscribers have access to precise buy and sell recommendations for stocks and ETFs. You can subscribe for $19/month or $190/year.

https://smartmoneypassport.substack.com

Glossary of Terms

Investing has a language all its own, but it doesn't have to be intimidating. The average investor only needs to know the basics, so if you understand the terms in this glossary, you're off to a good start.

annuity

A contractual financial agreement between you and an issuing company. You give the issuing company a certain amount of money, and in turn, the company promises to invest your money and repay you according to the option or payment method that you choose.

asset

Anything you own that has monetary value, including cash, stocks, bonds, mutual funds, cars, real estate, and other items.

asset allocation

The specific distribution of your money among several different asset classes within an investment portfolio. Investment funds may be split among several different asset classes, such as stocks, bonds, and cash funds, each of which has unique risk and return characteristics. Determining just how to allocate funds depends on the financial plans of the individual investor.

bankruptcy

A legal process where a party acknowledges that they are unable to pay their debts and plans for those debts to be legally (if not financially) settled. The party declaring bankruptcy either allows their assets to be sold to repay creditors to the extent possible (liquidation bankruptcy) or works with the court to set up a plan to pay all or some of their debt over a period of several years (reorganization bankruptcy).

bear market

A market in which a group of assets (normally securities) falls in price or loses value over a period. A prolonged bear market may result in a decrease of 20% or more in market prices. A bear market in stocks may be due to investors' expectations of economic trends; in bonds, a bear market results from rising interest rates.

beneficiary

A person (or other entity, like a charitable foundation) who is named in a legal document (like a will or a trust agreement) to receive specific assets or to have the right to use specific assets.

bid price

The price a prospective buyer is ready to pay for a security. The term is commonly used by traders who stand ready to buy or sell security units at publicly quoted prices.

blockchain

Computer code used to describe and quantify data. It is commonly used to record transactions and as the basis for cryptocurrencies.

blue chip

A term used to describe companies that have established themselves as reliably successful over time, often by demonstrating sound management and creating quality products and services. Such companies have shown the capability to function in both good and bad economic times and usually pay dividends to investors even during lean years. Most blue chips are large-cap, *Fortune* 500–type stocks like Amazon.com or Texas Instruments.

bonds

Loans from investors to corporations and governments given in exchange for interest payments and timely repayment of the debt. Interest rates are usually fixed.

budget

A detailed listing of income and expenses by category, usually prepared with an eye toward the future. Used by households and businesses alike to gain tighter control over incoming and outgoing cash.

bull market

An extended period of rising securities prices. Bull markets generally involve heavy trading and are marked by a general upward trend in the market, independent of daily fluctuations.

capital gains

The appreciation in the value of an asset that occurs when its selling price is greater than the original price for which the asset was bought. The tax rate on capital gains depends on how long the asset was held and is often lower than the rate on ordinary income.

capital gains distributions

Payments to the shareholders of a mutual fund based on profits earned from selling securities in the fund's portfolio. Capital gains distributions are usually paid once a year.

cash flow

Financial term referring to the amount of cash left over after all current expenses, excluding long-term debt and taxes, are covered.

certificate of deposit (CD)

Money deposited with banks for a fixed period, usually between one month and five years, in exchange for compound interest, usually at a fixed rate. At the end of this term, on the maturity date, the principal may either be repaid to the depositor or rolled over into another CD. Any money deposited into a CD is insured by the bank (up to FDIC limits), making these very low-risk investments. Most banks set heavy penalties for early withdrawal of monies from a CD.

commission

A fee charged by a stockbroker (and, in some cases, a financial advisor) who executes securities trade transactions for an investor. This fee is generally a percentage based on either the number of shares bought or sold, or the value of the shares bought or sold.

compound interest

Interest earned on the original investment (or deposit) amount plus any previously earned interest; effectively, new interest is paid on already-earned interest. This helps the investment grow more quickly than it would with simple interest, which is applied only to the original investment amount.

cost basis

The total original purchase price of an asset, which may include items other than just the asset price, such as sales tax, commissions, and delivery and installation fees. This total amount is subtracted from the sale price of the asset to compute the capital gain or loss when that asset is eventually sold.

credit risk

The risk that the principal you've invested through debt securities (like bonds) will not be repaid at all or on time. If the issuer of a debt security fails to repay the principal, the issuer is deemed to be in default.

creditor

Any person (or entity) to whom you owe money.

cryptocurrency

An asset class category based on blockchain. Common cryptocurrencies include Bitcoin and Ethereum.

cyclical

When applied to the duration of markets, cyclical means a bull or bear market that lasts a short period, usually less than twelve months. An example of a cyclical bear market is the bear market that started in October 1990 and ended in January 1991.

default

To fail to repay principal or make timely payments on a bond or other debt investment security as promised. More likely to happen with high-yield corporate bonds (a.k.a. junk bonds) than other types of bonds.

discount broker

Brokerage firms that offer cut-rate fees for buying and selling securities, usually online or over an automated teleservice, although some also offer fax trade order options. Among the most prominent are Fidelity, Charles Schwab, Robinhood, and E*TRADE.

diversification

The process of optimizing an investment portfolio by allocating funds to multiple different assets. Diversification minimizes risks while maximizing returns by spreading out risk across several investments. Different types of assets, such as stocks, bonds, and cash funds, carry different types of risk. For an optimal portfolio, it is important to diversify among assets with dissimilar risk levels. Investing in several assets allows for unexpected negative performances to balance out with or be superseded by positive performances.

dividend

A payment made by a corporation to its shareholders that represents a portion of the profits of the company. The amount to be paid is determined by the board of directors, and dividends may be paid even during a time when the company is not performing profitably. Dividends are paid on a set schedule, such as quarterly, semiannually, or annually. Dividends may be paid directly to the investor or reinvested into more shares of the company's stock. Even if dividends are reinvested, the individual is responsible for paying taxes on the dividends earned. Mutual funds also pay dividends, from the income earned on the underlying investments of the fund portfolio. Dividends usually are not guaranteed (except with certain types of preferred stock) and may vary each time they are paid.

dividend reinvestment plan (DRIP)

A plan allowing investors to automatically reinvest their dividends in the company's stock rather than receive them in cash. Many companies waive the sales charges for stock purchased under the DRIP.

dividend yield

The current or estimated annual dividend divided by the market price per share of a security. Used to compare dividend-paying shares of different corporations.

Dow Jones Industrial Average (DJIA)

An index to which the performance of individual stocks or mutual funds can be compared. It is a means of measuring the change in stock prices. This index is a composite of thirty blue chip companies. These thirty companies do not represent only the United States; rather, they are involved with commerce on a global scale. The DJIA is computed by adding the prices of these thirty stocks and dividing by an adjusted number that considers stock splits and other divisions that would interfere with the average. Stocks represented on the Dow Jones Industrial Average make up between 15%–20% of the total market.

earnings growth

A pattern of increasing rate of growth in earnings per share from one period to another, which usually causes a stock's price to rise.

equity

Equity is the total ownership or partial ownership of an asset minus any debts that are owed in relation to that asset (like a home with a mortgage). Equity also refers to the amount of interest shareholders hold in a company as a part of their rights of partial ownership. Equity is considered synonymous with ownership, a share of ownership, or the rights of ownership.

exchange-traded fund (ETF)

An investment pool, similar in principle to mutual funds, whose shares trade over an exchange much like shares of stock. ETFs often mirror benchmark indexes but also allow for trading in single stocks.

financial advisor

A financial planning professional (typically licensed and accredited) who helps people manage their wealth. Functions may include preparing a retirement savings plan, devising tax strategies, and preparing an estate planning strategy, among other financial services.

foreclosure

A legal process that terminates an owner's right to a property, usually because the borrower defaults on payments. Home foreclosures usually result in a forced sale of the property to pay off the mortgage.

fundamental analysis

An analysis of a company's current and past balance sheets and income statements used to forecast its future stock price movements. Fundamental analysts consider past records of assets, earnings, sales, products, management, and markets in predicting the future trends of a company's success or failure. By appraising a company's prospects, these analysts assess whether a particular stock or group of stocks is undervalued or overvalued at its current market price.

going public

When a company that has previously been wholly privately owned offers its stock to the public for the first time.

good 'til canceled

Buy or sell limit order that remains active until canceled.

hedge

Hedging is a strategy of reducing risk by offsetting investments with investments of opposite risks. Risks must be negatively correlated to hedge each other—for example, pairing an investment with high inflation risk and low immediate returns with investments with low inflation risk and high immediate returns. Long hedges protect against a short-term position, and short hedges protect against a long-term position. Hedging is not the same as diversification; it aims to protect against risk by counterbalancing that specific area of risk.

individual retirement account (IRA)

A retirement account that anyone who has earned income can contribute to. Amounts contributed to traditional IRAs are usually tax-deferred. Amounts contributed to Roth IRAs are not currently deductible, but taxes are never levied on the earnings.

inflation

A general increase in prices coinciding with a fall in the real value of money, as measured by the Consumer Price Index.

inflation risk

The risk that rising prices of goods and services over time will decrease the value of the return on investments. Inflation risk is also known as purchasing-power risk because it refers to increased prices of goods and services and a decreased value of cash.

junk bond

A high-yield bond that comes with a high risk of default. Junk bonds are generally low-rated bonds and are usually bought on speculation. Investors hope for the yield rather than the default. An investor with high risk tolerance may choose to invest in junk bonds.

leverage

The practice of using borrowed money to invest or trade. Common forms of leverage include margin loans and lines of credit.

liability

An amount owed to creditors or others. Common personal liabilities include mortgages, car payments, student loans, and credit card debt.

liquidity

The ease with which an asset can be converted to cash at its present market value. High liquidity is associated with a high number of buyers and sellers trading investments at a high volume.

load

A sales charge or commission paid to a broker or other third party when mutual funds are bought or sold. Front-end loads are incurred when an investor purchases the shares, and back-end loads are incurred when investors sell the shares.

margin

Trading financial assets with money borrowed from the broker who performs the transaction. Margin trading requires a special agreement between the investor and the broker and is regulated by the Federal Reserve. Brokers charge interest for margin trades.

market capitalization

The current market price of a company's shares multiplied by the number of shares outstanding, commonly referred to as "market cap." Large-cap corporations generally have over $10 billion in market capitalization, mid-cap companies between $2 billion and $10 billion, and small-cap companies less than $2 billion. These capitalization figures may vary depending upon the index being used or the guidelines used by the portfolio manager.

market risk

The risk that investments will lose money is based on the daily fluctuations of the overall market. Bond market risk results from fluctuations in prevailing interest rates. Stock market risk is influenced by a wide range of factors, such as the state of the economy, political news, and events of national importance. Though time is a stabilizing element in the markets, as returns tend to outweigh risks over long periods, market risk cannot be systematically diversified away.

market value

The value of an asset if it were to be immediately sold, or the current price of a security being sold on the market.

mutual fund

An investment that allows thousands of investors to pool their money to collectively invest in stocks, bonds, or other types of assets, depending on the objectives of the fund. Mutual funds are convenient, particularly for small investors, because they diversify an individual's portfolio among many investments, more unique securities than an individual could normally purchase on their own. Investors share in the profits of a mutual fund, and mutual fund shares can be sold back to the company on any business day at the net asset value price.

National Association of Securities Dealers Automatic Quotation (NASDAQ)

A global automated computer system that provides up-to-the-minute information on approximately 5,500 over-the-counter stocks. Whereas on the New York Stock Exchange (NYSE) securities are bought and sold on the trading floor, securities on the NASDAQ are traded via computer.

net worth

The value of all a person's assets (anything owned that has a monetary value) minus all the person's liabilities (amounts owed to others).

New York Stock Exchange (NYSE)

The best-known exchange in the United States, where securities are traded by brokers and dealers for customers on the trading floor at 11 Wall Street in New York City.

price/earnings (P/E) ratio

A measure of how much buyers are willing to pay for each dollar of a company's earnings, calculated by dividing the current share price by the stock's earnings per share. This ratio is a useful way to compare the value of stocks and helps to indicate expectations for the company's growth in earnings, most useful when comparing companies within similar industries. The P/E ratio is sometimes also called the "multiple."

price-to-book ratio

Current market price of a stock divided by its book value, or net asset value. Sometimes used to assess companies with a high proportion of fixed assets or heavy equipment.

quote

A listing of the current price and related pertinent information for assets, such as stocks, bonds, futures, and options. Quotes are listed in terms of Bid/Ask. Bid is the highest price a potential buyer is willing to pay for the security and Ask is the lowest price at which a seller is willing to sell the security.

reinvestment

The use of capital gains, interest, and dividends to buy more of the same investment. For example, the dividends received from stock shares may be reinvested by buying more shares of the same stock.

risk tolerance

An investor's ability to tolerate fluctuations (including sharp downturns) in the value of an investment in the expectation of receiving a higher return.

rollover

Immediate reinvestment of a distribution from a qualified retirement plan into an IRA or another qualified plan to retain its tax-deferred status and avoid taxes and penalties for early withdrawal.

secular

Term that refers to the length of a bull or bear market. A secular bull market is one that lasts several years. An example was the bull market in stocks, which started in 2020 and was still in place in 2024.

Securities and Exchange Commission (SEC)

A federal government agency that was established to protect individual investors from fraud and malpractice in the marketplace. The commission oversees and regulates the activities of registered investment advisors, stock and bond markets, broker/dealers, and mutual funds.

security

Any investment purchased with the expectation of making a profit. Securities include total or partial ownership of an asset, rights to ownership of an asset, and certificates of debt from an institution. Examples of securities include stocks, bonds, certificates of deposit, and options.

socially responsible investing

Investing in companies that meet an ethical standard by using a carefully employed screening process before purchasing any securities.

split

When a corporation increases its number of shares outstanding. The total shareholders' equity does not change; instead, the number of shares increases while the value of each share decreases proportionally. For example, in a 2-for-1 split, a shareholder with one hundred shares prior to the split would now own two hundred shares. The price of the shares, however, would be cut in half; shares that cost $200 before the split would be worth $100 after the split.

Standard & Poor's (S&P) 500 Index

A market index of five hundred of the top-performing US corporations. This index, a more comprehensive measure of the domestic market than the Dow Jones Industrial Average, indicates broad market changes.

stock

An ownership share in a corporation, entitling the investor to a pro-rata share of the corporation's earnings and assets.

technical analysis

The use of charts and indicators to predict movements in securities prices. Technical analysis uses manual charts and computer programs to identify and project price trends in a market, security, mutual fund, or futures contract.

total return

The change in value of an investment over a specific time, typically expressed as a percentage. Total return calculations assume all earnings are reinvested in additional shares of the investment.

underwriter

A person (or company) who distributes securities as an intermediary between the issuer and the buyer of the securities. For example, an underwriter may be the broker listing an IPO. Generally, the underwriter agrees to purchase the remaining units of the security, such as remaining shares of stocks or bonds, from the issuer if the public does not buy all specified units. An underwriter may also be a company that backs the issue of a contract by agreeing to accept responsibility for fulfilling the contract in return for a premium.

value investing

An investment approach that focuses on companies that may be temporarily out of favor despite strong success potential or whose earnings or assets are not fully reflected in their stock prices. Value stocks will tend to have a lower price-to-earnings ratio than growth stocks, and are currently undervalued, making them good investment "deals."

volatility

An indicator of expected risk, categorized by the range of price movement of a security. It demonstrates the degree to which the market price of an asset, rate, or index fluctuates from its average. Volatility is calculated by finding the standard deviation from the mean, or average, return.

yield

The return, or earnings, on an investment. Yield refers to the interest earned on a bond, or the dividend earnings on an equity investment. Yield does not include capital gains.

Index